CONTENTS

REGULATORY DISCLAIMERS

HYPOTHETICAL PERFORMANCE DISCLOSURE

The performance results included in this presentation are hypothetical returns. Past performance is no guarantee of future returns. The performance results are based upon a hypothetical model. Hypothetical performance results may have inherent limitations, some of which are described below. No representation is being made that anyone leveraging these strategies will or is likely to achieve profits or losses similar to those shown. One of the limitations of hypothetical performance results is that they are prepared with the benefit of hindsight. There are numerous other factors related to the markets in general or to the implementation of any specific trading strategy that cannot be fully accounted for in the preparation of hypothetical performance results and all of which can adversely affect actual trading results.

The results shown do not represent the results of actual trading but were achieved by means of the retroactive application of an investment process that was designed with the benefit of hindsight, otherwise known as back testing. Thus, the performance results noted above should not be considered indicative of a certain level of skill. The back-tested performance was compiled after the end of the period depicted. These results do not reflect the effects of material economic and market factors on decision-making. In addition, back-tested performance results do not involve financial risk, and no hypothetical trading record can completely account for the impact of financial risks associated with actual investing.

INDEXES

Any indexes and other financial benchmarks shown are provided for illustrative purposes only, are unmanaged, reflect reinvestment of income and dividends, and do not reflect the impact of advisory fees, commissions, or taxes. Investors cannot invest directly in an index. The Standard & Poor's 500 Index (S&P 500) is provided for illustrative purposes only, is unmanaged, and reflects reinvestment of income and dividends. The S&P 500 is a widely unmanaged index of market activity based on the aggregate performance of a selected portfolio of publicly traded common stocks, and the results of such an index are included to merely give you a perspective of the historical performance of the US equity market.

ADDITIONAL DISCLOSURE

The commentary in this book reflects the personal opinions, viewpoints, and analyses of the author and should not be regarded as a description of advisory services provided by Alpha Cubed Investments, LLC, or performance returns of any Alpha Cubed Investments, LLC client or strategy. The views reflected in the commentary are subject to change at any time without notice. Nothing in this book constitutes investment advice, performance data, or any recommendation that any particular security, portfolio of securities, transaction, or investment strategy is suitable for any specific person. Any mention of a particular security and related performance data is not a recommendation to buy or sell that security.

The opinions expressed in this book are for general informational purposes only and are intended to provide education about the financial industry. To determine which investments may be appropriate for you, consult your financial advisor prior to investing. Any past performance discussed during this book is no guarantee of future results. As always, please remember investing involves risk and possible loss of principal capital; please seek advice from a licensed professional.

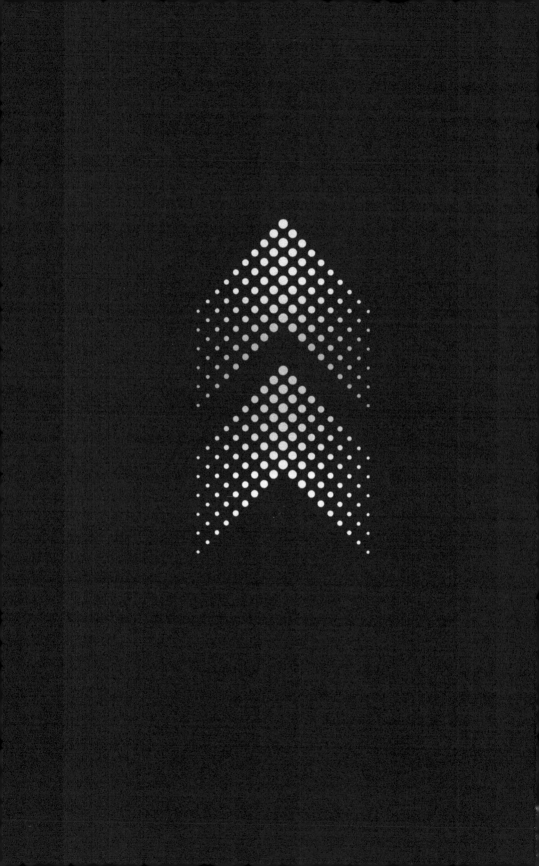

INTRODUCTION

IN 1956, THEN-SENATOR JOHN F. KENNEDY wrote *Profiles in Courage*, a book that describes acts of courage and strength exhibited by eight US senators throughout history. *Profiles in Courage* was a bestseller and earned JFK a Pulitzer Prize.

Tales of greatness and overcoming insurmountable odds have always inspired me. I find it amazing that in one short lifetime, one person can achieve things that are beyond the wildest dreams of most of the rest of us. I remember learning in elementary school about how Julius Caesar defeated Rome's enemies in Gaul (modern-day France), returned to Rome, then chased the reigning Roman Emperor Pompey all the way to Egypt and defeated him there. While in Egypt, Caesar formed an alliance with Cleopatra (yes, that Cleopatra) and installed her as ruler of Egypt, and they bore a child together. Caesar returned to Rome, consolidated his power, and made himself dictator. He did all that over the course of just four years, from 52 BC to 48 BC! I've remained curious about the seemingly unimaginable feats that can be accomplished in just one lifetime.

Throughout my thirty-five-plus-year career as an investment advisor, I have witnessed companies achieve seemingly impossible levels of success. The idea of building a company from nothing more than an idea to over a trillion dollars of market capitalization still strikes me as truly mind-boggling. In this book, I want to highlight the companies that have changed the landscape of modern capitalism and created massive value for investors. As Kennedy gave us *Profile in Courage* to showcase the common characteristics of great leaders, I want to look at some of the common characteristics of the greatest companies of the last sixty years, a *Profiles in Great Stocks*, if you will, so that today's investors can get a leg up as they try to identify the next great companies of the future.

My initial plan for this book was to undertake a high-level review of similar characteristics common to the greatest companies, but I began to notice that taking that approach felt extremely subjective. I have a lot of experience and knowledge informing my understanding and opinions, but I didn't just want to write a history report with some highly subjective guidelines. Instead, I wanted to be able to offer a clear and repeatable process that others could follow when they chose to speculate on the next great company. That's when I started applying the technical analysis tools I've created, borrowed, and refined over many decades. Once I integrated the technical component into an algorithm, I felt that I had created an objective process to complement the subjective characteristics we will review throughout the book.

Before we go any further, let's pause for a moment to talk about the meaning of market "speculation." I am the CEO of Alpha Cubed Investments. We are a registered investment advisory (RIA) firm specializing in managing investments for what are generally considered to be high-net-worth retail investors. These are typically individual investors who are building for retirement or who are already retired and are investing in roughly the $500,000 to $20 million range. Most of these investors want to be positioned for the long term with an allocation between stocks and bonds with moderate trading activity that is designed to keep them "on-cycle" with prevailing market conditions. In other words, they are not "speculators." That being said, even the most disciplined, conservative investors occasionally want to "take a flyer" on something they believe could be the next big thing. And it seems like almost everyone under twenty-five years old thinks speculating is actually investing if you look at the crypto, decentralized finance (DeFi), and meme stock phenomena of the last few years.

This book is designed to provide a clear-cut process to help investors who want to speculate with a portion of their investments. This book is *not* for the buy-and-hold, buy-and-manage, asset-allocation majority part of your portfolio. It is dedicated to helping investors when they are taking large risks with small portions of their portfolios in the interest of finding the next great company that may have material impacts on their total portfolios over time.

I stress this point here at the start because over the last thirty-five-plus years, I have seen this movie play out exactly the same way for investors. The market gets hot, and an exciting stock starts moving up at a frantic pace. As a result, an otherwise thoughtful and conservative investor will go out and buy it, and then six months to one year later, it will crater, and a lot of money will be lost. I have seen this cycle repeated over and over again during the course of my career. It's hard for people to resist throwing some money into a speculative idea when others seem to be making money hand over fist on some new and "obvious" winner. But it often ends in big losses. And when it does, it almost always comes down to investors' gut feelings leading them in the wrong direction.

My goal is that the next time an investor looks to chase the next big "sure" thing, they will apply the process laid out in this book to control risk and take some of the gut emotionality out of their decision-making. I hope my readers gain some insight into how to build their own process around finding and managing the next great stock by applying some of the lessons of this book.

More than anything else, I will always recommend the following: Make sure the majority of your investments are following a longer-term process with a financial plan designed to prudently meet your retirement or other investment goals. Never, *ever* speculate with money you can't 100 percent afford to lose. And when you do speculate, have a clear process to manage risk in case things don't work out.

With that advice in place, let's look at some of the greatest companies in history, the subjective lessons we can learn from them as we look for the next great companies, and an objective process for controlling the risk around these speculative names when they first show up on the investment horizon.

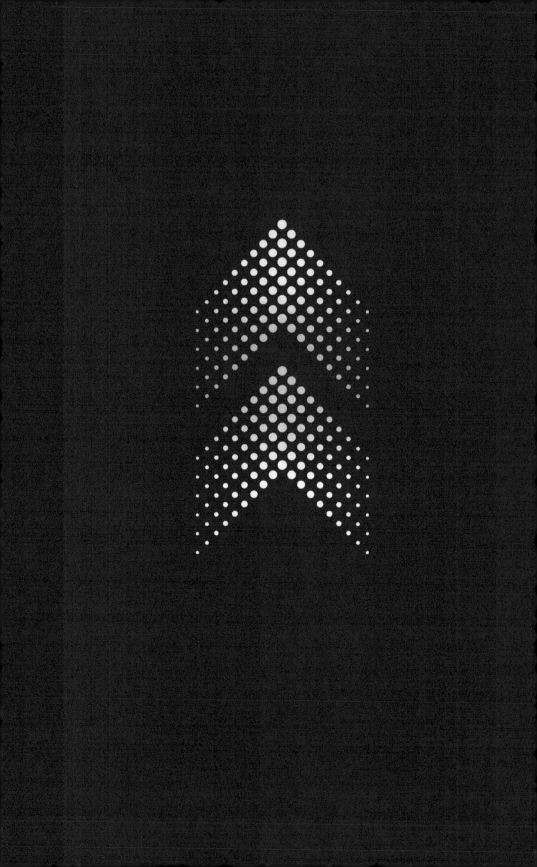

CHAPTER ONE

MY FRONT-ROW SEAT TO STOCK MARKET HISTORY

I BEGAN MY CAREER IN 1986, a twenty-two-year-old at the venerable white shoe firm of E. F. Hutton. The term "white shoe firm" even back then was an old-school term used to suggest that it was part of the established upper class. I grew up in a broken home on welfare and had to scratch and claw for everything I got. At E. F. Hutton, I was definitely far from my roots! So I did my best to try to blend in and kept my head down until I figured out what I was supposed to be doing and how to stay in the business. Needless to say, I had a lot to learn, and I had to learn fast. I understood that I was extremely fortunate to be hired by such a well-respected firm, and I worked more hours than anyone there during my first year (at least it felt that way). Terminations were frequent, so we were all under a lot of pressure.

I knew my position at the firm was by far the most tenuous and that I could be fired any day. Since I didn't have any connections or come from a wealthy family, I decided my strategy would be to outwork everyone else. I would arrive before 6:00 a.m. and generally stay until after 9:00 p.m. That first year was a wild ride. I was in a hypercompetitive environment, learning securities analysis, market behavior, general business skills (I was right out of college at UCLA), and, of course, I had to learn how to sell—and fast!

It was definitely sink or swim (or just plain get shown the door). We were held to production standards, and if you were not making the firm money, you got fired, plain and simple. At all my jobs prior to that one, I had kept a running list of my fellow employees to see how fast I was moving up. But by the end of that first year at E. F. Hutton, my list had so many scratch marks and new people added that it was a mess to look at. I saw at least thirty people lose their jobs by the end of that first year just in my office alone. Because I was only twenty-two years old (and a very young-looking twenty-two-year-old), I made a strategic decision to *not* see people in person until that person and I had established a working relationship over the phone. I figured I might be better off meeting people once they had some experience talking with me about investment concepts and the market.

That approach actually worked well. Although most were surprised by how young I was, they seemed to appreciate my depth of knowledge as well as the energy and enthusiasm I brought to the process. That was also the fateful year of 1987 when the market went straight up … until it didn't. On October 19, 1987, a day that would come to be known as "Black Monday," the market crashed and had the single largest one-day drop ever: 508 points, or -22.6 percent in one day on the Dow Jones Industrial Average. That was my welcome to Wall Street! Wow—what a shock … I thought I might have to actually give up the business and go to law school.

The Crash of '87

Stocks Plunge 508 Amid Panicky Selling

Percentage Decline Is Far Steeper Than '29; Bond Prices Surge

NEW YORK – The stock market crashed yesterday.

Source: The Wall Street Journal

I was so new I barely knew what happened! Over time, we came to understand that a number of things conspired to cause the crash. One was a strategy that involved selling stock index futures against stock market holdings, called portfolio insurance; it had become the rage on Wall Street, as the market had been in "bull mode" for many years at that point.[1] We have seen many "easy money," "get-rich-quick," and "guaranteed safe" strategies come and go over the history of the market. But there is never a free lunch. These ideas may work at first—or they wouldn't become fashionable. But then everyone piles in, serious risk materializes, and that risk is ultimately realized by the last investors in the door (and sometimes many others along with them).

Portfolio insurance in 1987 was essentially an algorithm that had computers sell stock futures on an index (like the S&P 500) when the market was dropping and use the proceeds from those sales

---

1   "Black Monday," corporatefinanceinstitute.com, December 20, 2022,
     https://corporatefinanceinstitute.com/resources/equities/black-monday/.

to offset market losses as a form of "insurance." Unfortunately, the computers running these programs overwhelmed the market with relentless selling on that fateful October day. A negative feedback loop developed, with lowered prices causing even more selling.[2] Additionally, a lot of wise guys in the business were selling their clients on strategies that involved selling naked puts and calls for just a few pennies, thinking the market could "never" move that much, and they would keep the "free money." Without getting too technical, they were engaging in a strategy that involved selling options way above or below the current market price on the presumption that the market couldn't go up or drop enough to cause the option strike prices to be exceeded. Theoretically, that meant they would take in the premium for the put or call and keep it because the market would never move enough for them to have to cover the option. Selling options above and below the market was called a "naked straddle," and when the market dropped a historic amount on Black Monday, they had to sell ever larger puts to cover the massive losses being generated by this so-called risk free strategy. A lot of investors got wiped out with huge unexpected losses. It was bedlam. Fortunately, I was not involved in any of these shenanigans. My basic approach was to only do things I understood. (That has kept me relatively safe throughout my career, by the way.)

We all suffered on Black Monday, but my strategy of keeping things simple and focusing on quality allowed for a speedier recovery. To this day, I recommend that when you hear the term "risk free," you should generally run for the hills unless there is FDIC insurance behind the investment. When you start shifting away from high-quality investments and basic blocking and tackling, the risk almost always goes up. And when some new scheme becomes pervasive in the

---

2   Ibid.

markets and gets utilized by too many participants, more than likely the risks go up. Then the risks get realized, and people lose a lot of money. The crash of 1987 was a great lesson for me not to follow the crowd but to be a contrarian and to keep heeding my own advice: if you don't understand it, don't do it.

One of the very senior brokers at E. F. Hutton pulled me aside shortly after the crash of '87 and showed me some technical statistics from a company called Investors Intelligence, which had developed a newsletter writer indicator. He showed me that when the majority of newsletter writers at any given time became bearish, it correlated with better times to enter the stock market. That was my first introduction to the concept of technical analysis—the process of looking at charts, chart patterns, internal metrics, sentiment, and other indicators to see possible future outcomes based on similar readings or patterns that had happened before.

> The crash of 1987 was a great lesson for me not to follow the crowd but to be a contrarian and to keep heeding my own advice: if you don't understand it, don't do it.

One way to think about technical analysis is to imagine flying through a rainstorm using only your instrument panel. The images you are seeing through the windshield during a storm can lead to bad judgments, so having an instrument panel with objective data can be a life saver. Technical analysis is very similar in that it looks at raw data around an individual security or the entire market and filters out all the emotional commentary that we are constantly bombarded with by analysts and television commentators (who may even have a hidden agenda). It can help remove the emotional component and lead to better entry and exit prices. Another way to look at it is this: the details of every bull market and every bear market are always, by definition, going to be different. But the way people react to fear and greed are similar and definitely rhyme over different periods of time. Money has always been important to people, and there are similarities to how people react even many decades apart and especially in periods of crisis when they are scared and losing money. Technical analysis can help objectively measure behavior like this, among other things.

After spending some time learning about the newsletter writer indicator, I could see there were strong correlations with better entry points into the market. Eventually, I wrote to Investor's Intelligence and purchased the raw data going back to the inception of their recordkeeping in the early 1960s. Computers were not ubiquitous at that time, but I used one to create a graphic showing the newsletter writer statistical data against the Dow Jones Industrial Average going all the way back to the beginning of the data set. Once the charts were completed, the pattern was obvious: extreme readings in this metric could have provided better entry points into the market.

Ultimately the charts ended up demonstrating that when the majority of "professional" investment newsletter writers were bearish, the market was probably low enough to consider entering. It was a very contrarian indicator. But it also made sense: Once everyone agrees that the market is a terrible place to be, the consensus has been to sell. Then, once markets have exhausted all the sellers and there is no one left willing to sell, they can start

> The details of every bull market and every bear market are always, by definition, going to be different. But the way people react to fear and greed are similar and definitely rhyme over different periods of time.

going back up again. As Jesse Livermore, the protagonist in Edwin Lefèvre's must-read 1923 classic *Reminiscences of a Stock Operator*, said, "The stock market is never obvious. It is designed to fool most of the people, most of the time."[3] So having some objective tools to sort through the emotions associated with volatile markets made a lot of sense to me. And so began my journey into the world of technical analysis. I've included here a modern version of that same technical tool (note the periods where the percentage of bulls—top line—crosses below the percentage of bears and think about what those markets were like at that time):

BULLS & BEARS

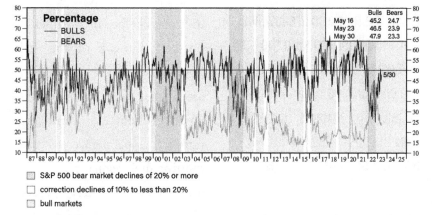

June 7, 2023 | Stock Market Indicators: Bull/Bear Ratios | Yardeni Research Inc. | www.yardeni.com

Source: Yardeni Research

Over the years, my knowledge of stock fundamentals grew, but my interest in technical analysis grew as well. It seemed to me that having a tool that could objectively help me counter all the emotional inputs the stock market throws at us on a daily basis could give me a huge advantage in managing money. I have come to see the process of investing as the crucible of fear and greed: when the markets are

---

3   Edwin Lefèvre, *Reminiscences of a Stock Operator* (Hoboken, NJ: Wiley, 2006).

low, we want to get out to stop the pain, and when they are high, we are encouraged to get in and accelerate the gains. But isn't that the opposite of what we are supposed to be doing?

Fascinated by this contradiction, I began adding to my knowledge base day by day, year by year, in an ongoing effort to counteract the powerful emotions we are all subjected to during wild market swings up and down. I read everything I could and began building a collection of different technical analysis metrics that seemed to help identify better entry points into the stock market at more opportune times. Constant research and countless late nights of studying different technical indicators helped me weather the dot-com blowup of the early 2000s. Back in the year 2000, it seemed like everyone belonged to an investment club, and large numbers of people were actually quitting their regular nine-to-five jobs to become "day traders."

> When the markets are low, we want to get out to stop the pain, and when they are high, we are encouraged to get in and accelerate the gains. But isn't that the opposite of what we are supposed to be doing?

There were even day-trading businesses set up around the country where these newly minted traders could go to work at their trading jobs, trying to make their fortune during the dot-com mania.[4] It was a wild time. Having a set of objective technical metrics to look at really helped sort through all of the "irrational exuberance" of the day (that phrase was coined in late 1986 by Alan Greenspan, then the chairman of the Federal Reserve). By 2008, when the Global Financial Crisis hit, I had developed a combination of even more technical indicators for tactically trading the stock market and helping to filter out the extreme emotions

---

4   Alex Frew McMillan, "Day Trading Loses Its Shine," CNNMoney, August 9, 2000, https://money.cnn.com/2000/08/09/investing/q_daytradewhere/.

that accompanied the large market moves of that period. A lot of the work I did back then led to the development of a hypothetical process-based algorithm that I will introduce in this book to help investors who choose to speculate.

The magazine-cover indicator is a somewhat irreverent economic indicator with interesting correlations to extreme levels of market sentiment, which implies that the cover stories on the more widely circulated magazines—particularly *TIME, BusinessWeek, Forbes,* and *Fortune* in the United States—can be contrary indicators.

TIME magazine is a good example, as it generally captured the attention of the greatest number of people in its prime. People tend to buy more magazines when they are interested in the topic, and once everybody believes in a particular narrative, it is probably priced into the market (and may even be about to reverse). No indicator is perfect, but we believe there is some merit to it, and it is certainly an interesting sociological phenomenon.

At Alpha Cubed Investments, we have original magazine-cover "indicators" displayed in our headquarters. We believe that we have one of the largest private collections of original historical magazine-indicator covers anywhere in the world. We have great respect for the history of our business, so when you see extreme headlines and pervasive consensus, remember the old contrarian saying: "The market attempts to confuse the majority of the people the majority of the time."

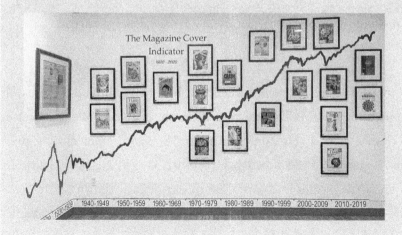

Like I said, it has been a wild ride, and through it all I have been a witness to history through the prism of the stock market. Since 1986 I have had a front-row seat to the birth and maturation of some of the greatest and most revolutionary companies ever created. I was there when some of the most innovative and transformative companies of all time came public, and I watched them go through all their massive growth cycles, navigate challenges and market-related problems, and go on to execute succession plans that ensured their continued success into the future. Here are some of the greatest companies of the last sixty years and the total return percentage of each since the first day they went public through December 31, 2022, with each compared to the price change in the S&P 500 over the same period (both excluding dividends).

Ticker	IPO Date*	Split-Adjusted IPO Price	Price on 12/31/22	Price Return through 12/31/22**	S&P 500 Price Return since IPO*
AAPL	12/12/80	$0.10	$129.93	129,830%	2,915%
AMZN	5/15/97	$0.08	$84.00	111,900%	359%
GOOGL	8/19/04	$2.13	$88.23	4,052%	251%
MSFT	3/13/86	$0.07	$239.82	328,796%	1,551%
TSLA	6/29/10	$1.13	$123.18	10,769%	257%

*These dates are the same for calculation purposes.
**These results do not consider the impact of dividends that have been paid.

Source: Bloomberg Finance L.P.

The total return of the S&P 500 (including dividends) is approximately 3347.26 percent since the first day of my career as a trainee at E. F. Hutton on August 18, 1986 (from closing price on August 15, 1986 through December 31, 2022). Not a bad total return, but it pales in comparison to the gigantic returns, potentially life-changing returns, available from some of the great companies listed above.

From my perspective on the front lines since 1986, I am going to take you on a trip through history to look at the biggest winning stocks of the last couple of generations. We will see if we can build a road map or process you can follow as you try to identify and manage the next great stock winners that will appear on the landscape over the years and decades to come.

What these companies have in common is that they all have exciting stories of revolutionary business undertakings, massive success, and huge investment returns. But their paths were not one-way streets. There were bumps and challenges along the way for each. Companies like these fall into the realm of speculation and need to be treated as such generally—especially when they are young and have just had an initial public offering. We only know that they are successful now with the benefit of hindsight. When they first went public, they were not for everyone and certainly not for the majority of a solid long-term investment plan. But if you're going to speculate with a portion of your money, you should have a plan around it and not just go by the seat of your pants or how you feel. That's what this book is about.

Hopefully, by the end of it, you will have learned a lot about the characteristics of great companies and have a process-based plan to help manage future possible candidates if you choose to speculate. There is a big difference between speculating on big returns and investing conservatively for retirement or other goals over the long haul. Most investors prefer to take a long-term approach to investing and that generally makes the most sense. Having a core of great long-term securities, bonds, and stocks is not very sexy but it is the core of any great long-term investment plan (ask Warren Buffet). However, when we are talking about finding the next great new company, that almost always involves taking on a much higher degree of risk. When taking larger amounts of risk, the first issue is to only use money you may be comfortable losing. Speculating in new, high-growth companies is very risky by definition, so it is important to never jeopardize your long-term investment plan at the altar of speculation. You don't want to ever risk money that you cannot afford to lose. But if you are going to go down this path and periodically speculate with money you can afford to lose, it makes sense to have an investment process to manage around the companies that work and also the ones that inevitably do not work. That involves short-term, or tactical, trading. We will review one possible approach to managing the risk in speculative, high-growth companies like this in the upcoming chapters.

As we move forward, we will discuss a possible three-step process to help manage speculation in individual companies, where a tactical approach may be more appropriate than buying-and-holding dividend-paying blue-chip stocks.

Step One: Fundamental Analysis

The analysis of fundamentals has macro- and microcomponents. Assessing the macrocomponents involves looking at big-picture data (like the expectation for Gross Domestic Product [GDP]—a measure of the health and growth rate of the US economy) and is also called "top-down" analysis. We also want to look closely at the earnings estimates for the S&P 500 for the coming year. Are they increasing or decreasing? The market will generally correlate to that data. Another big-picture metric to consider is what the overall valuation of the stock market is relative to those earnings (using information like the classic p/e or price-to-earnings ratio). Is it high (maybe a good time to be cautious), or is it historically low (maybe take more risk)?

Once we have a good reading on these and other macrocomponents, we want to assess microcomponents, which involves looking at the individual stocks and is also called "bottom-up" analysis. Things like the p/e ratio, price-to-sales, price-to-book, dividend coverage ratio, and many other data analytics are all available to analyze and then rank each individual stock. The best part is that the executives who run any company you own are required to report on their performance, their earnings, and their success on executing the business plan every quarter. It's just like in high school when the report cards are due, and you find out who is keeping their nose to the grindstone. Back in high school, it was all fun and games until report cards went out and you had to answer to your parents. Getting As was good; getting Ds might mean you lost your driving privileges—or worse! Owning stocks is no different. The management teams for each of the companies you own are required to answer every single quarter for the earnings they generate, and it is pretty easy to determine if the results are As, Bs, Cs, Ds, or Fs.

The stock market is littered with former great companies like Sears, JCPenney, Eastman Kodak, Enron, Bear Stearns, Lehman Brothers, and so many others that have failed over the years. Many former blue-chip stocks are now gone or have become mere shadows of their former selves. But they didn't disappear in one day. They started missing their quarterly earnings estimates, and it was generally death by a thousand cuts—a painful process that, in some cases, took many years to play out. Looking at the quarterly earnings and reading their 10Qs to analyze their "report card" would have given you a good opportunity to sell those companies and perhaps find another, better-managed company long before they cratered.

Investing is a uniquely egalitarian pursuit in that you can easily sell an underperforming company and buy a different one, right along with the best investors of the world. It is a true meritocracy if you have a robust investment process, continue to follow it, and build on it over time. Very often, the price action at the time earnings are announced tells you all you need to know about the management team for any given stock. This is especially true when it comes to managing newer speculative companies.

Step Two: Technical Analysis

I mentioned earlier that technical analysis is like flying through a rainstorm and filtering out the bad inputs by looking at the instrument panel. The "bad inputs" in this case are all the fear, greed, and general consternation created by our twenty-four-seven nonstop financial news cycle. Everyone is looking to increase web hits or viewership, usually by having the most outrageous or extreme opinion, and technical analysis can give us an opportunity to filter out all that noise. It looks at metrics like relative strength, momentum, money flow, stochastics, moving averages, and many others that can help determine whether a stock is healthy at any given moment in time.

Step Three: Risk Management

Risk management involves looking at the simple price action of younger, more speculative companies. Price is a beautiful thing in concept. It generally takes all of the known information that investors actually know at any given point and expresses it in terms of a number that investors agree at that instant most accurately represents the correct valuation of any given stock. For newer, speculative companies, it's imperative to consider price as a source of information. When it is down and we don't understand why, that compels us to look a little deeper to see if there is something other than market conditions going on beneath the surface. Most new, speculative companies run the risk of not being able to execute their business plan against formidable competition and overwhelming odds. Sometimes price alone can be a good indication of trouble in paradise (or of the executive team not being able to execute their business plan).

Using this three-step process, we are going to look together at fundamental factors like earnings reports and technicals indicators—and how price action alone can help inform our decisions—for some of the greatest companies in the past sixty years. Let's see if we can uncover some of the secrets to finding and managing the next great speculative companies that will change the investment landscape of the future. Buckle up. It's going to be a wild ride.

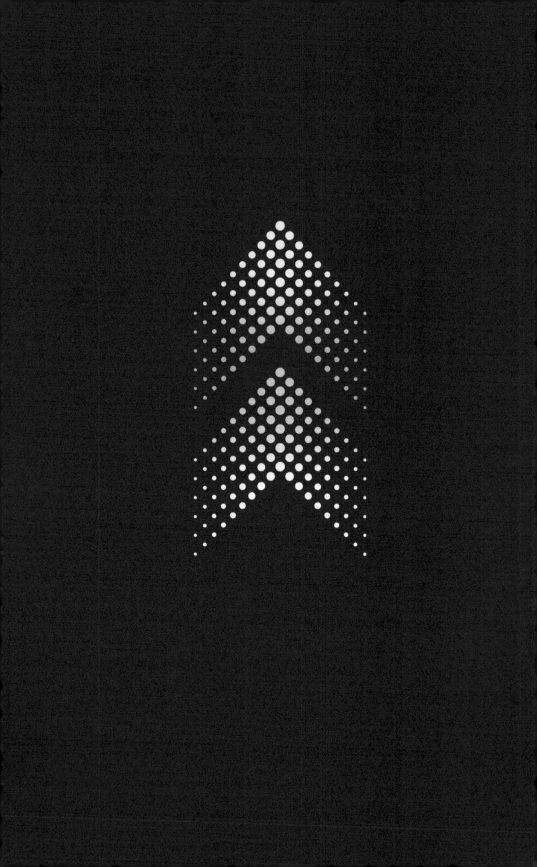

CHAPTER TWO

AMAZON

An investment of $1,000 in AMZN stock the day it came public on May 15, 1997, at the split-adjusted IPO price of $0.075 was worth ~$1,120,000 on December 31, 2022, for a return of ~111,900 percent.

We are stubborn on vision. We are flexible on details.... We don't give up on things easily.... If you're not stubborn, you'll give up on experiments too soon. And if you're not flexible, you'll pound your head against the wall, and you won't see a different solution to a problem you're trying to solve.

—JEFF BEZOS

Timeline from Formation through Initial Public Offering

- **1994:** Cadabra.com (as in "abracadabra") is established by Jeff Bezos in his garage in Bellevue, Washington.

- **1995:** "Cadabra" is quickly dropped in favor of "Amazon" after Bezos's lawyer reveals he misheard the original moniker as "cadaver." Bezos decides to go with a more authoritative name—referencing the largest river basin in the world—to suggest the business's potential scale. (Amazon's launch tagline was "Earth's biggest bookstore.")

- **1996:** Amazon increases to eleven employees and moves out of the garage and into a small warehouse—its second official headquarters.

- **1997:** Amazon completes its initial public offering (IPO) of stock at $18 per share on May 15, 1997.

Origin Story

Jeff Bezos was first recognized as the wealthiest man in the world in October 2017. How did the journey of Amazon and its founder unfold? Bezos was born on January 12, 1964, in Albuquerque, New Mexico. His mom was only a teenager when she gave birth to him, and his parents got divorced shortly thereafter. Three years later, his mother married a Cuban immigrant, Mike Bezos, who ended up adopting Jeff. They raised Jeff in Houston, Texas, and later moved to Miami, Florida, where he would end up graduating high school in 1982. After developing a passion for computers during his childhood, he studied electrical engineering and computer science at Princeton University. After graduating in 1986, he took his talents to a tele-communications start-up called Fitel, where he stayed for two years before moving on to become a product manager at Bankers Trust. In 1990, Bezos decided to try his luck on Wall Street and took a job at the hedge fund D. E. Shaw. He excelled and became a vice president at D. E. Shaw within two years, the youngest ever VP at the firm, in charge of researching the investment possibilities of the internet. Through his work at D. E. Shaw, he saw that the World Wide Web was growing 2,300 percent annually. That was in 1994, and he knew he needed to act.

Bezos sensed the potential of this meteoric growth and began working on an idea for the best way to participate in it. He started by making a list of twenty different items that he could sell online. Through this research, he realized that there are more items in the book category than in any other. Using this insight, Bezos decided to start an e-commerce business that focused solely on books. The vast number of titles that exist not only means they attract a wider customer base but also creates potential economies of scale. Instead of stocking retail stores across the country with millions of books (which was impossible), he would create a natural central inventory hub that could be distributed across the country via mail. At the time, this distribution process wasn't an option for mail-order companies, because to include all the books available, their catalogs would have become too big. This competitive advantage, or what some in the investment world would call a "moat," is what made Amazon's business model thrive almost immediately: better product logistics allowing more efficiencies at a better price. In short, an all-encompassing bookstore could only exist and succeed in the form of an online store. Bezos had built a better mousetrap!

Bezos quit his Wall Street job, packed up his things, and drove out to the West Coast in 1994. The decision came together so quickly that he didn't even draft a business plan until he was in the car on his way to Seattle. Bezos started Amazon out of his garage in Seattle on July 5, 1994. Among his first and earliest investors were his parents; he told them they had a 70 percent chance of losing everything. On July 16, 1995, the website Amazon.com was launched and opened for business. Within the first few days, Bezos "knew this was going to be huge," and within the first month, Amazon had sold books to people in all fifty states and in forty-five different countries. In the early days, a bell would go off in the office every time an order was placed. It didn't take long for the automatic bell to get turned off, as the constant ringing became overwhelming. Bezos would help box up the orders and drive them to the post office in the ten-year-old Chevy Blazer he borrowed from his father. A story that Bezos frequently tells about this time period is that when he was packing boxes kneeling on the cement floor, he suggested to one of his employees that the team should get kneepads. It was uncomfortable to be shifting around on your knees all day while packing. That's when another employee had the brilliant idea to get tables, so they no longer had to pack boxes on the ground all day. That simple idea would end up doubling Amazon's productivity. Clearly, revolutionary innovation ran through the core of Amazon's early business (humor intended).

State of the Industry

Of course, back in 1994, the main way to get books was to go to a physical bookstore. In 1994, companies with large physical locations like Barnes & Noble dominated the bookselling industry. Scaling the business from day one was critical to Amazon's long-term success, along with an almost hyperfocus on customer service. Bezos has always stressed that customer obsession is a much better approach than competitor obsession, business model obsession, product obsession, or technology obsession. He believes that if you focus on the customer experience—such as selection, ease of use, low prices, etc., along with great customer service—then you'll have a good chance of succeeding. From the very beginning, Bezos wanted Amazon's identity to involve excessive attention to the customer experience from end to end.[5]

---

5   S. Bavister, "Customer Obsession: The Secret to Amazon's Success, Lead Generation for Consultants with Guaranteed Results," Lexis Click, accessed March 10, 2023, https://www.lexisclick.com/blog/customer-obsession-the-secret-to-amazons-success.

In fact, Bezos believed that providing customers with the best experience would be the key to successfully scaling an extremely complicated business. Just as well, he knew that if he could achieve scale, he would be able to offer the best prices, the best product, and in turn, the best customer experience. This is called the "flywheel" effect, which has become a buzzword in the investment industry, especially for unprofitable companies seeking funding. As Amazon gained scale, they could provide better products and prices, which then attracted more customers, which then allowed them to scale further, which then allowed them to offer even better products and prices. For example, as Amazon gets more customers, they build more distribution centers, which speeds up delivery times and lowers delivery costs to the customers near those distribution centers. This "flywheel" leverages the size of the business into an asset. Passing the savings along to the customer creates a moat around the business, thereby making it more difficult for the competition to compete and new entrants to disrupt.

Source: Feedvisor

Here's how Bezos puts it:[6]

There are two ways to build a successful company. One is to work very, very hard to convince customers to pay high margins. The other is to work very, very hard to be able to offer customers low margins. They both work. We're firmly in the second camp. It's difficult—you have to eliminate defects and be very efficient. But it's also a point of view. We'd rather have a very large customer base and low margins than a small customer base and higher margins.

As Bezos was building the company by providing customers with the best experience possible, Amazon was forgoing short-term profits. However, it was also extending the relationship with its customer and thus the life of the business and the value of that relationship. Many of us will be lifelong Amazon customers for just this reason.

Within two years, Amazon had grown so fast that it was ready to go public with and initial public offering of stock (an "IPO"). After launching the website in 1995, Amazon hit $15.7 million in revenues by 1996 and $147.8 million in 1997. On May 15, 1997, Amazon went public. That same week, Barnes & Noble sued Amazon and launched their own bookselling website. Barnes & Noble was obviously late to the party, but nevertheless, a major competitor had entered the online bookselling business.

As Amazon gets more customers, they build more distribution centers, which speeds up delivery times and lowers delivery costs to the customers near those distribution centers. This "flywheel" leverages the size of the business into an asset.

---

6   Senthil, "Go It Alone on the Last Mile?," operationsworklife.com, February 14, 2018, https://www.operationsworklife.com/all-alone-on-the-last-mile/.

Going Public

In 1997, Madeleine Albright became the first female US secretary of state. Diana, Princess of Wales, was killed in a car crash in Paris. Steve Jobs returned to run Apple Computers. Hong Kong returned to Chinese rule. The average price of a new car was $16,900.

The year 1997 was a very interesting year for the markets. The S&P 500 was up ~31.01 percent and stayed above the one-hundred-day moving average (and the fifty-day moving average), except when it didn't, as you can see from the chart on the following page! There were two bouts of volatility. The first came after the market sailed into 1997 on the tailwinds of a strong 1996. In March '97, the market took a breather and had a garden variety correction of less than ~10 percent. It never broke the two-hundred-day moving average (generally considered to be the sign of a healthy market), and then went right back to going up. By October 1997, the frothy market had doubled in value over the prior thirty months and was set to lock in solid gains for the year. But on October 27 and 28, 1997, the nation's securities markets fell by a record absolute amount on then-record trading volume. On Monday, October 27, the Dow Jones Industrial Average ("DJIA") declined 554.26 points (-7.18 percent) to close at 7,161.15. This represented the tenth-largest percentage decline in the index since 1915. However, the market was unable to close below the two-hundred-day moving average and closed the year out just below the all-time high. In hindsight, this was just another garden variety correction in the midst of the raging bull market of the 1990s.[7] Much ado about nothing, as

---

7   S. Bavister, "Customer Obsession."

S&P 500, JANUARY 1997 TO DECEMBER 1997

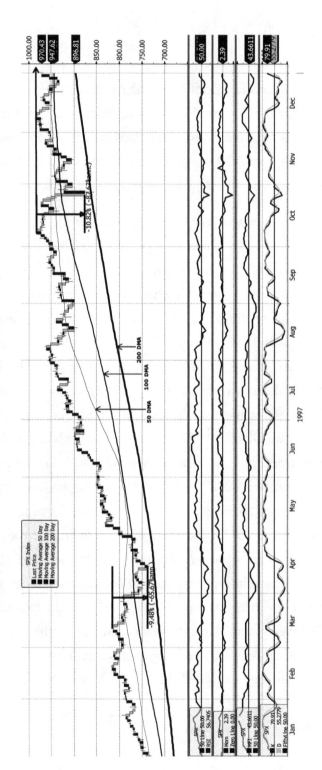

Shakespeare would say. (I could ask why it never feels that way when you're in the middle of one of these corrections, but that is why we are going to build a process to manage around the fear and greed we are all subjected to.)

By the time of the IPO, Amazon had eighty thousand daily visits to its website, and revenues had grown almost 3,000 percent in 1996 alone. Although at $15.75 million, Amazon's revenues still only represented a tiny fraction of the approximately $26 billion in revenues of the worldwide book industry at that time. Today's Amazon looks very little like the company that went public at a price of $18 per share in May 1997. Long before Alexa, Amazon Prime, Streaming, and the Kindle, Amazon's business was much more focused: "Amazon.com is the leading online retailer of books," the company said succinctly in its S-1 IPO filing.

Amazon was the essence of what's called a "hot" IPO, so the public got almost no shares. "Hot" IPOs generally get allocated to the largest institutional clients of the underwriting group, while the small fish (individual investors) generally got scraps, if anything. Trading was wild on the first day. Huge demand pushed the opening trade from $18 to $29¼ (back then they quoted stock prices in fractions and not in decimals), about 50 percent higher than the stated IPO price. The innovative online bookstore hit a high of $30 that first day before settling down to close at $23½. That was more than 30 percent higher than the $18 IPO price set by underwriters just the night before. Even the $18 pre-IPO price had been raised twice before the market opened. Initially, it had been set for a $12 to $14 range, but because of the high demand, it got bumped up to $14, then to $16, before the company's investment bankers settled on the $18 price. The IPO raised $54 million for Amazon, giving the company a market capitalization of $438 million. From there, AMZN followed a fairly typical "hot-IPO" trading pattern of blasting off well above the pre-IPO price, falling back to at or near that price; finding a base; then reasserting a more sustainable organic move up as the core business continued to succeed. As you can see in the following chart, AMZN spent the first few months of trading consolidating the initial excitement around the IPO and then started to rise above that level through the end of the year (all charts throughout the book are adjusted for stock splits).[8]

Once the IPO was complete, the company had to do the hard part—execute organic growth over the long run! Let's dig into what happened and see if we can draw out any lessons to help find other great companies in the future.

Achievements and Milestones

Things were moving quickly for Amazon. A second distribution facility opened in November 1997 in New Castle, Delaware, in order to serve customers on the East Coast. The large, two-hundred-thousand-square-foot facility was just the beginning of what would become a national network designed to efficiently fulfill orders across the United States. In 1998, Amazon expanded into music sales, selling CDs and DVDs, while using a similar strategy

> Once the IPO was complete, the company had to do the hard part—execute organic growth over the long run!

to its industry-disrupting bookselling approach. The music division launched with 125,000 titles, substantially more than the average physical music store could carry. And music lovers could listen to song

---

8   A. Wilhelm, "A Look Back in IPO: Amazon's 1997 Move," *TechCrunch*, accessed March 10, 2023, https://techcrunch.com/2017/06/28/a-look-back-at-amazons-1997-ipo/.

AMZN, MAY 1997 TO DECEMBER 1997

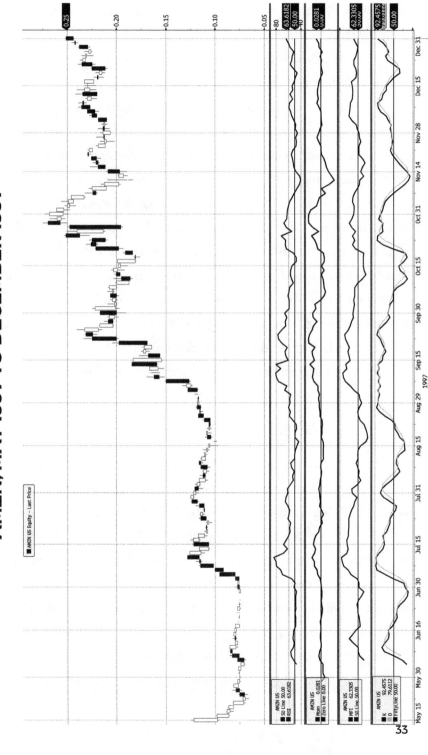

clips in the comfort of their own homes. In 1999, Amazon secured the "1-Click" patent, creating the ability to purchase an item online with the click of a mouse.

Then the company created its third-party seller marketplace, which would transform the company into the Amazon that we know today. Originally conceived as a way for shoppers to find rare and collectible books and other specialty items, Amazon allowed third-party sellers to sell items in what it called zShops (now known as the Marketplace), and it put in place the infrastructure to evolve from a "bookseller" to an "everything seller." Transaction volume increased dramatically, with over one-quarter of a million customers using the new service in the first few months. By the end of 1999, Jeff Bezos had been named *TIME* magazine's Person of the Year and "the king of cybercommerce." At age thirty-five, he was the youngest recipient of the honor. Things were going as good as they could possibly go. But underneath the surface, the stock market had turned into a mania that was about to burst and create serious challenges for Amazon.

Dealing with Adversity

In 1999 and early in the year 2000, the stock market was in the full grip of the dot-com mania. People were quitting their jobs to "day-trade" or joining "investment clubs" by the thousands to get their share of the dot-com riches the market promised. On March 10, 2000, the NASDAQ stock market index (where most of the dot-com names were traded) peaked at 5,132.52. Then, over the next three years, the index traded down by ~90 percent (!). AMZN was no exception. Its stock price ultimately dropped about the same amount. Most of the unprofitable companies from that era were wiped out. Even companies with solid business models were under intense pressure as market prices tumbled, funding sources dried up, and the contagion from the excesses of the dot-com bull market mania bled into the real economy and caused a recession. It would take sixteen years for the NASDAQ index to get back to the highs reached in 2000.

Call it serendipity, great foresight, or just prudent management, but Amazon may have been saved from failure in that moment due to a very timely financing decision. Bezos biographer Brad Stone explained in his 2013 book, *The Everything Store: Jeff Bezos and the Age of Amazon*, how close Amazon came to going bankrupt in the wake of the 2000 market crash:

> *Early in 2000, Warren Jenson, the fiscally conservative new chief financial officer from Delta and, before that, the NBC division of General Electric, decided that the company needed a stronger cash position as a hedge against the possibility that nervous suppliers might ask to be paid more quickly for the products amazon sold. Ruth Porat, co-head of Morgan Stanley's global-technology group, advised him to tap into the European market, and so in February, Amazon sold $672 million in convertible bonds to overseas investors. This time, with the stock market fluctuating and the global economy tipping into recession, the process wasn't as easy as the previous fund-raising had been. Amazon was forced to offer a far more generous 6.9 percent interest rate and flexible conversion terms—another sign that times were changing. The deal was completed just a month before the crash of the stock market, after which it became exceedingly difficult for any company to raise money. Without that cushion, Amazon would almost certainly have faced the prospect of insolvency over the next year.*[9]

---

9   Brad Stone, *The Everything Store: Jeff Bezos and the Age of Amazon* (New York, NY: Back Bay Books, 2014).

If Bezos and his team had waited a few weeks longer to raise those extra funds, people today may have had to lump Amazon in with other dot-com-era failures like Webvan, Kozmo, and Pets.com—big-spending companies that collapsed under their own weight along with the lack of available financing. While Amazon clearly had a stronger business model than most, raising working capital right before the dot-com collapse gave them some much needed breathing room. This episode also drives home the risk surrounding most new companies as they scratch and claw their way to success. If they fail to execute at any point they can be relegated to the dustbin of stock market history.[10]

The company would lay off 15 percent of its workforce during these difficult years for the equity markets and the economy in general, but it was able to continue growing, expanding, and diversifying. Amazon was aggressively reinvesting its revenue and began experimenting with and investing in big new ideas that would pay off later, including selling clothing (2002), Web Hosting Services (2003), Amazon Prime (2005), and Kindle (2007). The company never lost focus during these difficult years in the market.

As of 2022, Amazon has made ninety-eight acquisitions and ninety-five strategic investments over the years. Some worked and others didn't. But many have gone on to transform and secure Amazon's place as a leader in multiple sectors. Amazon acquired the shopping site Zappos in 2009. It acquired robotics company Kiva Systems in 2012 as part of an ongoing effort to make its distribution systems state of the art. In 2017, Amazon acquired Whole Foods markets to strengthen and integrate its food delivery capabilities. And

---

10   T. B. Lee, "The Little-Known Deal That Saved Amazon from the Dot-Com Crash," Vox, accessed March 10, 2023, https://www.vox.com/new-money/2017/4/5/15190650/amazon-jeff-bezos-richest.

outside Amazon, Bezos acquired the *Washington Post* for $250 million in August 2013.

Course Correction and Dealing with Failures

It is important to note that Amazon has experienced a lot of failures throughout its existence. Every company has to have a plan to deal with things that don't work, and Amazon has embraced that process. Of the ninety-eight acquisitions, many completely failed and were ultimately valued at $0. Failure at some level is a part of all businesses, but Amazon has a unique culture of embracing failure to encourage new and innovative ideas. Remember the Amazon Fire Phone? It was launched in June of 2014. It fell flat with consumers and critics and was discontinued about a year later. There was Amazon Auction, Amazon WebPay, Amazon Destinations, Quidsi, Amazon Tickets, Pop-Up Stores, Haven … these and many other business lines were launched with much fanfare and then shuttered. Encouraging innovation and then listening to the market (by shutting down what doesn't work) has been one of Amazon's strengths since its founding. It is this same process that led to successes like Amazon Web Services, Amazon Prime Video, Alexa, the Whole Foods Market acquisition, and many other businesses that actually had legs, worked well, and continue to transform the company to this day.[11]

> Encouraging innovation and then listening to the market (by shutting down what doesn't work) has been one of Amazon's strengths since its founding.

11   D. Green, "Jeff Bezos Famously Embraces Failure: Here Are the Biggest Flops Amazon Has Overcome under His Watch," Business Insider, accessed March 10, 2023, https://www.businessinsider.com/amazon-products-services-failed-discontinued-2019-3.

Right Place, Right Time

Amazon continued to grow and innovate from 2014 through 2020 with offerings like Prime Pantry, Dash Button, and Prime Day, expanding its private label, and then acquiring Whole Foods in 2018. When the world was turned upside-down by COVID-19 in 2020, Amazon was there to help pick up the pieces. Up until the COVID-19 pandemic hit, many people were resistant to using digital platforms. They were used to, and enjoyed, the process of physically going somewhere to do their shopping. That all changed once the world went on lockdown. Millions of people who may have never used platforms like Amazon were forced to order goods online for basic survival.

Amazon's sales and profits surged during the pandemic. Shoppers turned to the online giant to deliver basic necessities to their homes, and by the third quarter of 2020, Amazon said its sales grew 37 percent, compared to the same period the prior year, to $96.1 billion, and profit increased 197 percent to $6.3 billion. Sales at online stores, which include items Amazon sells directly to customers on its website, grew 38 percent in the third quarter. Amazon's sales from third-party sellers increased 55 percent. Revenue from Amazon Web Services, the company's cloud computing business and largest profit driver, grew 29 percent, and its advertising business grew 51 percent.[12]

Preparing for Succession and Continued Growth

With Amazon's place secure as a leader or dominant player in many industries, Jeff Bezos announced plans to step down as Amazon CEO as of July 2021. He established a clear path for a positive succession

---

12   N. Meyersohn, "Amazon Had a Blowout Quarter as People Flocked to Online Shopping," CNN Business, accessed March 10, 2023, https://www.cnn.com/2020/10/29/business/amazon-earnings/index.html.

across all business sectors that Amazon was involved with as he moved to his new role of executive chair. Bezos had been Amazon's CEO since its founding in 1995. He oversaw its growth from an online bookseller into a $1.7 trillion global retail and logistics behemoth, which has also made Bezos into one of the world's richest people.

Let's take a look under the hood to see what we can learn about Amazon's stock price and valuations over the years.

Revenue Growth

Amazon has always been considered a high-growth company or a "growth" stock. Despite not turning a profit for years, it was at the heart of the internet bubble hysteria. You can see the annual earnings progression for AMZN on the following page.

AMZN REVENUE AND NET INCOME HISTORY, 1997 TO 2022 ($ IN MILLIONS)

Fiscal Year	Revenue	Net Income
1997	$ 147.79	$ (31.02)
1998	$ 609.82	$ (124.55)
1999	$ 1,639.84	$ (719.97)
2000	$ 2,761.98	$ (1,411.27)
2001	$ 3,122.43	$ (567.28)
2002	$ 3,932.94	$ (149.13)
2003	$ 5,263.70	$ 35.28
2004	$ 6,921.12	$ 588.45
2005	$ 8,490.00	$ 359.00
2006	$ 10,711.00	$ 190.00
2007	$ 14,835.00	$ 476.00
2008	$ 19,166.00	$ 645.00
2009	$ 24,509.00	$ 902.00
2010	$ 34,204.00	$ 1,152.00
2011	$ 48,077.00	$ 631.00
2012	$ 61,093.00	$ (39.00)
2013	$ 74,452.00	$ 274.00
2014	$ 88,988.00	$ (241.00)
2015	$ 107,006.00	$ 596.00
2016	$ 135,987.00	$ 2,371.00
2017	$ 177,866.00	$ 3,033.00
2018	$ 232,887.00	$ 10,073.00
2019	$ 280,522.00	$ 11,588.00
2020	$ 386,064.00	$ 21,331.00
2021	$ 469,822.00	$ 33,364.00
2022	$ 513,983.00	$ (2,722.00)

Source: Bloomberg Finance L.P.

Revenues were climbing fast from the beginning but as the company was plowing money into its growth, there were no net profits.

So how do we objectively determine what to do? There are lots of companies that generated large and growing revenues but ultimately never made any money, so we can't just rely on revenues alone. After all, making net profits is what investing or running a business is all about. It is easy to look at earnings from a very simplistic standpoint: If the net earnings are up, then that is good, and vice versa. Sadly, it is not anywhere close to that simple. And as Benjamin Graham said, "In the short run, the market is a voting machine but in the long run it is a weighing machine."[13] The market "weighs" the actual net earnings and values them as the return on your investment in the stock. However, in the short term (and sometimes the short term lasts for years), the market will act as a voting machine, frequently looking at other metrics that might only be in favor for a period of time. In the dot-com era, one of those wonky metrics was called "eyeballs," or how many people were visiting a website. The theory of this particular metric was that if a website had a lot of traffic, it would eventually be able to make money. In other words, to understand what is considered a "good" earnings report at any time in history, there is only one metric to consider, and that is price. If the price moved up substantially immediately after the earnings were reported, it is clear that the earnings report was viewed as a positive surprise and very good news. Alternately, a big drop meant that the earnings report was a negative surprise and constituted bad news.[14]

---

13   "The Timeless Parable of Mr. Market," fs.blog, October 28, 2019, https://fs.blog/mr-market/#:~:text=As%20Ben%20said%3A%20%E2%80%9CIn%20the,increasing%20at%20a%20satisfactory%20rate.

14   Informit, accessed March 10, 2023, https://www.informit.com/articles/article.aspx?p=30351&seqNum=2.

Applying the Three-Step Process

The early go-go days of the dot-com bubble, the eventual market blowup that followed, and all the positive and negative news reports about Amazon over the years would have made the average investor's head spin. But what happens when we take a look at Amazon over the years through the prism of an objective hypothetical three-step process that incorporates fundamentals, technicals, and risk management based on price movement?

STEP 1: FUNDAMENTAL ANALYSIS/EARNINGS

The following quarterly earnings table goes back to the IPO, and the darker shaded boxes indicate large price movements in reaction to the earnings announcement. For the purposes of creating a hypothetical process around which to manage high-risk stocks (like Amazon was at the beginning), we will consider a positive "surprise" announcement if the stock moved up immediately after the announcement by more than 10 percent and code it with a black box. A 10 percent drop based on a negative surprise is coded a dark gray box. We will look more carefully into the quarterly earnings and develop a hypothetical scoring approach later to see if that can help us manage around all the volatility.

AMZN FISCAL YEAR QUARTERLY EARNINGS HISTORY, 1997 TO 2022 (PER SHARE)

Fiscal Year	Q1	Q2	Q3	Q4	Annual
1997	-$0.0007	-$0.0013	-$0.0017	-$0.0020	-$0.0057
1998	-$0.0017	-$0.0037	-$0.0075	-$0.0075	-$0.0204
1999	-$0.0100	-$0.0215	-$0.0295	-$0.0480	-$0.1090
2000	-$0.0450	-$0.0455	-$0.0340	-$0.0765	-$0.2010
2001	-$0.0330	-$0.0235	-$0.0230	$0.0005	-$0.0790
2002	-$0.0030	-$0.0125	-$0.0045	$0.0005	-$0.0195
2003	-$0.0015	-$0.0055	$0.0020	$0.0085	$0.0035
2004	$0.0130	$0.0090	$0.0065	$0.0410	$0.0695
2005	$0.0090	$0.0060	$0.0035	$0.0235	$0.0420
2006	$0.0060	$0.0025	$0.0025	$0.0115	$0.0225
2007	$0.0130	$0.0095	$0.0095	$0.0240	$0.0560
2008	$0.0170	$0.0185	$0.0135	$0.0260	$0.0750
2009	$0.0205	$0.0160	$0.0225	$0.0425	$0.1015
2010	$0.0330	$0.0225	$0.0255	$0.0455	$0.1265
2011	$0.0220	$0.0205	$0.0070	$0.0190	$0.0685
2012	$0.0140	$0.0005	-$0.0300	$0.0105	-$0.0050
2013	$0.0090	-$0.0010	-$0.0045	$0.0255	$0.0290
2014	$0.0115	-$0.0135	-$0.0475	$0.0225	-$0.0270
2015	-$0.0060	$0.0095	$0.0085	$0.0500	$0.0620
2016	$0.0535	$0.0890	$0.0260	$0.0769	$0.2454
2017	$0.0740	$0.0200	$0.0260	$0.1875	$0.3075
2018	$0.1635	$0.2535	$0.2875	$0.3020	$1.0065
2019	$0.3545	$0.2610	$0.2115	$0.3235	$1.1505
2020	$0.2505	$0.5150	$0.6185	$0.7045	$2.0885
2021	$0.7895	$0.7560	$0.3060	$1.3875	$3.2390
2022	-$0.3780	-$0.2000	$0.2800	$0.0300	-$0.2680
Key:	Positive	Negative			

Source: Bloomberg Finance L.P.

STEP 2: TECHNICAL ANALYSIS

Before we dive into technical analysis relative to AMZN, I want to discuss the relevance of time frames when using technical analysis. You can perform the same technical analytics in almost any time frame: minute segments, five-minute segments, hourly, daily, weekly, monthly, and so on. Given that in this book we are focusing on the characteristics of long-term winners and how to manage them, it makes the most sense to look at longer-term time frames, like monthly periods, which capture all the trading activity within that frame in a single data point. Looking at all the trading activity for an entire month is a very powerful indicator. Over the course of a month, everyone has had a chance to vote by their actions, and so the results tend to have more weight. Shorter time frames, like one-minute bars, are only useful for things like day trading and often contain a lot of useless noise when it comes to making longer-term decisions. The other benefit of using monthly bars is that it allows you to *calm down* and helps remove some of the emotion from investing. Remember, when it comes to investing, emotional responses are your sworn enemy. That's why having an investment process, especially around the speculative portion of your portfolio, is so important.

We are going to look specifically at five technical elements of AMZN stock over the years, concentrating on monthly data. This next part is going to get a little wonky, but bear with me, because you will see how these five elements may work together and can help you become a better investor. Feel free to skim the definitions since many of these indicators come preprogrammed into most trading systems. My final caveat: I have added my own mathematical "tweaks" over the years to some of the standard metrics, but the general definitions that follow here still apply.

Here are the five technical metrics we will be using (OK, six if you include price):

- **Price.** We will be using the monthly bar charts of the price action of AMZN since the IPO in 1997.

- **The twenty-one-period monthly exponential moving average (EMA).** What the heck is this? You've no doubt heard of the fifty-day, one-hundred-day, and two-hundred-day moving averages. But the twenty-one-period exponential moving average has some very interesting characteristics, one of which is that healthy stocks tend to stay above it.

  Investopedia defines the following formula used to calculate the current EMA:

  EMA = Closing price x multiplier + EMA (previous day) x (1-multiplier)[15]

  The EMA gives a higher weight to recent prices, while the SMA (simple moving average) assigns equal weight to all values. The weighting given to the most recent price is greater for a shorter-period EMA than for a longer-period EMA. For example, an 18.18 percent multiplier is applied to the most recent price data for a ten-period EMA, while the weight is only 9.52 percent for a twenty-period EMA.

  Yuck! But let's not get bogged down in formulas. I will display the indicator on a chart as we move forward, and I promise it will make more sense. But here is the standard formula to determine the twenty-one-period exponential moving average.

---

15   James Chen, "What Is EMA? How to Use Exponential Moving Average with Formula," Investopedia.com, March 31, 2023, https://www.investopedia.com/terms/e/ema.asp.

Formula for Exponential Moving Average (EMA)

$$EMA_{Today} = \left(Value_{Today} * \left(\frac{Smoothing}{1 + Days} \right) \right)$$

$$+ \; EMA_{Yesterday} * \left(1 - \left(\frac{Smoothing}{1 + Days} \right) \right)$$

where: EMA = Exponential Moving Average

- **Monthly Relative Strength Index (RSI).** Again, according to Investopedia, the relative strength index (RSI) is a momentum indicator that measures the magnitude of recent price changes to evaluate overbought or oversold conditions in the price of a stock or other asset. The RSI is displayed as an oscillator (a line graph that moves between two extremes) and can have a reading from 0 to 100. The indicator was originally developed by J. Welles Wilder Jr. and introduced in his seminal 1978 book, *New Concepts in Technical Trading Systems*. It reflects how a stock is doing relative to the overall market. (See Appendix A for the standard RSI formula.)

- **Momentum.** Momentum is the rate of acceleration of a security's price—that is, the speed at which the price is changing. Market momentum refers to the aggregate rate of acceleration for the broader market as a whole. (See Appendix B for the standard momentum formula.)

- **Money flows.** The money flow index (MFI) is a technical oscillator that uses price and volume data for identifying overbought or oversold signals in an asset. It can also be used to spot divergences that warn of a trend change in price. The oscillator moves between 0 and 100.

    Unlike conventional oscillators such as the relative strength index (RSI), the money flow index incorporates both price and volume data, as opposed to just price. For this reason, some analysts call MFI the volume-weighted RSI. After all, knowing what the volume is can be a huge factor, and this indicator helps capture it. (See Appendix C for the standard money flow index formula.)

- **Stochastics.** The word "stochastic" indicates some sort of random process. This randomness can be measured probabilistically but cannot be known completely in advance. Adding randomness, or "noise," to understanding the movement of stock prices was seen as a major innovation.

  The stochastic oscillator was developed in the late 1950s by George Lane and presents the location of the closing price of a stock in relation to the high and low range of the price of a stock over a period of time, typically a fourteen-day period. Over the course of numerous interviews, Lane said that the stochastic oscillator does not follow price or volume or anything similar. He indicated that the oscillator follows the speed or momentum of price.

  Lane also revealed in interviews that, as a rule, the momentum or speed of the price of a stock changes before the price itself changes. In this way, the stochastic oscillator can be used to foreshadow reversals when the indicator reveals bullish or bearish divergences.

  There are two components to stochastics generally: the "fast," %K, and the "slow," %D. I use the stochastics differently than most technicians and focus primarily on the fast line (K) (you will see how it is used in the charts that follow). (See Appendix D for the stochastic momentum oscillator formula.)

Thanks for hanging in there with all this detail! Now let's see the indicators in action! (I promise this will be a lot more fun.)

A quick note about how charts are displayed. We will be looking at companies that spanned decades, and many split their stock multiple times over their history. For the sake of consistency, we will be displaying all stock charts using their split-adjusted prices as of December 31, 2022.

On page 49 is the stock price chart for AMZN from the IPO in June 1997 to 2006. Now that we've identified the technical metrics we will be focusing on, I have labeled them on this first chart for future reference throughout the book. This time period also captures the dot-com bubble, tech wreck, and recovery. You can see the price initially shot out of a cannon and traded as high as a split-adjusted +$100 in just a few short years during the dot-com bubble and right before the bust. Following this initial run, AMZN dropped as much as 90 percent and had not recovered even one-half of its all-time high as of 2007.

Let's look at some of the technical signals to see if we could have had a smoother investment experience.[16] The solid black line that you see in the price chart is the twenty-one-period exponential moving average (EMA). Do you notice anything interesting about it? First, the stock never traded below it until it finally broke down in May of 2000 (gray down arrow), almost three full years after it went public. Then it stayed below the EMA until October 2002, more than two full years later. And when it crossed back up (dark up arrow), it was at a much lower price than when it crossed down. That's a pretty interesting fact. Actually, you'll notice very similar activity around

---

16   Please note that the arrows illustrating possible technical signals on this chart and all the charts in this book are for illustration purposes only and will not precisely reflect other calculations for the hypothetical algorithm contained in this book.

AMZN, MAY 1997 TO DECEMBER 2006

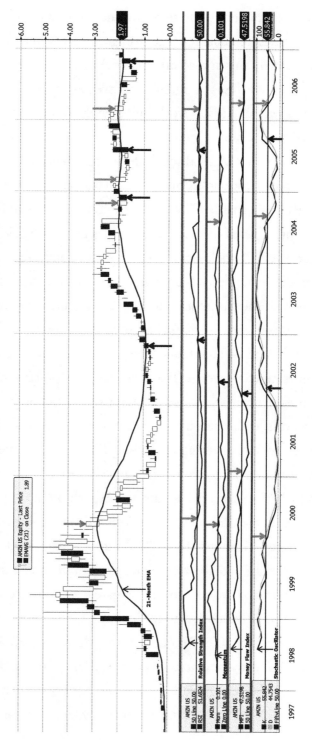

relative strength (RSI), momentum, money flows, and stochastics (for stochastics, remember we are using the fast K line illustrated by the black line in this and all other charts). As each of these technical metrics crossed below the midline, it served as a warning that maybe all was not well for AMZN stock, and then the reverse when they each recovered one by one.

The high for AMZN through the year 2000 was ~$100 (adjusted for subsequent stock splits on the next chart at about $5—the gray horizontal line). That level became technical resistance and was tested in 2007, but it failed there and could not get above the old level from the year 2000. It took until late 2009 to finally break above this long-term resistance level. It ultimately took over nine years for AMZN to get above the high price set in the year 2000—an interesting reminder that even one of the best stocks in history can go nowhere for years.

It took Amazon about nine long years to recover, and many other companies never recovered. That's why having a process around all of your investments makes sense. Without some kind of formal investment process, could you have held on to this huge winner for nine long years without making any money? Very few people have that kind of patience. That's why a mechanical process can be a big help.

Now back to our original timeline. We left off in the period from 2007 to 2012: the Global Financial Crisis (GFC) and recovery. You can see in the next chart that from 2007 through about 2009, the stock churned sideways and also had to grapple with the effects of the GFC. The indicators we have been looking at gave lots of possible sell and buy indications while the stock churned back and forth. But that all changed in about March of 2009. You can see that the stock price went above the EMA. RSI had already turned positive. Money flows and stochastics were next. And then momentum joined the party. All these metrics went positive in 2009 and generally stayed that way for a few years.

AMZN, MAY 1997 TO DECEMBER 2010

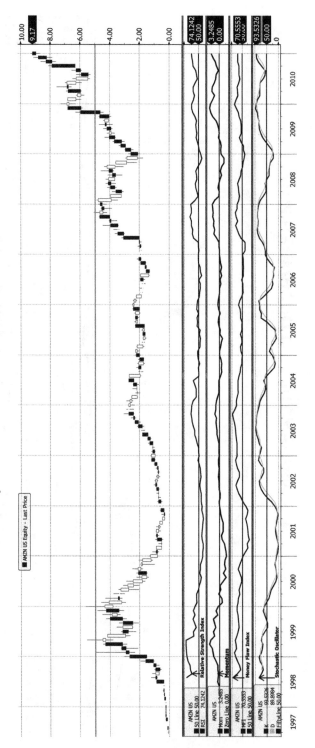

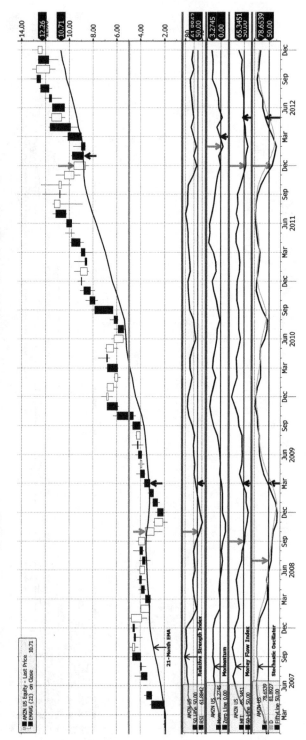

AMZN, JANUARY 2007 TO DECEMBER 2012

Those of you who watched TV in the 1990s will remember that Ron Popeil used to sell an electric oven on TV with the tagline, "Set it and forget it!" The previous chart reminds me of that after 2009. There were a few close calls on a couple of the metrics in 2011 but without the universality we saw when they all went positive in 2009. The stock went almost straight up.

When we move on to the period from 2013 to 2017, we can see that it was mostly smooth sailing as the stock had another good run. From late 2014 through 2016, the Federal Reserve had attempted to reverse the quantitative easing they had initiated during the GFC. They needed to shrink their balance sheet back down, and it was a huge headwind for the market—with low annualized stock market returns and more volatility than usual during 2014 to 2016. I actually coined the term "investor fatigue" during this period as people grew ever more tired of seeing their accounts go nowhere quarter after quarter. AMZN stock was not immune to the pressures of the overall stock market environment, and in the following chart, you can see some of the metrics triggering red flags or caution signals in this period. But you can also see it was not as unanimous as the signals given back in 2009. After 2015, it was off to the races again, as all the metrics we are looking at stayed well in the positive zone, and the stock skyrocketed about 200 percent.

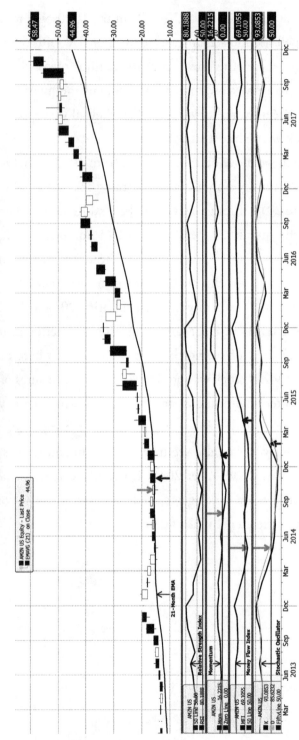

AMZN, JANUARY 2013 TO DECEMBER 2017

This next and final chart, tracking the period from 2018 to 2022, is a bit fascinating, as it captures the massive dislocation that occurred at the beginning of the COVID-19 pandemic and subsequent recovery and the market hangover that followed. The stock market's initial response to the pandemic was one of the most vicious drops the market had seen since the Great Depression in the 1930s, with the Dow Jones Industrial Average (DJIA) dropping almost 35 percent in just a few weeks. And while the overall market was in freefall the monthly technical metrics for AMZN, amazingly, stayed relatively strong!

During that period, fear was at a level ten out of ten. A lot of people were making decisions about selling stocks based on what they were hearing and seeing on TV. While that's understandable, it certainly could have helped to have these technical metrics in front of you to help stay the course and know that it was not a situation where all the metrics were unanimously negative. Of course, as the Federal Reserve and the US government adopted a "whatever it takes" approach to stimulate the economy (and the stock market), AMZN shot straight up over 100 percent from its pandemic low price in a matter of five short months. Technology companies were taking off and companies that offered a digital delivery solution were at the forefront. AMZN was in the right place at the right time. By 2022 it was clear that the inflation genie had been let out of the bottle by the Federal Reserve leaving rates "too low for too long." The postpandemic stimulus hangover had begun, and we started to see the technical metrics deteriorate. Observing the technical metrics since the IPO could have provided valuable insight into a mechanical trading strategy.

It is clear that when the EMA, RSI, momentum, money flows, and stochastics all turn positive or negative, a strong signal is given for

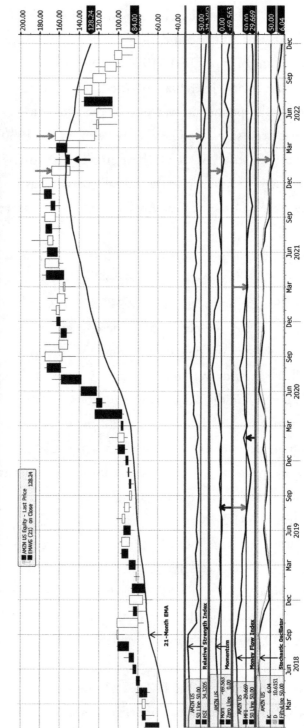

AMZN, JANUARY 2018 TO DECEMBER 2022

the technical trader about the health or lack thereof for the underlying stock. We will do a deeper dive on all this later and flesh out a possible system for managing trading signals (including avoiding false signals).

STEP 3: RISK MANAGEMENT

Since all available information ends up reflected at every moment in the price, it is a valuable tool when managing speculative companies. All stocks move up and down according to the vagaries of everyday information flow. You don't want to be trading in and out of a stock with every positive or negative story. But using the old standard definition of a bear market—when the market trades down 20 percent below the fifty-two-week high—could be helpful in providing some risk management around a position that is dropping before the news becomes public or when the news is more serious than it may seem to the average investor.[17] I can't say I agree with the definition 100 percent, at the very least because it's highly inelegant. But it is a good place to start when it comes to managing the speculative portion of your portfolio. Let's see what happens if we apply this metric to our stocks.

The Fifty-Two-Week High Indicator chart illustrates one possible application of this risk management approach. It looks at the idea of trading out of a stock (or at least to some degree) when the price gets more that 20 percent below the fifty-two-week rolling high (defined by the rolling dotted black lines in the chart above). And then when the stock recaptures that level or lower over time, maybe consider that the coast is clear for trading back in. It has to be a "rolling" fifty-two-week high, because over time that number can move up or down as the stock trades. I've highlighted a possible signal to trade out of at

---

17   "What Next for Travel and Tourism? 2 Experts Explain," World Economic Forum, accessed March 10, 2023, https://www.weforum.org/agenda/2022/06/what-next-for-travel-and-tourism-industry-experts-explain/.

FIFTY-TWO-WEEK HIGH INDICATOR: AMZN

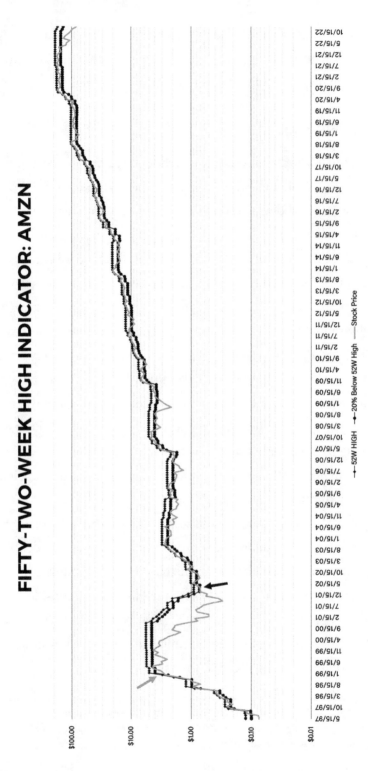

Source: Bloomberg Finance L.P.

least some of the stock for illustration purposes only. The gray down arrow marks a possible sell signal before the dot-com crash. You can see the fifty-two-week high lines started coming down precipitously as the stock dropped the following years as lower prices over many years pulled the "rolling" level down. The black arrow up illustrates when the indicator switched back to a trading buy. There were many other signals given, but I selected these two points to clearly illustrate the indicator at work. A couple of clear takeaways follow:

- The indicator works well in situations where there are large drops that last a long time.

- It does not work so well in sideways or choppy markets (this is true of most longer-term technical indicators too).

We will add this component to our other hypothetical indicators later to see if it can help manage speculative companies (or control risk in those companies that fail to execute).

Applying a Process to Manage AMZN Stock

What if things didn't work out for the company you selected? We are analyzing Amazon here, which we already know was a huge winner. Only with the benefit of hindsight do we "know" the stock should have been held and never have been sold. But nothing is guaranteed for any company you select in the future. So let's apply some rules to the case of AMZN and see if we can smooth out the ride even for one of the most successful investments of the past thirty years.

Here is one possible version of applying components of a three-step process for trading a speculative stock like AMZN since the initial public offering in 1997:

- Analysis of fundamentals

- Positive or negative earnings surprise announcements and market reaction

- Technical analysis

- Twenty-one-period monthly Exponential Moving Average

- Monthly Relative Strength Index

- Monthly momentum

- Monthly money flows

- Monthly stochastics

- Risk management

- 20 percent below the rolling fifty-two-week high price

Let's try assigning a weighting and management system around all of these metrics and see if it can help. Remember, we want to maximize the returns of the best companies, but also have a process in place for when we inevitably pick a stinker (that's a technical term for a bad stock). Let's assign a 10-point system to our metrics, give them different weightings, and see what could have happened using this approach with AMZN stock:

- Movement of stock after earnings announcement: Negative price movement >-10% = (-1), Positive price movement >+10% = (+1)

- Twenty-one-period monthly Exponential Moving Average (EMA): Price closing monthly below = (-2), above = (+2)

- Relative Strength Index (RSI): Monthly close below 50 = (-2), above 50 = (+2)

- Momentum: Monthly close below 50 = (-1), above = (+1)

- Money flows: Monthly close below 50 = (-1), above = (+1)

- Stochastics (K): Monthly close below 50 = (-1), above = (+1)

- Fifty-two-week high indicator: 20% below = (-2), recapturing the < 20% level of the rolling fifty-two-week high = (+2)

The first good thing about this approach is that it will help you get rid of companies that just aren't working on every level. A score of (10) means you are 100 percent in the stock. When -1 shows up, it means you need to sell 10 percent of your holdings. If the negatives add up to -10, then you are out of the stock and in cash (we will also assume a 0 percent return on the cash for simplicity's sake). I am adding a buffer of 5 percent for the RSI, momentum, money flows, and stochastics indicators to minimize false signals. In other words, when dropping, the RSI signal will not trigger until it has a monthly close 5 percent below the 50 indicator line at 47.5. On the way up, it won't trigger a positive change until it hits 52.5. On a long-term winner like AMZN, this approach could have cost you some money to the upside and definitely would have cost some money in taxes. But let's see what would have happened if we applied it theoretically and, of course, in hindsight to the actual management of AMZN over the years. We are going to use the IPO price and assume $1,000 was invested. We will also adjust the table for stock splits.

Below is a sample of the algorithm showing when changes were proposed during 1999 (the end column, "Position Level," shows total holdings for that position based on the algorithm). The entire algorithm is contained in the appendix:

Date	% Below 52W High Score	21-Month EMA Score	RSI Score	Momentum Score	Money Flow Score	Stochastics Score	Earnings Score	Technical Score	Position Level
1/29/99	0	2	2	1	1	1	1	8	80%
2/26/99	0	2	2	1	1	1	1	8	80%
3/31/99	2	2	2	1	1	1	1	10	100%
4/30/99	0	2	2	1	1	1	0	7	70%
5/31/99	0	2	2	1	1	1	0	7	70%
6/30/99	0	2	2	1	1	1	0	7	70%
7/30/99	0	2	2	1	1	1	0	7	70%
8/31/99	0	2	2	1	1	1	0	7	70%
9/30/99	0	2	2	1	1	1	0	7	70%
10/29/99	0	2	2	1	1	1	0	7	70%
11/30/99	0	2	2	1	1	1	0	7	70%
12/31/99	0	2	2	1	1	1	0	7	70%

And on page 63 is a chart comparing this hypothetical algorithm to buying and holding all the way through (the gray line is buy-and-hold, and the black line is our hypothetical algorithm).

Remember, $1,000 invested in Amazon and held until December 31, 2022, grew to about $1,120,000, which is an amazing performance. It's true that most people don't have the patience or the stomach to hold a security over that long a period, but for those who did (and were lucky enough to pick the exact right stock), they were handsomely rewarded. Using our hypothetical scoring approach and adjusting the position size over the years resulted in the original $1,000 potentially growing to about the same level, $1,668,263.15. This hypothetical (and backward looking only) algorithm approach ended up resulting in superior potential performance over the selected time frame (not factoring in taxes for taxable accounts or money market interest earned while out of the stock as will be the case for all illustrations of the hypothetical algorithm throughout this book). This approach also significantly decreased the volatility for the investor who managed around the position and the many difficult events and bad

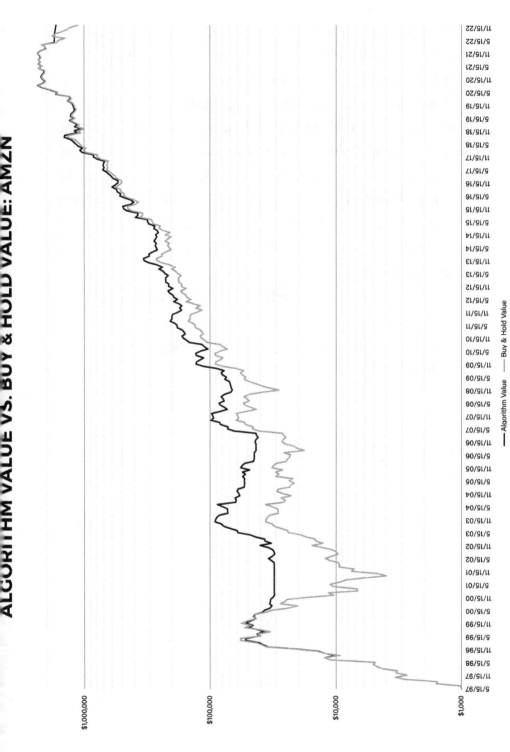

ALGORITHM VALUE VS. BUY & HOLD VALUE: AMZN

—— Algorithm Value   —— Buy & Hold Value

$1,000,000
$100,000
$10,000
$1,000

5/15/97
11/15/97
5/15/98
11/15/98
5/15/99
11/15/99
5/15/00
11/15/00
5/15/01
11/15/01
5/15/02
11/15/02
5/15/03
11/15/03
5/15/04
11/15/04
5/15/05
11/15/05
5/15/06
11/15/06
5/15/07
11/15/07
5/15/08
11/15/08
5/15/09
11/15/09
5/15/10
11/15/10
5/15/11
11/15/11
5/15/12
11/15/12
5/15/13
11/15/13
5/15/14
11/15/14
5/15/15
11/15/15
5/15/16
11/15/16
5/15/17
11/15/17
5/15/18
11/15/18
5/15/19
11/15/19
5/15/20
11/15/20
5/15/21
11/15/21
5/15/22
11/15/22

markets over the decades since Amazon stock went public (including the nine years after the dot-com bust, when the stock went nowhere). Our hypothetical approach also gives the investor looking for the next great winner a process for weeding out the bad picks. In other words, not every stock you think will be the next great winner will actually accomplish that feat, so you should consider having a plan in place for when that occurs too. In the case of Amazon, you could have hypothetically had your cake and eaten it too—superior pretax returns and much less volatility, even with one of the best performing stocks of all time for the buy-and-hold investor (at least through the end of 2022).

With our process established, let's move to the next case study— another household name and dominant worldwide brand that started out small, with just two young friends tinkering with computer programming.

CHAPTER THREE

MICROSOFT

A total of $1,000 invested in MSFT stock the day it came public March 3, 1986, at the IPO price of $21 was worth $3,288,960 on December 31, 2022, for a compounded return of 328,796 percent.

Success is a lousy teacher. It seduces smart people into thinking they can't lose.

—BILL GATES

Timeline from Formation through Initial Public Offering

- 1975: Microsoft is founded.

- 1979: Microsoft moves from Albuquerque, New Mexico, to Bellevue, Washington.

- 1981: Microsoft incorporates.

- 1981: IBM introduces its personal computer with Microsoft's sixteen-bit operating system, MS-DOS 1.0.

- 1986: Microsoft moves to corporate campus in Redmond, Washington.

- 1986: Microsoft stock goes public at $21 per share on March 3, 1986.

Origin Story

Bill Gates has evolved into an almost legendary figure in the computer industry. He is considered central to bringing personal computing into the mainstream. He is also well known to have a giant intellect (I saw a documentary on him in which he said he read about one book per week and took additional steps to absorb and retain the information).

Gates was born in Seattle, Washington, on October 28, 1955, to a successful family that also encouraged and rewarded competition. Gates showed early signs of competitiveness when he coordinated family athletic games at the family's summer house on Puget Sound. He also loved playing board games (Risk was his favorite, along with Monopoly).[18] He was always a very gifted student and wrote his first computer program at the age of thirteen. Remember, this was 1968, when you turned your TV channel by getting up off the couch and rotating the dial among a handful of channels—ten or twelve, if you were lucky. And if you wanted to create a bit of formal correspondence, it had to be typed by hitting metal keys on a typewriter that inked individual letters onto the page and would often get jammed. It was truly a different world, and Gates was on the cutting edge of a future he would help design.

---

18   Biography.com, accessed March 11, 2023. https://www.biography.com/business-figure/bill-gates.

Along with his friend Paul Allen and some other early programming enthusiasts, Gates formed the Lakeside Prep Programmers Club (named after the school they both attended). They took on whatever projects both interested them and would allow them to earn some money, or at least allow them some free time using computer systems, which were then very rare. To say that Bill Gates was a prodigy might be something of an understatement. At seventeen, Gates and Paul Allen formed a company called Traf-O-Data to make traffic counters based on the Intel 8008 processor. He also served as a congressional page in the House of Representatives in his spare time. He was a National Merit Scholar when he graduated from Lakeside Prep School in 1973.[19] He scored an almost perfect 1590 out of 1600 on the Scholastic Aptitude Tests (SAT) and enrolled at Harvard College that fall. While he initially enrolled as a prelaw major, he also studied mathematics and took graduate-level computer science courses. It's at Harvard where he met fellow student Steve Ballmer,

> To say that Bill Gates was a prodigy might be something of an understatement.

who, many years later, would rise to the CEO position at Microsoft. Gates eventually left Harvard after two years, while Ballmer stayed and graduated magna cum laude.[20]

State of the Industry

Prior to 1977, there was no such thing as a "personal computer" (PC). Computing was almost exclusively performed by large corporations or

---

19 "Bill & Melinda Gates Foundation." Wikipedia. Wikimedia Foundation, accessed March 8, 2023. https://en.wikipedia.org/wiki/Bill_%26_Melinda_Gates_Foundation.

20 "Microsoft Founded—History," accessed March 11, 2023, https://www.history.com/this-day-in-history/microsoft-founded.

academic institutions in very large rooms, and computers were housed on racks that were built about two feet above floor level to accommodate the massive cooling systems that early computers required to run properly. I learned BASIC programming in one of these "computer rooms" in 1983 while at UCLA. International Business Machines (IBM) dominated the computer industry at that point. And it made sense that a huge company like IBM was the dominant player. Until then, computing required massive up-front and ongoing investments in equipment and personnel, so it was primarily suited to larger enterprises. But that all changed one fateful day in April 1977 at the first West Coast Computer Faire. This is the now-famous event where Steve Jobs introduced the Apple II and Commodore unveiled its PET computer. Both machines were designed for the public. The personal computer revolution had begun in earnest.

By 1975, Bill Gates was at Harvard, and Paul Allen (who had dropped out of Washington State University after two years—and had a perfect 1600 SAT score, by the way) was a programmer at Honeywell in Boston. As legend goes, they were inspired by the January 1975 issue of *Popular Electronics* magazine, which featured Micro Instrumentation and Telemetry Systems (MITS) Altair 8800 microcomputer. Allen convinced Gates that they could program a BASIC interpreter for the system. Gates then called MITS and told them that he had a working BASIC interpreter, even though the pair did not yet have a working prototype. MITS liked the idea and requested to see a demonstration. Allen and Gates worked furiously over the next month and were able to demonstrate a working interpreter to MITS in March 1975. MITS agreed to distribute it, so Allen left Honeywell to join MITS at its headquarters in Albuquerque, New Mexico, and by November of that year, Gates left Harvard to join Allen. Allen and Gates initially named their partnership Micro-soft. Micro-soft became independent of MITS and officially registered the name "Microsoft" with the Secretary of the State of New Mexico on November 26, 1976. Microsoft expanded by developing programming language software for various systems and had revenues of over $1 million by 1978. The company moved its headquarters from Albuquerque to Bellevue, Washington, on January 1, 1979.

By 1980, it was clear to everyone that the personal computer was here to stay. More and more companies wanted in on this fast-growing market sector. IBM was not about to let this sector be dominated by anyone else, so they made a plan. Getting projects to market at a large, bureaucratic company like IBM could, and had, taken years in the past. That was OK in the large-enterprise computer space they had dominated but not in the super-fast-growing personal computer market. They could not afford to go slowly or risk being permanently shut out of the market, so they developed a plan to work outside of IBM's normal development channels to deliver a working PC to the market in one year or less. The plan called for outsourcing existing hardware components and, critically, outsourcing the operating software.

Bill Gates met with IBM in July 1980, as Microsoft was one of two teams being seriously considered to provide the operating software for the new IBM PC. Microsoft ended up getting the contract after the other competitor bungled the negotiations by having someone else vet the IBM team rather than meeting directly with them himself from the beginning. Microsoft had just landed the contract that would set the course for the rest of the corporation's history.[21]

---

21   "This Man Should Have Been Bill Gates. He Missed One Meeting and It Cost Him the Largest Fortune in the World," Celebrity Net Worth, March 7, 2018, https://www.celebritynetworth.com/articles/entertainment-articles/man-bill-gates-missed-one-meeting-cost-largest-fortune-world/.

IBM made the decision to entrust Microsoft with sole responsibility for making the operating system work as well as to allow Microsoft to retain all rights to that operating system. It was a controversial decision within IBM but, in the interest of time, IBM leadership allowed it to proceed. It is unlikely that even IBM understood the size that the PC market would eventually develop into. With no time to write the code for a new operating system from scratch, Microsoft went out and bought the rights to QDOS for $75,000 with the intention of modifying and building on its framework. This eventually would become MS-DOS and put Microsoft in a position to license the dominant operating system for much of the personal computing world as the industry exploded.

IBM Personal Computer
Source: Rama & Musée Bolo, CC BY-SA 2.0 FR <https://creativecommons.org/licenses/by-sa/2.0/fr/deed.en>, via Wikimedia Commons

The first shipments of the new IBM PC occurred in October 1981, and in its first year, the IBM PC generated $1 billion in revenue, far exceeding company projections. The IBM PC immediately dominated the market and set the standard for other competitors who began to enter the fray. That meant that Microsoft's operating system was now the standard for almost the entire PC industry and companies looking to compete with the IBM PC needed to license their software directly through Microsoft. One significant and noteworthy exception was Apple Computers, which made the decision to use its own proprietary operating system, or what is called closed-source, as opposed to the open-source MS-DOS. Microsoft was now in a position to print money by licensing out their operating system across the fast-growing PC industry. The company continued to grow on all fronts.

In 1983, Microsoft sold its first mouse and released the Microsoft Word program that is now ubiquitous. Then in 1985, it started selling a spreadsheet program called Microsoft Excel. Microsoft Word and Excel were called "killer apps" at the time. Killer apps were computer programs, or applications, that changed the game and made other approaches obsolete. There were complicated mathematical functions you could perform quickly on an Excel spreadsheet that were almost impossible to accomplish efficiently without it. And Microsoft Word transformed document production. Anyone want to type a paper on a typewriter anymore? I used to do it and it was not fun (especially when I mistyped something). Microsoft did not invent either of these applications, by the way. VisiCalc, for the Apple II computer, was launched in 1979 and is considered the first "killer app." People would buy Apple computers just to run the VisiCalc spreadsheet program. Lotus 1-2-3 was hugely popular at the time and ran well on the IBM PC. When Lotus 1-2-3 was launched in early 1983, it quickly overtook VisiCalc. Microsoft Excel didn't launch until 1985, but it overtook the others and then became even more dominant once Microsoft bundled it with Word and other office efficiency programs in late 1990.[22]

IBM poured millions of dollars into a collaboration with Microsoft beginning in 1985 to develop OS/2. IBM wanted to create a protected operating system that it controlled and that would help the company differentiate its PCs from the army of clones that had flooded the market. The overnight success of the IBM PC had also led IBM to abandon the strike team culture that it initially used to storm the PC market in favor of the more bureaucratic, institutional approach it applied to the rest of its business. IBM went back to its stodgy old management playbook, but Microsoft and most of the new companies in the PC industry operated from a much nimbler entrepreneurial culture. Cultural and bureaucratic differences continued to grow over the years between IBM and Microsoft. Meanwhile, Microsoft was also developing Windows to compete with the graphical user interface (GUI) that Apple had pioneered. Windows was launched in November 1985 and would go on to become the PC industry standard.[23]

---

22   "What Is the Difference between Open Source and Closed Source?," Linode Guides & Tutorials, Linode, accessed March 9, 2023, https://www.linode.com/docs/guides/open-source-vs-closed-source/.

23   Jeremy Reimer, "Half an Operating System: The Triumph and Tragedy of OS/2," Ars Technica, November 29, 2019, https://arstechnica.com/information-technology/2019/11/half-an-operating-system-the-triumph-and-tragedy-of-os2/.

Going Public

On April 26, 1986, the Soviet nuclear reactor at Chernobyl exploded, causing the release of radioactive material across much of Europe. That same year, the space shuttle Challenger disintegrated seventy-three seconds after launching, killing all seven astronauts on board. The Oprah Winfrey Show debuted nationally. The average price of a new car was $9,255.

Overall stock market conditions in 1986 were favorable as you can see on the next page. It was an interesting year for the stock market in that almost all of the returns for the year happened in the first half of the year. The S&P 500 went up about 20 percent by the beginning of July 1986 and then churned sideways for the rest of the year. This was a relatively positive and calm market environment for Microsoft to go public in.[24]

Through the 1980s, and after winning the operating system contract for the IBM PC and then licensing out the operating system to competitors making PC clones, Microsoft's revenue grew quickly. The firm booked just under $25 million in revenues in 1982, which roughly doubled in 1983, and then doubled again in 1984. Microsoft's meteoric growth slowed a bit in 1985 when the company reported a still-impressive 40 percent increase in revenues at $140.4 million. By June of 1986, revenues had grown to almost $200 million with net income of $39.3 million.

---

24 Alex Wilhelm, "A Look Back in IPO: Microsoft, the Software Success," *TechCrunch*, August 8, 2017. https://techcrunch.com/2017/08/08/a-look-back-in-ipo-microsoft-the-software-success/. See also: "Microsoft to Make Initial Stock Offer," *New York Times*, February 4, 1986, https://www.nytimes.com/1986/02/04/business/microsoft-to-make-initial-stock-offer.html.

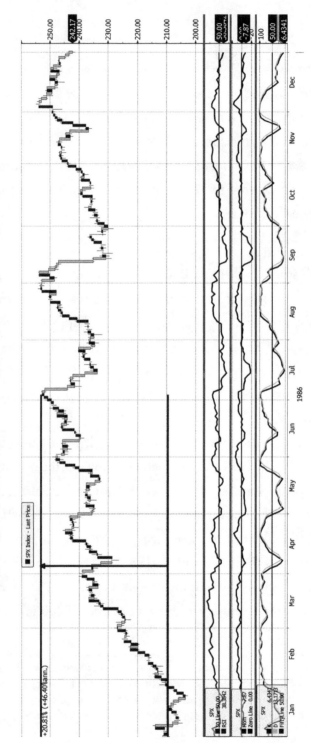

S&P 500, JANUARY 1986 TO DECEMBER 1986

MICROSOFT INCOME STATEMENT IN 1986

Selected Consolidated Financial Information
(In thousands, except per share data)

	Year Ended June 30,				Six Months Ended December 31,	
	1982	1983	1984	1985	1984	1985
					(Unaudited)	
Income Statement Data:						
Net revenues	$ 24,486	$ 50,065	$ 97,479	$ 140,417	$ 62,837	$ 85,050
Income before income taxes	5,595	11,064	28,030	42,843	18,219	29,048
Net income	3,507	6,487	15,880	24,101	9,996	17,118
Net income per share	$ .17	$ .29	$ .69	$ 1.04	$ .43	$ .72
Shares used in computing net income per share	21,240	22,681	22,947	23,260	23,253	23,936

	December 31, 1985	
	Actual	As Adjusted
Balance Sheet Data:	(Unaudited)	
Working Capital	$ 57,574	$ 96,502
Total Assets	94,438	133,366
Total long-term debt	—	—
Stockholders' equity	71,845	110,773

Source: Begin to Invest[25]

This was back in the days when companies that went public were generally already making money, unlike now when unicorns have an IPO years before they have a chance to make money if their

25   "March 13th—This Day in Stock Market History," begintoinvest.com, March 13, 2019, https://www.begintoinvest.com/march-13/#:~:text=March%2013th%2C%20 1986%20%E2%80%93%20Microsoft%20Corp,adjusted%20for%20splits%20 and%20dividends.

business plan actually works. Microsoft also had the advantage of not having large venture capital ownership of the company demanding to cash out and take a profit by going public. Instead, Microsoft had only taken on one investment at just 5 percent of the company. This allowed Gates to maintain control of the process much more than companies with large venture capital partners. Microsoft (MSFT) went public on March 13, 1986, in the middle of the early 1986 20 percent run-up the overall market was experiencing.

The market was strong, and interest in the IPO was high, so the underwriters wanted to price the offering between $17 and $20 per share, a bit higher than the preliminary prospectus, which indicated a possible offer price of $16 to $19 per share. Gates favored an initial price of $16 per share, which would put Microsoft's market value at what he felt was a more reasonable level. But institutional demand was so high that the stock eventually priced at $21 per share.[26]

Trading on the open market on the first day was frenetic. The stock opened at $27.75 per share and zoomed as high as $35.50 before settling back to close at the same level as the first publicly available trade, $27.75, a ~32 percent gain from the IPO price.[27] Microsoft and its shareholders raised $61 million that day for a total market cap of approximately $777 million. Bill Gates ended up with only $1.6 million for the shares he sold, but going public put a market value of $350 million on the 45 percent stake he retained.[28] Microsoft's IPO would make Bill Gates a household name—and ultimately the world's richest person.

---

26 "1986: IPO of the Year Puts Goldman Sachs on the Map with Tech Companies," Goldman Sachs, accessed March 11, 2023, https://www.goldmansachs.com/our-firm/history/moments/1986-microsoft-ipo.html.

27 "Going Public—Microsoft, 1986," Aabri.com, accessed March 11, 2023, https://www.aabri.com/manuscripts/09226.pdf.

28 Alex Wilhelm, "A Look Back in IPO."

MSFT MARCH 1986 TO DECEMBER 1986

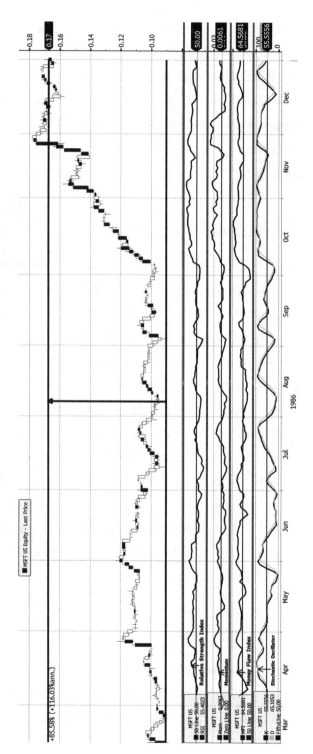

After the initial excitement of the IPO, the stock spent the next six months essentially trading sideways and consolidating the big first-day gains. The share price began its long march higher in October 1986, as investors started paying attention to the ever-improving financial performance of the company. By the end of that year, the stock had risen ~70 percent above the IPO price, and the growth trajectory was just getting going.

Achievements and Milestones

MSFT grew its revenues to $198 billion by the end of its fiscal year in 2022. That represented a long term compounded growth rate of ~16.79 percent from 1990 on. It accomplished this impressive feat through many different economic cycles—both favorable and challenging—and while facing difficult business environments. At the core was a commitment to innovation and execution.

After the IPO, Microsoft continued to assert its dominance in the IBM PC clone market. Sales grew every year as the overall market for computers continued to grow. In 1990, the company expanded its footprint by bundling office applications like Word, Excel, and PowerPoint together into a one-stop-shop office efficiency solution called Microsoft Office. It also continued to improve the Windows operating system platform with Windows 3.0 in May 1990 and Windows 95 in August 1995.

Right Place, Right Time

The early version of the internet was created through government and academic research to connect computer systems at different locations. UCLA and SRI International in Menlo Park were first connected

MICROSOFT REVENUE, BY FISCAL YEAR

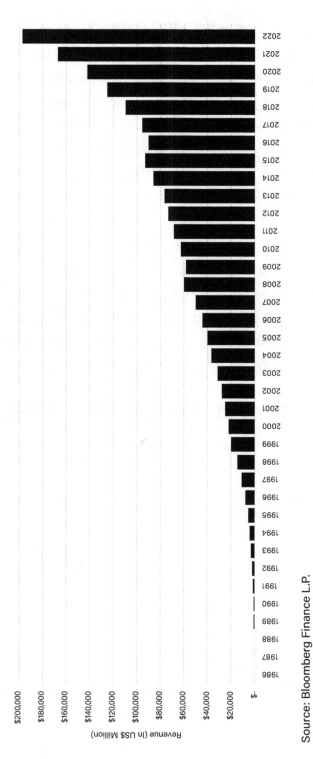

Source: Bloomberg Finance L.P.

through what was called ARPANET in October 1969. Access to ARPANET continued to expand slowly through 1981. By 1982, the Internet Protocol Suite (TCP/IP) was standardized. Incremental improvements to the network continued through the 1980s until it evolved into the early form of the internet that we know today. When the first commercial internet service providers (ISPs) were launched in 1989, the internet became available to businesses and consumers.

Major product innovations or technologically driven consumer products tend to grow along what is called an S-curve. The curve typically illustrates a few years of slow initial growth followed by years of aggressive growth until the product or service becomes ubiquitous, and there is almost universal adoption and therefore slower growth. The television followed this path, as did the automobile, radio, cell phones, and many other revolutionary developments. Here is a representation of the S-curve adoption path of the internet.

INTERNET ADOPTION S-CURVE

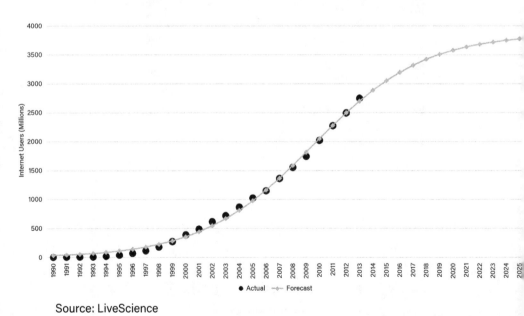

Source: LiveScience

In the early 1990s, when Microsoft dominated the IBM-PC clone market and had successfully branched out into other operating systems like Windows NT and software products like Microsoft Office, they were not focused on the growth potential associated with consumer and business adoption of the internet. Netscape is generally considered the first company to target the business opportunities associated with the early internet. Netscape's Jim Clark and Marc Andreessen launched the first browser for the internet in October 1994, and within four months, it had captured 75 percent of the browser market. Gates and Microsoft quickly realized that they were missing the boat by not having exposure to the new and fast-growing internet, so Microsoft launched Internet Explorer almost a year later, in August 1995. But Microsoft made Internet Explorer available free of charge and leveraged its dominant position in the PC market by lobbying computer makers and ISPs to distribute Internet Explorer exclusively. By contrast, Netscape was not free to the public until 1998.

Microsoft eventually bundled Internet Explorer into their operating system, ensuring that the majority of consumers would be using their service exclusively. This was truly a competition-crushing approach. Internet Explorer eventually became the most widely used web browser, attaining a peak of about 95 percent market share by 2003. Microsoft was flexing its muscles as the dominant player in the PC world and the competition decided to push back.[29]

Dealing with Adversity

It was 1992 when the Federal Trade Commission began looking at Microsoft potentially asserting monopolistic control over the PC

---

29   Matt Blitz, "Later, Navigator: How Netscape Navigator Won and Then Lost the World Wide Web," *Popular Mechanics*, April 4, 2019. https://www.popularmechanics.com/culture/web/a27033147/netscape-navigator-history/.

operating system market. These early inquiries did not amount to much of a problem for Microsoft, but as time went on and Microsoft's dominance across multiple sectors continued to grow, so, too, did the government's interest in potential antitrust violations by Microsoft. Then in 1996, Netscape accused Microsoft of violating the US Justice Department's 1994 antitrust consent decree. The DOJ consent decree mandated that Microsoft not use its dominance in the operating system market to hinder competition and consumer choice.

In Netscape's letter to the DOJ, it charged that Microsoft did the following:

- Made PC manufacturers pay $3 extra for each personal computer using Windows 95 if those manufacturers wanted both Microsoft's Internet Explorer and Netscape Navigator included. Netscape estimated that Microsoft sold forty million copies of Windows 95 in the product's first year, meaning that manufacturers paid an extra $120 million.

- Offered corporate customers free operating system upgrades and consulting. Netscape also alleged that Microsoft paid international telecommunications customers $5 for every Netscape Navigator browser that they dropped and replaced with Internet Explorer.

- Offered to buy out contracts that large internet service providers had with Netscape. Netscape alleged that Microsoft offered $400,000 if the providers promised not to sell Netscape or other internet software.[30]

These aggressive business tactics, along with years of monopolistic accusations, persuaded the Justice Department to reopen a broad

---

30 "Netscape: Microsoft Breaking Law," CNNMoney, Cable News Network, accessed March 11, 2023, https://money.cnn.com/1996/08/20/technology/netscape/.

investigation of Microsoft that resulted in antitrust charges being filed against the company in May 1998. The DOJ and the attorneys general of twenty different states were involved in determining whether the company's bundling of additional programs into its operating system constituted monopolistic actions.[31] Microsoft had an aggressive competition-based internal culture and may have failed to realize the implications of an all-out war with the US government.

Microsoft's culture of competitiveness was not well suited to dealing with an omnipowerful political adversary. Microsoft, and Gates specifically, approached the concept of government regulation and antitrust consideration with disdain. Gates had cut his teeth on the razor's edge of daily competition within the fast-moving PC world. His competitiveness and aggressiveness in the marketplace had been handsomely rewarded, ultimately making him the world's richest person by the age of thirty-nine. He expected to apply the same approach to fighting the government. But this was a completely different venue that required a dramatically different approach.

Gates's decision to take on the government is generally considered to have failed spectacularly. As one commentator observed,

> *During three days of intense questioning, Gates often feigned ignorance of his own company's policies and actions. He parsed everyday words or phrases such as "concern," "support," and "piss on." Gates seemed to use the strategy to evade tough questions about whether his company abused its entrenched Windows franchise to kill off emerging competitors, such as Navigator and Java. To the surprise of his many attorneys and image*

---

31   Andrew Beattie, "Why Did Microsoft Face Antitrust Charges in 1998?," Investopedia, December 19, 2022, https://www.investopedia.com/ask/answers/08/microsoft-antitrust.asp.

handlers, Gates came off as argumentative, petty, and someone badly losing ground to a more formidable rival.[32]

The trial lasted thirty months. In the end, Microsoft was found in violation of the Sherman Antitrust Act and ordered to break up the company. In 2001, an appeals court overturned the order to break up the company but still found Microsoft guilty of trying to maintain an illegal monopoly. This result then led to similar actions in the European Union. All of it collectively resulted in billions of dollars of fines and years of serious distractions to running the company.

Preparing for Succession and Continued Growth

Gates was Microsoft CEO until 2000, chief software architect until 2006, and chairman until 2014. He remained on the board until March of 2020, when he resigned to focus on philanthropy and serve as advisor to CEO Satya Nadella.

Steve Ballmer, whom Gates had met while at Harvard, joined Microsoft in 1980, eventually became president in 1998 and replaced Gates as CEO on January 13, 2000. On February 4, 2014, Ballmer retired as CEO and was replaced by Satya Nadella. Under Nadella's leadership, Microsoft has continued to grow and dominate the various sectors in which it operates, including a newer growth area for the company: cloud services.

---

32   Dan Goodin, "Revisiting the Spectacular Failure That Was the Bill Gates Deposition," Ars Technica, September 10, 2020, https://arstechnica.com/tech-policy/2020/09/revisiting-the-spectacular-failure-that-was-the-bill-gates-deposition/.

Course Correction and Dealing with Failures

At an event in October 2020, Bill Gates remarked, "Everybody saw what I did and knows better now." Taking on the US government as though it were just another competitor had been a long and costly strategic mistake. But while Gates's approach to working with the government evolved after this significant failure, the Microsoft culture of competition and laser focus continued.

GROWTH OF XBOX MARKET SHARE OVER TIME

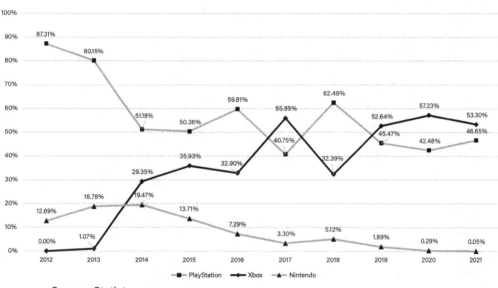

Source: Statista

By the late 1990s, Microsoft was a very large corporation with about thirty-one thousand employees. Even when Gates was distracted by the antitrust case(s), the company was still able to innovate and grow. In 2001, Microsoft released the electronic gaming console Xbox. Although it struggled to gain market share at the beginning,

Xbox eventually went on to become a dominant player in the gaming industry, with a 53 percent market share in the United States by 2021.

In June 2009, Microsoft launched Bing decision engine—a less than successful effort to compete with Google. Bing's market share peaked in 2014 at 3.63 percent and stood at ~2.47 percent as of 2022.[33] Then in November 2010, Microsoft introduced the Windows Phone 7 with similar lackluster success. (The Windows phone peaked at 3.6 percent market share in 2013.) With diminishing interest and application development for the platform, Microsoft discontinued active development of Windows 10 Mobile in 2017, and the platform was discontinued on January 14, 2020.[34] In June 2011, Microsoft launched the enhanced web version of its Microsoft Office product, Office 365 (later renamed Microsoft 365). As of February 2022, Microsoft 365 controlled about 48 percent of the market share for major office suite technology solutions worldwide.[35]

In October 2011, Microsoft acquired the dominant video over internet (VoIP) company, Skype. At the time, Skype was the largest player in its market, with a market share of ~32 percent in February 2020 (until Zoom came along and literally stole the market). Recent figures show Skype at only 4.4 percent market share and Zoom at 59.9

---

33 "Microsoft Bing Usage and Revenue Stats (New Data)," Backlinko, October 25, 2021, https://backlinko.com/bing-users.

34 Petroc Taylor, "Windows Phone OS Market Share of Sales 2011–2016," Statista, January 18, 2023. https://www.statista.com/statistics/236034/global-smartphone-os-market-share-of-windows-mobile/.

35 Lionel Sujay Vailshery, "Office Productivity Software Global Market Share 2022," Statista, February 6, 2023. https://www.statista.com/statistics/983299/worldwide-market-share-of-office-productivity-software/#:~:text=Office%20productivity%20software%20market%20share%20worldwide%202022&text=As%20of%20February%202022%2C%20Microsoft's,the%20lead%20to%20Office%20365.

percent.[36] Talk about the need to be competitive and laser focused in the technology business! Maybe Microsoft can be forgiven for its generally hypercompetitive business practices in light of the lightning-fast collapse in market share of its Skype acquisition. Microsoft launched its Teams video communication application in March 2017 to continue to compete in this space and has had some success there with a ~15 percent global market share. Of course, Teams is bundled with the Microsoft 365 product and available for … free.

Other innovations, acquisitions, and launches include the following:

- Microsoft launched the Surface laptop in October 2012 and in 2022 could lay claim to about a 4 percent global market share in the tablet business as well as a top-five status in tablet vendors.[37]

- Microsoft acquired the Nokia Devices and Services business in 2014 and then opened its flagship store in New York City in 2015; this was an effort to compete directly with Apple's successful physical stores.

- In July 2016, Microsoft acquired the influential business networking site LinkedIn for $26.2 billion.

- The internet hosting and software development company GitHub was acquired by Microsoft in 2018, and in January

36   Robert Brandl, "The Most Popular Video Call Platforms in 2023," EmailTool-Tester.com, January 4, 2023, https://www.emailtooltester.com/en/blog/video-conferencing-market-share/.

37   "Strategy Analytics: Microsoft Breaks into Top Five Tablet Vendors amid Strong Productivity Demand," Business Wire, January 28, 2022, https://www.businesswire.com/news/home/20220128005257/en/Strategy-Analytics-Microsoft-Breaks-into-Top-Five-Tablet-Vendors-amid-Strong-Productivity-Demand.

2022, Microsoft announced plans to acquire leading digital gaming developer Activision Blizzard.[38]

I've intentionally left the best for last. Microsoft entered the cloud computing business with Windows Azure in February 2010. Microsoft is the number-two player in this rapidly growing business sector, with a 21 percent market share as of Q1, 2022.[39] Cloud services has now become the number-one revenue generator for the company.

MICROSOFT REVENUE BY MAJOR PRODUCT LINE

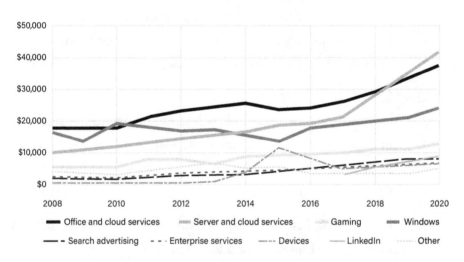

Source: Tech Behemoths

---

38 "Microsoft to Acquire LinkedIn," Stories, June 13, 2016, https://news.microsoft. com/2016/06/13/microsoft-to-acquire-linkedin/.

39 Joe Panettieri, "Cloud Market Share 2022: Amazon AWS, Microsoft Azure, Google Cloud—ChannelE2E: Technology News for MSPS & Channel Partners," ChannelE2E, April 29, 2022, https://www.channele2e.com/news/ cloud-market-share-amazon-aws-microsoft-azure-google/.

Cloud services revenue is at about 29 percent of total revenue and growing fast at over 32 percent year over year in 2022 alone.[40] Only Amazon Web Services has a stronger market share, at about 33 percent as of 2022.[41] Google is in third place. Let the never-ending fierce competition continue!

Finally, and like a blast from the past, there is talk of new antitrust action against Microsoft—this time because of its dominance in cloud services.[42] Microsoft has a built-in advantage in this area, as Windows is the most used in desktop and laptop computers at 75 percent, followed by Apple's macOS at 15 percent and Linux-based operating systems at 5 percent.[43] Maybe it's true that you can't teach a laser-focused competitor new tricks … but hopefully, Microsoft's history with antitrust violations will help the company steer clear of future mistakes.

40   "Microsoft Cloud Strength Fuels Third Quarter Results," Stories, April 26, 2022, https://news.microsoft.com/2022/04/26/microsoft-cloud-strength-fuels-third-quar-ter-results-2/#:~:text=%E2%80%9CContinued%20customer%20commitment%20 to%20our,chief%20financial%20officer%20of%20Microsoft.

41   Roberto Torres, "Cloud Market Makeup Entrenched as AWS Holds Lead," CIO Dive, May 2, 2022, https://www.ciodive.com/news/aws-microsoft-google-cloud-market-share/623004/#:~:text=AWS%20remains%20atop%20competitors%20 in,Synergy%20Research%20Group%20released%20Thursday.

42   Richard Waters, "Microsoft's Tactics to Win Cloud Battle Lead to New Antitrust Scrutiny," Ars Technica, April 13, 2022, https://arstechnica.com/tech-policy/2022/04/ microsofts-tactics-to-win-cloud-battle-lead-to-new-antitrust-scrutiny/.

43   Petroc Taylor, "Desktop Operating System Market Share 2013–2023," Statista, February 27, 2023, https://www.statista.com/statistics/218089/ global-market-share-of-windows-7/.

Revenue Growth

MSFT REVENUE AND NET INCOME HISTORY, 1986 TO 2022 ($ IN MILLIONS)

Fiscal Year	Revenue	Net Income
1986	$ 197.51	$ 39.25
1987	$ 345.89	$ 71.88
1988	$ 590.83	$ 123.91
1989	$ 803.53	$ 170.54
1990	$ 1,183.45	$ 279.19
1991	$ 1,843.43	$ 462.74
1992	$ 2,758.73	$ 708.06
1993	$ 3,753.00	$ 953.00
1994	$ 4,649.00	$ 1,146.00
1995	$ 5,937.00	$ 1,453.00
1996	$ 8,671.00	$ 2,195.00
1997	$ 11,358.00	$ 3,454.00
1998	$ 15,262.00	$ 4,490.00
1999	$ 19,747.00	$ 7,785.00
2000	$ 22,956.00	$ 9,421.00
2001	$ 25,296.00	$ 7,346.00
2002	$ 28,365.00	$ 7,829.00
2003	$ 32,187.00	$ 7,531.00
2004	$ 36,835.00	$ 8,168.00
2005	$ 39,788.00	$ 12,254.00
2006	$ 44,282.00	$ 12,599.00
2007	$ 51,122.00	$ 14,065.00
2008	$ 60,420.00	$ 17,681.00
2009	$ 58,437.00	$ 14,569.00
2010	$ 62,484.00	$ 18,760.00
2011	$ 69,943.00	$ 23,150.00
2012	$ 73,723.00	$ 16,978.00
2013	$ 77,849.00	$ 21,863.00
2014	$ 86,833.00	$ 22,074.00
2015	$ 93,580.00	$ 12,193.00

2016	$	91,154.00	$	20,539.00
2017	$	96,571.00	$	25,489.00
2018	$	110,360.00	$	16,571.00
2019	$	125,843.00	$	39,240.00
2020	$	143,015.00	$	44,281.00
2021	$	168,088.00	$	61,271.00
2022	$	198,270.00	$	72,738.00

Source: Bloomberg Finance L.P.

The revenue and net income history table shows that revenues grew aggressively over the years. There were only two years out of thirty-six where revenues did not grow! That's an impressive record for such a long time period and one that covers a lot of economic turmoil. Net income was a little choppier at times, so let's dig into the actual quarterly earnings to get a little more help.

Applying the Three-Step Process

STEP 1: FUNDAMENTAL ANALYSIS / EARNINGS

Microsoft stock went public in 1986, so it has seen dramatic changes in market conditions along with multiple raging bull and bear markets. Let's see how the market reacted to earnings and look for patterns that might be helpful in managing a hypothetical position.

MSFT FISCAL YEAR QUARTERLY EARNINGS HISTORY, 1986 TO 2022 (PER SHARE)

Fiscal Year	Q1	Q2	Q3	Q4	Annual
1986	$0.0009	$0.0016	$0.0015	$0.0015	$0.0054
1987	$0.0020	$0.0024	$0.0024	$0.0022	$0.0090
1988	$0.0026	$0.0044	$0.0046	$0.0038	$0.0154
1989	$0.0046	$0.0058	$0.0050	$0.0056	$0.0210
1990	$0.0060	$0.0088	$0.0086	$0.0090	$0.0323
1991	$0.0099	$0.0126	$0.0136	$0.0152	$0.0513
1992	$0.0156	$0.0187	$0.0187	$0.0219	$0.0749
1993	$0.0219	$0.0244	$0.0250	$0.0269	$0.0982
1994	$0.0244	$0.0297	$0.0262	$0.0369	$0.1172
1995	$0.0319	$0.0375	$0.0394	$0.0362	$0.1450
1996	$0.0487	$0.0562	$0.0550	$0.0544	$0.2143
1997	$0.0594	$0.0712	$0.1000	$0.1000	$0.3306
1998	$0.0600	$0.1050	$0.1250	$0.0625	$0.3525
1999	$0.1550	$0.1800	$0.1750	$0.2000	$0.7100
2000	$0.2000	$0.2200	$0.2150	$0.2200	$0.8550
2001	$0.1835	$0.2350	$0.2200	$0.0050	$0.6435
2002	$0.1150	$0.2050	$0.2450	$0.1400	$0.7050
2003	$0.0950	$0.0850	$0.2000	$0.1300	$0.5100
2004	$0.2400	$0.1400	$0.1200	$0.2500	$0.7500
2005	$0.2300	$0.3200	$0.2300	$0.3421	$1.1221
2006	$0.2900	$0.3400	$0.2900	$0.2746	$1.1946
2007	$0.3500	$0.2600	$0.5000	$0.3100	$1.4200
2008	$0.4500	$0.5000	$0.4700	$0.4600	$1.8800
2009	$0.4800	$0.4700	$0.3300	$0.3400	$1.6200
2010	$0.4000	$0.7400	$0.4500	$0.5100	$2.1000
2011	$0.6200	$0.7700	$0.6100	$0.6900	$2.6900
2012	$0.6800	$0.7800	$0.6000	-$0.0600	$2.0000
2013	$0.5300	$0.7600	$0.7200	$0.5900	$2.6000
2014	$0.6200	$0.7800	$0.6800	$0.5500	$2.6300
2015	$0.5400	$0.7100	$0.6100	-$0.4000	$1.4600
2016	$0.6300	$0.7400	$0.5400	$0.6600	$2.5700
2017	$0.7200	$0.8000	$0.7000	$1.0300	$3.2500
2018	$0.8400	-$0.8200	$0.9500	$1.1400	$2.1100

2019	$1.1400	$1.0800	$1.1400	$1.7100	$5.0700
2020	$1.3800	$1.5100	$1.4000	$1.4600	$5.7500
2021	$1.8200	$2.0300	$2.0300	$2.1700	$8.0500
2022	$2.7300	$2.4800	$2.2200	$2.2300	$9.6600
2023	$2.3500	$2.2000			$4.5500
Key:	Positive	Negative			

Source: Bloomberg Finance L.P.

The quarterly earnings history is shaded boxes to reflect the price movement after the announcement of 10 percent or more up or down. Since the IPO in 1986 there were only eight instances where a signal was given using this approach. We will add this data to our algorithm later to see how and whether it could have helped us manage around the stock.

STEP 2: TECHNICAL ANALYSIS

Let's go back to the beginning in 1986 and take a long-term look at how some of the technical indicators we discussed earlier (the twenty-one-period EMA, RSI, momentum, money flows, and stochastics) behaved. The following chart illustrates the amazing first ten-plus years of trading in MSFT.

The prices are split adjusted, and you can see the strong upward trajectory of the stock. Relative strength (RSI) stayed positive on a monthly basis for the entire ten years! And there were only a couple of brief hiccups in the twenty-one-period EMA (up and down arrows). The same is true for momentum, money flows, and stochastics, which only had minor breakdowns. It appears that the majority of these occurred in late 1993 through early 1994, while the stock was mostly moving sideways and consolidating the earlier large gains. From a technical perspective, this is a pretty amazing display of strength over such a long

MSFT, MARCH 1986 TO DECEMBER 1996

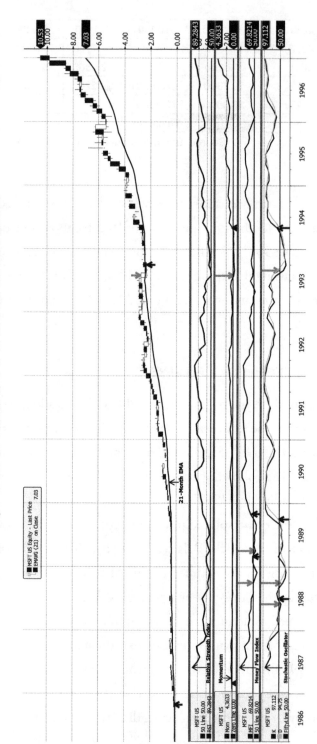

period of time. We will apply the technical scoring approach later in this chapter, but it is clear that this would have been an "easy" stock to hold over the first ten years—at least in theory from a technical standpoint.

Moving on to the next ten years, things get a little more interesting, as this time period covers the great dot-com bull market and subsequent bust. No stocks were immune to these massive market pressures. Let's see how a huge market leader like MSFT fared in this wild boom-bust period. As we can see from the chart on page 98 tracking from 1997 to 2006, MSFT was not spared during this wild ride. After peaking at a split-adjusted price of about $60 in early 2000, the stock got hit hard with the overall market collapse and stayed in a lower range for some time.

You can see that the twenty-one-period EMA, RSI, momentum, and stochastics all went negative at the same time in April of 2000. Money flows had already turned negative a few months earlier—in January 2000. This unanimity of negative metrics was a strong indication of the difficult markets to come during the dot-com bust between 2000 and 2003; it was a long three-year bear market. The stochastics and twenty-one-period EMA both gave some false buy/sell indications, but RSI, momentum, and money flows generally stayed negative after the initial drop in early 2000 and generally stayed that way for many years—through to about 2006. There wasn't much, if any, decisive positive movement in either the stock or these technical metrics over the whole of those years.

In fact, as the chart on page 99 tracking the twenty-year period from 1997 to 2016 illustrates, it took until the start of 2017 for MSFT to eclipse the $60 split-adjusted high price of ~$60 set in late 1999. Valuations matter. That's almost seventeen full years of waiting on one of the greatest stocks of all time. Most investors don't have anywhere near that kind of patience.

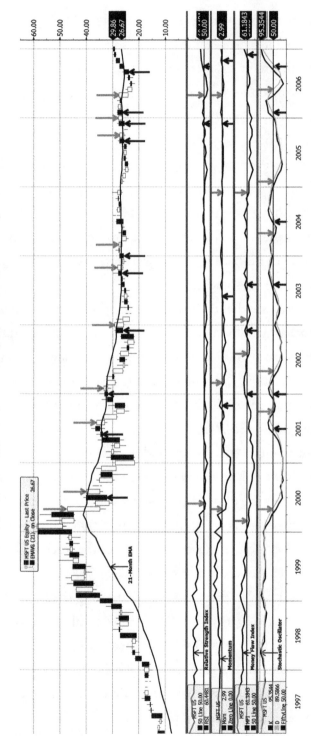

MSFT, JANUARY 1997 TO DECEMBER 2006

MSFT, JANUARY 1997 TO DECEMBER 2016

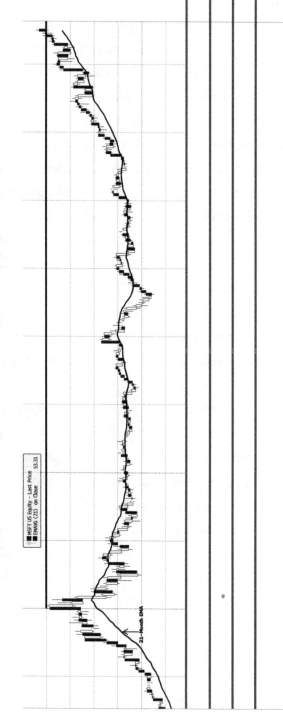

MSFT US Equity - Last Price   53.31
EMAVG (21)   on Close

21-Month EMA

Now let's get back to the technical picture to see what was happening and maybe glean some possible advantages to managing around this seventeen-year hiatus in stock price growth. In particular, let's get back to the analytics for the decade from 2007 to 2016. 2007 through 2016 saw tremendous economic and stock market volatility, especially during the Global Financial Crisis (GFC), or the "Great Recession," when the overall market as measured by the S&P 500 dropped by over 50 percent between late 2007 and early 2009.

Something very interesting happened in January 2008. Right at the beginning of what would come to be called the Great Recession, the EMA, RSI, momentum, and stochastics all went negative at the same time on the monthly chart. Money flow followed a few months later. This was certainly a technical "red flag." Then they all started going positive in June of 2009, generally signaling the "all-clear" alert. There were some minor breaks and false signals given after that, but nothing like the universal breaks and recoveries entering and leaving the GFC.

In the five-year period covering 2017 to 2021 shown in the chart on page 102, all the technical metrics we have been focusing on stayed in the positive range—all the way through December 2021. This illustrates the phenomenon of "overhead supply." I added a horizontal line indicating the price high hit all the way back in late 1999 during the dot-com boom. Once that level was finally eclipsed, there was no overhead supply to fight. In other words, no one had purchased the stock at a higher price and was hoping to get out and "break even." There was no one left holding a loss from the old high price, so the price was free to move up without the theoretical "overhead supply" selling pressure.

The stock launched forward from the old resistance of ~$60 originally established all the way back in 1999 and ran up to as high as

MSFT, JANUARY 2007 TO DECEMBER 2016

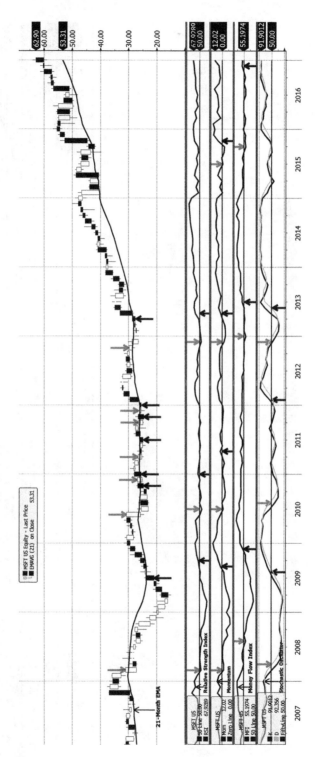

MSFT, JANUARY 2017 TO DECEMBER 2022

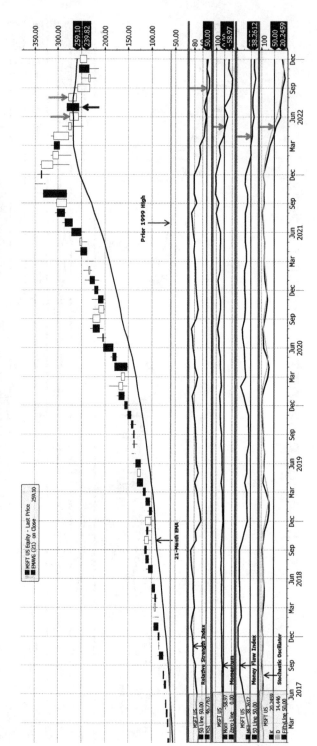

~$350 (an almost 600 percent return!) over a relatively short five years, which included the pandemic-related collapse of the stock market in March 2020. MSFT powered through all of it technically. These technical metrics could have allowed an investor to stay the course through what were extremely emotional and scary times during the pandemic. At least until 2022 it was "set it and forget it," as the great Ron Popeil used to say! By 2022 we see some of the indicators breaking down, reflecting the inflation battle the Federal Reserve undertook in 2022. When volatility strikes, even the market leaders can be impacted.

> **When volatility strikes, even the market leaders can be impacted.**

STEP 3: RISK MANAGEMENT

The next chart on page 104 illustrates when the stock price of MSFT dropped below the rolling fifty-two-week high.

The two dotted black lines represent the rolling fifty-two-week high and where a 20 percent price drop would be. Crossovers are illustrated by the down arrow (showing breakdown and causing a sell signal) and then the up arrow crossing back up (issuing a buy signal). When we look at the fifty-two-week high indicator, we immediately notice a few things:

1. The stock demonstrated relatively low volatility.

2. There were only a few periods of major volatility, including the late 1980s, the dot-com bust, and the Global Financial Crisis.

3. Relatively few buy/sell signals were given over the decades, which would have allowed an investor using this indicator to have less activity managing the stock.

FIFTY-TWO-WEEK HIGH INDICATOR: MSFT

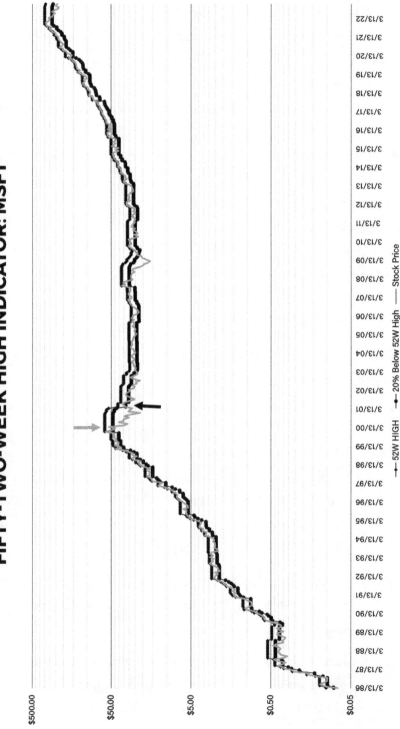

Applying a Process to Manage MSFT Stock

The next chart on page 106 combines all of these indicators into the hypothetical algorithm to show the difference between hypothetically managing the stock (the black line) versus buying and holding all the way through (the gray line).

Microsoft has turned out to be one of the greatest stocks of all time as we saw in the earlier table reflecting approximately a 328,796 percent return excluding dividends since the IPO in 1986. So in hindsight, it should likely never have been sold. However, even though the returns were significantly lower over the same time period (~104,269 percent return on a price basis), the hypothetical algorithm approach helped remove the emotion from the equation over the decades and managed to also show profits. With a gigantic winner like MSFT, nothing could be expected to beat a buy-and-hold approach, though. Unfortunately, all stocks are not MSFT …

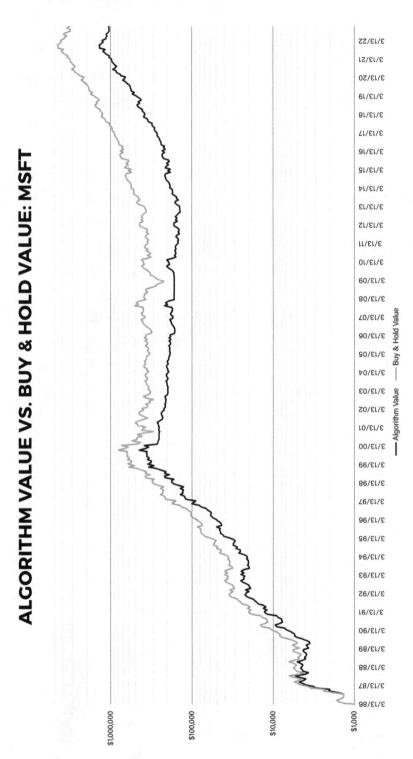

ALGORITHM VALUE VS. BUY & HOLD VALUE: MSFT

—— Algorithm Value   —— Buy & Hold Value

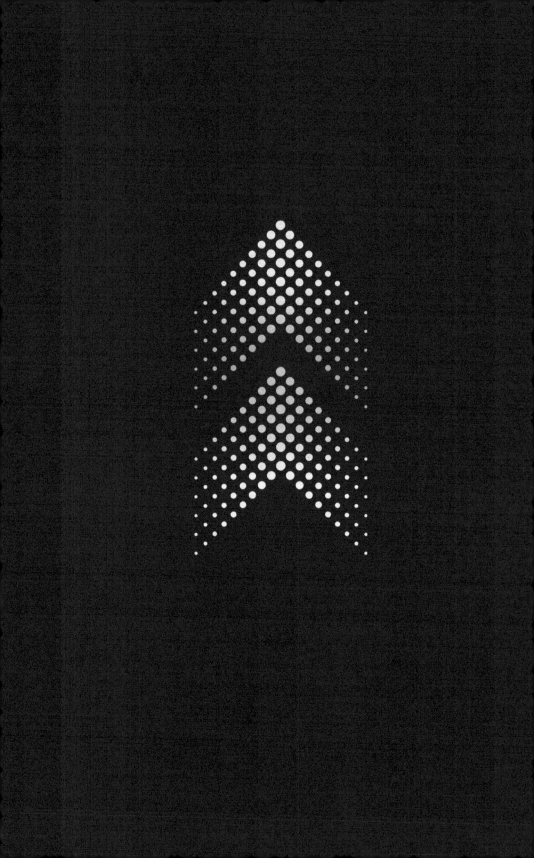

CHAPTER FOUR

APPLE

A total of $1,000 invested in AAPL stock the day it came public on December 12, 1980, at the IPO price of $22 was worth $1,299,300 on December 31, 2022, for a compounded return of 129,830 percent.

Your work is going to fill a large part of your life, and the only way to be truly satisfied is to do what you believe is great work. And the only way to do great work is to love what you do. If you haven't found it yet, keep looking. Don't settle. As with all matters of the heart, you'll know when you find it.

—STEVE JOBS

Timeline from Formation through Initial Public Offering

- 1976: Apple Computer Company is founded on April 1, 1976, as a business partnership between Steve Jobs, Steve Wozniak, and Ronald Wayne. The Apple I computer, designed by Steve Wozniak, is launched.

- 1977: Apple Computer, Inc. is incorporated on January 3, 1977, without Wayne, who left and sold his share of the company back to Jobs and Wozniak for $800 just twelve days after having cofounded Apple. The Apple II, also invented by Wozniak, is introduced on April 16, 1977, at the first West Coast Computer Faire.

- 1979: In June 1979, the Apple II+ launches for $1,195.

- 1979: The project to develop the Apple Lisa is started. The computer is supposed to be ready in March 1981. It takes until January 1983 because of delays.

- 1979: VisiCalc, a computer spreadsheet program and the first "killer app," is available exclusively on Apple computers for the first twelve months. In many cases, people are buying the Apple II+ just to run the VisiCalc spreadsheet software.

- 1979: A research project for a new low-cost computer is started under the direction of Jeff Raskin. This would later become the Macintosh project.[44]

- 1980: On December 12, 1980, Apple goes public, offering 4.6 million shares of stock at $22 per share.

Origin Story

Steve Jobs stands out among the other successful leaders we are looking at in this book. Many of the people driving the growth in other companies had similar personality characteristics like competi-

---

44   "Timeline: The History of Apple Since 1976," Mac History, accessed March 11, 2023, https://www.mac-history.net/2022/12/16/timeline-the-history-of-apple-since-1976/.

tiveness, high-level academic intelligence, and being at the forefront of the development of their industry. Steve Jobs certainly had these traits, but he also had the soul of an artist, which he combined with an uncompromising need for stylistic perfection. This combination was the foundation of Apple and remains so to this day. As we will see, this rare combination created one of the most influential companies in history but also contributed to one of the bumpiest rides of any of the companies we review here. Tracking these leaders in relation to their companies suggests that there's a clear lesson we might draw about the connections between great leadership and company success: a great company demands a great leader to drive execution.

Steve Wozniak first met Steve Jobs while both were working at Hewlett Packard in 1971. Wozniak was twenty-one, and Jobs was only sixteen. Wozniak was designing calculators for HP and Jobs was working there for the summer. They both had an interest in computing; Wozniak was even designing his first computer at the time. Their first project together was selling what were called "blue boxes" that allowed people to (illegally) make long distance phone calls for free. Wozniak was the primary builder of the boxes, Jobs sold them, and they split the profits.

Steve Jobs's early academic path included a deep interest in electronics and computing along with an eclectic mix of literature, the arts, music, philosophy, and even a class in calligraphy that would go on to influence the development of Apple products (like the fonts available in the Macintosh

> Tracking these leaders in relation to their companies suggests that there's a clear lesson we might draw about the connections between great leadership and company success: a great company demands a great leader to drive execution.

computer). Jobs attended Reed College but dropped out after one semester in early 1973. By 1974, he was working with the video game maker Atari but soon left for a seven-month pilgrimage to India to immerse himself in learning about Buddhism. Jobs did not follow the traditional path by any standard. By mid-1975, Jobs was back at Atari and collaborating with Wozniak.

Early in 1976, Wozniak created a computer, which would later become known as the Apple I. The early computer design that Wozniak created was a circuit board more appropriate for computer hobbyists with a knack for electronics. He offered the design to his employer, HP, but they were not interested. Jobs was convinced that there was a market for the machine and urged Wozniak to go into business with him and start a new company to market the computer. Jobs famously sold his VW minibus, and Wozniak sold his HP-65 programmable calculator to raise a few hundred dollars each. They founded Apple Computer on April 1, 1976, and delivered their first order for fifty units of this early version of the Apple I computer in July 1976 at a retail price of $666.66. Their first customer, Byte Shop in Mountain-view, California (a local computer enthusiast/hobbyist shop), accepted the deconstructed units but insisted that the next version should have a complete package including a keyboard, case, and display … in other words, that it should look more like a finished and ready-to-use consumer product.[45]

---

45 "Timeline: The History of Apple Since 1976."

Apple I, 1976
Source: ArnoldReinhold, CC BY 4.0 <https://creativecommons.org/licenses/by/4.0>, via Wikimedia Commons

State of the Industry

As we covered in the last chapter, there was no personal computer industry in 1976. Jobs and Wozniak were among a small group of pioneers carving out what would become an entirely new industry over the following decade. The original Apple I was built in Steve Jobs's parents's garage with the help of a few friends and family and went on to sell two hundred units. Mike Markkula, already a successful tech investor, contributed $92,000 (along with securing a $250,000 line of credit for the

> There was no personal computer industry in 1976. Jobs and Wozniak were among a small group of pioneers carving out what would become an entirely new industry over the following decade.

company) for one-third of Apple Computer Inc. and joined Jobs and Wozniak to officially incorporate the company on January 3, 1977. Wozniak was already working on what would become known as the Apple II. The Apple II computer was introduced at the now famous West Coast Computer Faire on April 16, 1977. The more consumer-friendly Apple II was launched at a retail cost of $1,295. This version came with a sleek case that included a keyboard and would eventually evolve into the PC, as it would come to be known in the decades ahead, complete with a case, keyboard, and monitor. Apple was starting to develop the "cool factor" that would become its hallmark for decades to come.

Apple II, 1977
Source: FozzTexx, CC BY-SA 4.0 <https://creativecommons.org/licenses/by-sa/4.0>, via Wikimedia Commons

The Apple II was an immediate success. But it took a serendipitous development to drive the Apple II to the top of the new PC business. In 1979, the Apple II was chosen to be the desktop platform for the first "killer app" ever, VisiCalc's spreadsheet program. I mentioned earlier that VisiCalc allowed people to perform complicated mathematical spreadsheeting functions that were otherwise impossible or at least impractical. Mike Markkula at one point described the Apple II as a "VisiCalc accessory." Because the program was so powerful, it created a whole new market for Apple and turbo charged sales. Before VisiCalc, Apple had been a distant third-place competitor to Commodore and Tandy. The Apple II was a great product, but its selection by VisiCalc as the exclusive provider for the first twelve months certainly didn't hurt its prospects. In other words, it never hurts to have a little luck.

Sales began to rise at a meteoric rate, driving revenues at Apple Inc. from about $773,000 in 1977 to almost $118 million in 1980. By the time the Apple II line of computers was discontinued in 1993, approximately six million units had been sold.[46]

Selected Consolidated Financial Information

	January 3, 1977 (inception), to September 30, 1977	Fiscal Year Ended		
		September 30, 1978	September 30, 1979	September 30, 1980
Income Statement Data:				
Revenues	$773,977	$7,883,846	$47,938,981	$117,901,543
Net income	$41,575	$793,497	$5,072,812	$11,697,983
Earnings per common and common-equivalent share	Less than $.01	$.03	$.12	$.24
Shares used to calculate per-share data	16,640,000	31,544,000	43,620,000	48,412,000

Source: Fast Company

---

46 "Apple II Explained: Everything You Need to Know," *History-Computer*, November 30, 2022, https://history-computer.com/apple-ii-guide/.

Going Public

In 1980, the US ice hockey team defeated the Soviet Union in what was labeled the "Miracle on Ice." Mount Saint Helens in Washington State erupted on May 18, killing fifty-seven people. CNN began broadcasting, 3M introduced Post-it Notes, and former Beatle John Lennon was killed in New York City. The average price of a new car was about $7,000.

Overall stock market conditions in 1980 were historically difficult. Interest rates along with inflation had skyrocketed, and the public was focused on concepts like the "misery index," reflecting the general malaise at the time. Paul Volcker, chairman of the Federal Reserve, was undertaking historic rapid increases in the federal funds rate to staunch the threat of inflation. History shows that his interventions worked, but there was a price to pay in the real economy and the stock market. After going nowhere for a decade during the 1970s, the market now faced radically hawkish Fed policy as a major headwind. The markets were volatile, to say the least.

S&P 500 PRICE INDEX: 1968-1980

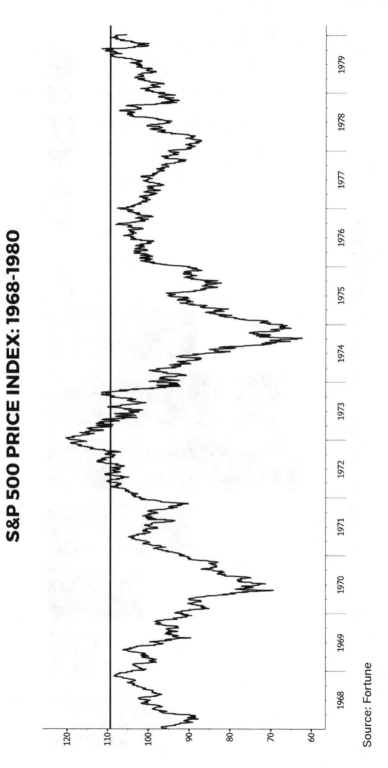

Source: Fortune

117

ANNUAL INFLATION RATE 1975-1985

Source: Bloomberg Finance, L.P.

There were two recessions within the first three years after Volcker took over as chairman of the Federal Reserve in August 1979. To combat the runaway inflation, Volcker led the Federal Reserve to raise the federal funds rate from about 11.2 percent in 1979 to a peak of 20 percent in June 1981. There was a six-month recession in 1980, then another recession in 1981 that lasted sixteen months. From the start of 1980 through the end of 1982, the United States was in a recession for twenty-two out of thirty-six months, or more than 60 percent of the time.[47] This was a relatively difficult and volatile market environment for Apple Computer to go public in. Between December 1980 and August 1982, the overall stock market as measured by the S&P 500 had dropped about 25 percent. The old saying that a rising tide lifts all boats works in the opposite direction too. Apple Computer (AAPL) was no exception and felt the pressure exerted by overall market conditions.

Despite challenging market conditions, AAPL was considered a hot IPO due to the rapid earnings growth it was enjoying in the brand-new personal computer business. Again, this was a different time in stock market history, where hot IPOs were generally launched with strong earnings. Apple's IPO filing showed almost $118 million in revenues and a rapid rate of organic growth.

47   Ben Carlson, "These Charts Show How Bad the Economy Was When Paul Volcker Took Over as Fed Chair in 1979," *Fortune*, December 9, 2019, https://fortune.com/2019/12/09/charts-1973-19174-economy-paul-volcker-fed-chair/.

S&P 500, DECEMBER 1980 TO AUGUST 1983

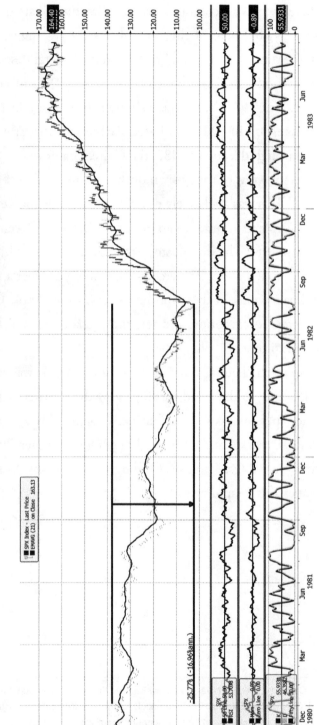

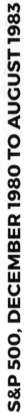

Apple stock originally filed to sell at $14 per share but interest was huge, and the offering price kept rising. The AAPL IPO priced on December 12, 1980, at $22 per share, raising about $100 million through the offering. The stock rose 32 percent that day, closing at $29 per share and representing a total market capitalization of $1.78 billion. The Apple Computer IPO was the single largest IPO since Ford Motor Company in 1956, and many of the early employees and investors became instant millionaires.

From there, the stock followed a typical hot IPO pattern as you can see on the next page—it went up a bit more over the first few weeks and then settled down after all the excitement as investors waited to see how the management of the new company would execute a follow-up to successful early products like the Apple II. The stock then traded along with the general market and didn't bottom out until the overall market did in August 1982. Because the overall market was dropping, AAPL did not eclipse the highs set in those first few weeks for over two years. It was up to the company to manage growth, innovate, and generally build on their wild early success.[48]

48　Luke Dormehl. "Today in Apple History: Apple IPO Mints Instant Million-aires," Cult of Mac, December 12, 2022, https://www.cultofmac.com/457878/tiah-apple-goes-public/.

AAPL, DECEMBER 1980 TO AUGUST 1983

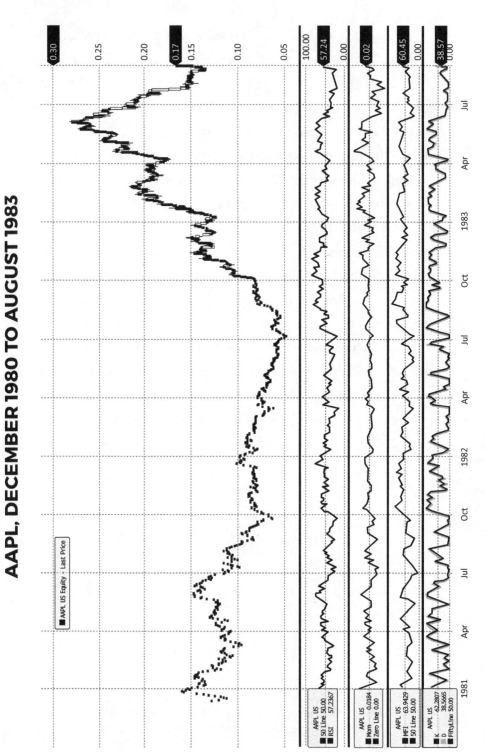

Overcoming Adversity, or "A Strange Thing Happened on the Way to Greatness"

At the time of the successful IPO, things could not have been going better for the rapidly growing Apple Computer company. Sales of the Apple II series were continuing to grow, so the company worked on next-generation systems like Macintosh and Lisa while bringing in more help in the form of professional corporate management.

APPLE III

The Apple III was the first Apple computer not designed by Steve Wozniak. The Apple III project started in late 1978 under the management of Dr. Wendell Sander, with specifications contributed by a committee of Apple engineers with input from marketing. Apple wanted the Apple III completed in ten months, but because of extra features constantly being added by the committee approach, it took two years. The Apple III ended up having numerous design flaws, including limited software availability, hardware that would often crash when using the Save command, and a motherboard with a propensity to get too hot and warp (causing chips to pop out of their sockets), which resulted in severe problems with the entire system.[49] These issues led Apple to recommend that the computer be periodically dropped onto the physical desktop to reset the chips (this really was a thing). Approximately 120,000 units of the Apple III series were sold before the computer line was discontinued in 1985. Steve Wozniak was quoted as saying that the Apple III failed because it was

---

49   "Main Menu," Low End Mac, accessed March 11, 2023, https://lowendmac.com/2015/apple-iii-chaos-apples-first-failure/.

developed by Apple Computer's marketing department instead of the engineering team.[50]

LISA

Steve Jobs was a visionary with a perfectionist's nature. Beginning in 1978, twenty-four-year-old Jobs began developing the concept of the Lisa computer as a successor to the Apple II line. He assembled the best ideas from within the new computer industry, including making a now famous visit to Xerox's PARC research facility in late 1979 (for which Xerox was granted the right to buy one hundred thousand shares of pre-IPO stock for $1 million). Jobs wanted Lisa to be the ultimate business computer solution of its day. Lisa was to be Apple's first computer with a real Graphical User Interface (GUI, or what we now know as a "desktop"), networking capability, and a mouse. In his quest for perfection, the costs of development soared. Over five years, development costs were about $50 million.[51] This occurred against the backdrop of a maturing company that had to answer to Wall Street with quarterly earnings expectations and a more professional management team than just Jobs and Wozniak selling their latest invention. Jobs was eventually forced out of the Lisa program in September 1980 because of ongoing cost concerns and friction with Apple Computer's management team.[52] Jobs was generally considered extremely demanding and difficult to work with at the time because of his exacting performance and design standards and because he

---

50 "IWoz: Computer Geek to Cult Icon: How I Invented the Personal Computer, Co-Founded Apple, and Had Fun Doing It," Internet Archive, New York: W. W. Norton & Co., January 1, 1970, https://archive.org/details/iwozcomputergeek00wozn.

51 Stephen Hackett, "The Lisa," MacStories, accessed March 11, 2023, https://www.macstories.net/mac/the-lisa/.

52 "Apple Lisa," Mac History, accessed March 11, 2023, https://www.mac-history.net/2007/10/12/apple-lisa/.

could be abrasive when he wasn't getting the results he expected.[53] The original Lisa computer was launched in January 1983 at a retail price of $9,995, a price that was prohibitively high for the average computer buyer used to spending around $1,000. The Lisa ultimately sold only ten thousand units over several years against development costs of approximately $150 million and was completely shuttered in just three short years.[54]

53   Luke Dormehl, "Today in Apple History: Apple Launches Ill-Fated Lisa Project," Cult of Mac, July 30, 2022, https://www.cultofmac.com/565721/apple-lisa-project/#:~:text=Even%20more%20notable%20was%20the,ultimately%20launched%20in%20January%201983.

54   Matt Milano, "The Reason Why the Apple Lisa Computer Failed," SlashGear, March 11, 2022, https://www.slashgear.com/796249/the-reason-why-the-apple-lisa-computer-failed/.

Steve Jobs and Macintosh computer, January 1984
Source: Bernard Gotfryd—Edited from tif by Cart, Public domain, via Wikimedia Commons

MACINTOSH

The Macintosh project started under the leadership of Jeff Raskin (employee number 28 at Apple) in 1979. The goal was to build a low-cost computer that would be easy for the average consumer to use. After being booted off the Lisa team in late 1981, Steve Jobs decided to join, and lead, the Macintosh team. Raskin and Jobs did not see eye to eye on many things, as Jobs considered Raskin an engineering functionary with little to no vision or innovative capability.[55] Raskin, on the other hand, felt Jobs's extremely demanding management style was imperious and counterproductive. One month after Jobs joined the Macintosh team, Raskin sent a memo to Apple CEO Mike Scott, complaining that Jobs was often late, showed bad judgment, interrupted coworkers, didn't listen, and was a bad manager. Raskin was later quoted as saying that Jobs "would have made a great king of France."[56] Over the years, Raskin was not alone in viewing Jobs's management style as extreme. But none of that mattered in the short run, as Raskin was pushed off the Macintosh project and then left the company a year later.

Jobs brought a lot of the goals and lessons from the Lisa project to the Macintosh project, from overall style, functionality, desktop, and mouse interaction—all with the idea to achieve these things more cheaply and elegantly.

The Macintosh was launched with the seminal *1984* commercial, directed by Ridley Scott of *Bladerunner* fame, and debuted during Super Bowl XVIII on January 22, 1984. This splashy and expensive

55 "Steve Jobs Discovers the Macintosh Project," Mac History, October 19, 2008, https://www.mac-history.net/steve-jobs-discovers-the-macintosh-project.

56 Drake Baer, "Here's the Angry Memo That Macintosh's Original Developer Sent to Apple after Steve Jobs Forced Him Out," Business Insider, accessed March 11, 2023, https://www.businessinsider.com/jef-raskin-steve-jobs-firing-memo-2015-3.

launch was driven by then-CEO John Sculley and was followed up with what would become the standard Steve Jobs–centric in-person product launch. The entire launch was a reminder that Apple products weren't just the cutting edge of technology; they were cool and independent. That ethos would eventually help Apple become the most valuable company in the world. Apple also ran a "Test Drive a Macintosh" promotion, which allowed buyers to take home a Macintosh for twenty-four hours and return it to their dealer afterward if they did not want to keep it. About two hundred thousand people participated, but there wasn't enough inventory to support the promotion and, of course, many computers were returned in suboptimal condition, making them unsalable as "new." This marketing campaign caused Sculley to raise the price from $1,995 to $2,495—the high end of computer pricing at the time.

The Macintosh computer got off to a splashy start but was ultimately not a huge success relative to the amount of money spent on development and the over-the-top launch campaign. That said, Jobs remained supremely confident about the success of the machine and predicted that Apple would sell 50,000 Macs in its first one hundred days. By day one hundred, Apple had sold 72,000 Macs. Initial success led Apple to ramp up production, which it did just as demand started to wane. The company ramped up manufacturing to a rate of 110,000 Macs per month, but sales slowed dramatically, and Apple did not hit the one million sales mark until March 1987, over three years after the launch. Granted, this was not a repeat of the Apple III failure, but the Macintosh was considered yet another setback for the company at the time.[57]

---

57   Luke Dormehl, "Today in Apple History: Mac's First 100 Days Prove a Roaring Success," Cult of Mac, May 3, 2022, https://www.cultofmac.com/479113/today-apple-history-first-100-days-mac-roaring-success/.

Eventually, the market did grow, and by 1985, the combination of the Mac, Apple's LaserWriter printer, and Mac-specific software like Boston Software's MacPublisher enabled users to design, preview, and print page layouts complete with text and graphics. These combined applications would later come to be known as desktop publishing.[58] Despite a bumpy start, the Macintosh forever changed the face of personal computing by combining a graphic user interface (desktop), the mouse, and a general ease of usability. The Macintosh line continued to grow so much that later generations would go on to form the backbone of Apple Computer's PC success. But there was trouble in paradise when all of these short-term failures compounded in the moment.

IBM Enters the Market

By August 1981, Apple Computer was among the three largest micro-computer companies worldwide, and revenues for the first half of the year had already exceeded 1980's $118 million. *InfoWorld* reported that lack of production capacity was constraining growth at the time. It was into this fast-growing environment that IBM entered the personal computer market with the IBM PC.

On August 12, 1981, at a press conference in the Waldorf Astoria ballroom in New York City, IBM's Don Estridge announced the company's PC at a price of $1,565. This was much lower than the release price of the Apple III, which started at $4,340 and went as high as $7,800 with added features. IBM, the computer giant, had demonstrated the seriousness and potential of personal computing in

---

58 "Macintosh by Apple—Complete History of Mac Computers," *History Computer*, November 23, 2022, https://history-computer.com/macintosh-by-apple-complete-history-of-mac-computers.

the business arena by offering a powerful machine at a very affordable price. Sales started off slowly, but by 1984, IBM PC and clones were selling two million units a year and growing fast.

As you might suspect from all of the different design projects, Apple Computer had become siloed into various power fiefdoms. A serious company needs serious and experienced management. After Mike Markkula helped incorporate the company in 1977, he worked quickly to bring in a world class management structure. Jobs was only twenty-two years old, and Wozniak was only twenty-six at the time, and neither one had much interest in corporate management anyway. In February 1977, Markkula recruited Michael Scott from National Semiconductor to serve as the first president and CEO of Apple Computer. When Apple Computer went public in 1980, Jobs became chairman while Markkula took on the role of president. Apple Computer had made the Fortune 500 by 1983 and was the fastest company to do so in history. That same year, the company recruited John Sculley, president of PepsiCo, Inc., to be CEO and hoped that he would become young Steve Jobs's mentor when it came to learning the finer points of running a large corporation. Jobs famously convinced Sculley to accept the position by challenging him: "Do you want to sell sugar water for the rest of your life?"[59]

Of course, Steve Jobs still held sway over the maverick soul of the company, but other factions grew as Apple Computer management evolved into a more traditional corporate and conservative culture focusing on bottom lines, budgets, and quarterly results. After the early and wild success of the Apple II, the mounting misfires of the Apple III, Lisa, and a fast start for the MacIntosh followed by disappointing sales, Apple Computers lost market share as well as valuable

---

59   "Steve Jobs," *Encyclopaedia Britannica*, February 20, 2023, https://www.britannica. com/biography/Steve-Jobs.

time and money. That all occurred against the meteoric rise of the IBM PC, the eight-hundred-pound competitor, which had just entered the room and was taking over the industry.

By 1982, IBM had come to dominate the PC market with an 80 percent market share.[60] Sculley and Apple Computer senior management faced a serious dilemma: should they continue pouring money into thus-far-unsuccessful innovation projects, or should they extract revenues now from existing products that were actually making money, like the successful Apple II series? Should they prioritize aggressive innovation or pursue traditional business management solutions, given the IBM threat? Sculley believed he knew exactly what needed to happen. But innovation coursed through Steve Jobs's blood, and he believed that innovation coupled with the pursuit of product perfection were essential to the very essence of Apple Computer's existence. Tensions continued to rise between the two leaders, and in April 1985, Sculley's logical and practical business approach won out. Steve Jobs was forced out of the company with the full support of the board of directors, including original partner Mike Markkula. Practicality had won out over innovation, and Apple Computer would never be the same ... at least for a while.

Dealing with More Adversity

Steve Jobs didn't let any grass grow under his feet after his shocking removal from Apple Computer. He quickly formed NeXT, Inc. and focused on designing powerful workstation computers for the education market. NeXT evolved over time to designing an innovative software system called NeXTSTEP. Jobs also acquired a control-

---

60   James W. Cortada, "How the IBM PC Won, Then Lost, the Personal Computer Market," IEEE Spectrum, August 30, 2022, https://spectrum.ieee.org/how-the-ibm-pc-won-then-lost-the-personal-computer-market.

ling interest in a computer animation company called Pixar, which would go on to produce the first completely computer-animated full-length feature film, *Toy Story*, in 1995. Pixar ultimately became the foundation of a new extremely profitable genre of the motion picture industry, and when it went public in 1995, Steve Jobs became a billionaire.

Over at Apple, and as I mentioned earlier, Macintosh sales got off to a hot start but declined quickly. Consumers avoided the machine for three reasons: (1) it was low powered, (2) it was relatively expensive (~$2,495), and (3) there were very few Macintosh-compatible programs. Apple had decided to use a closed-architecture approach, limiting applications available for its machine. By contrast, the IBM PC used an open-architecture approach, encouraging industry participants to create enhanced or expansion products for the IBM PC and to create new software used by the computer. This approach spawned literally hundreds of companies creating products for the IBM PC and writing thousands of different programs across the business and personal application spectrums.[61]

By firing Steve Jobs, Apple had made a strong commitment to the status quo. It forged ahead with improvements in the Apple II series, continued developing the new Macintosh series, and created compact versions of its top-selling Apple II line and early portable versions of the Macintosh. The company created peripheral devices, like printers, to try to build an ecosystem around its main product lines. In the early 1990s, Macintosh was split into multiple lines to try to generate consumer interest. Centris, Performa, and Quadra were new names for Macintosh variants, but these models differed little from the original in terms of functionality and did little to drive

---

61   "Open and Closed: Debating the Macintosh's Closed Architecture," accessed March 11, 2023, https://web.stanford.edu/dept/SUL/sites/mac/primary/docs/open.html.

sales in a meaningful way. Revenues and net sales continued to suffer throughout this period.[62]

AAPL, REVENUE AND NET INCOME HISTORY 1980 TO 1997 ($ IN MILLIONS)

Fiscal Year	Revenue	Net Income
1980	$ 117.13	$ 11.70
1981	$ 335.00	$ 39.42
1982	$ 583.00	$ 61.00
1983	$ 983.00	$ 77.00
1984	$ 1,516.00	$ 64.00
1985	$ 1,918.00	$ 61.00
1986	$ 1,902.00	$ 154.00
1987	$ 2,661.07	$ 217.50
1988	$ 4,071.37	$ 400.26
1989	$ 5,284.01	$ 454.03
1990	$ 5,558.44	$ 474.89
1991	$ 6,308.85	$ 309.84
1992	$ 7,086.54	$ 530.37
1993	$ 7,976.95	$ 86.59
1994	$ 9,188.75	$ 310.18
1995	$ 11,062.00	$ 424.00
1996	$ 9,833.00	$ (816.00)
1997	$ 7,081.00	$ (1,045.00)

Source: Bloomberg Finance L.P.

By the end of fiscal year 1996, Apple had lost $816 million, and things were looking to get worse. Revenue growth was slowing, and the company was floundering badly. By the early 1990s, John

---

62   Applelizados, "What Happened at Apple during Steve Jobs' Absence?," Soy de Mac, August 1, 2016. https://www.soydemac.com/en/apple-ausencia-steve-jobs/. See also: "1980 to Now: The Journey of Apple's Market Cap," Apple Maven, accessed March 11, 2023, https://www.thestreet.com/apple/stock/1980-to-now-the-journey-of-apples-market-cap.

Sculley had ascended to total control over Apple as chairman, CEO, and CTO (that's chief technical officer). It's worth noting that Sculley had no formal technical or engineering expertise. He'd received a bachelor's degree in architectural design from Brown University and an MBA from the Wharton School of the University of Pennsylvania. He was eventually forced to resign in October 1993 due to rising tensions over Apple's ongoing poor performance in the market and the serious deterioration of its balance sheet. After Sculley, longtime Apple employee Michael Spindler was installed as CEO, but little changed.

Then, in February 1996, Gil Amelio replaced Spindler as Apple's CEO. As an Apple board member, Amelio was aware that there were balance sheet problems, including a serious cash shortage, low-quality products, and lack of a viable operating system strategy. He could see that with the success of Windows NT and Windows 95, the Mac operating system was falling behind and holding the company back. Apple had been looking at various solutions for a new, modern operating system to keep them competitive in the current market and provide a foundation for the future. Amelio focused Apple's attention on Steve Jobs's company NeXT and its strong operating system NeXTSTEP. That system was built on top of UNIX, an operating system dating back to the 1960s. Using UNIX as its base gave NeXTSTEP several key advantages over Mac OS, like object-oriented programming and protected memory—a feature that translated into fewer system crashes. NeXTSTEP also used developer tools like Interface Builder, which made creating programs much more intuitive.

As a company, NeXT wasn't doing very well. Jobs originally wanted to create powerful computers for universities, education, and research. He accomplished that goal, but the computers were extremely expensive for the time, about $6,500, when the average PC clone was around $1,000 (and getting more powerful all the time, given the rapid evolution of technology and programming). NeXT computers never found a mass market, and the company had stopped producing them altogether in 1993 in order to focus solely on developing the NeXTSTEP operating system. Despite NeXT's computer struggles, the operating system was very powerful.[63] In December 1996, Apple acquired NeXT for $429 million and 1.5 million shares of Apple stock.[64]

With that, Steve Jobs was back working with Apple Computer.

Right Place, Right Time

When Steve Jobs came back to run Apple, he was a different man— still a demanding maverick and perfectionist innovator with the soul of an artist, but also a leader with the benefit of an additional decade building and running large businesses. Remember, he was only thirty years old when he was forced out of Apple, and that was the only corporate experience he had up to that point. He brought his more mature self fully to bear when he regained the reins at Apple and embarked on what would become one of the greatest comebacks in the history of business.

---

63   Clancy Morgan, "Steve Jobs Left Apple to Start a New Computer Company. His $12 Million Failure Saved Apple," Business Insider, accessed March 11, 2023, https://www.businessinsider.com/steve-jobs-12-million-dollar-failure-saved-apple-next-2019-8.

64   Jack Nicas, "Apple Is Worth $1,000,000,000,000. Two Decades Ago, It Was Almost Bankrupt," New York Times, August 2, 2018, https://www.nytimes.com/2018/08/02/technology/apple-stock-1-trillion-market-cap.html. See also: Joe Rossignol, "25 Years Ago, Apple Acquired next and Brought Back Steve Jobs," MacRumors, December 22, 2021, https://www.macrumors.com/2021/12/22/apple-acquiring-next-25th-anniversary/#:~:text=%22The%20acquisition%20of%20NeXT%20is,was%20announced%20December%2020%2C%201996.

Jobs initially returned to Apple as an advisor, then realized he had walked back into a company that was in extremely dire straits. For the fiscal year ending in September 1997, Apple reported a loss of $1.04 billion and was within ninety days of being insolvent. The company's stock price hit a new low, and the total market capitalization dropped to about $2.3 billion (just barely above the market capitalization on the day of the IPO seventeen years earlier). Apple needed a leader who could turn things around fast, and just like that, Steve Jobs showed up. Gil Amelio had been forced out in July 1997, and Jobs was installed as the interim CEO. Jobs cemented his position by announcing an investment into Apple Computer of $150 million from none other than Microsoft.

Microsoft was facing serious antitrust scrutiny by the US government at the time, so letting Apple Computer go bankrupt and losing the number-two operating system competitor by market share would not have helped their case. Many think this investment was a self-serving attempt by Microsoft to keep a competitor in the mix so as to dampen antitrust inquiries. Regardless of motivations, Microsoft helped save one of its fiercest competitors in the decades ahead. Jobs cleaned house by removing almost all the existing board of directors, including Mike Markkula, his original partner, who had gone along with the ouster of Jobs back in 1985. The path was cleared for Jobs to run the company his way, and that's just what he did.

Jobs immediately fired about three thousand employees and cut 70 percent of Apple's highly redundant product lines to focus on four key computers for professionals and consumers, two desktops and two portable versions: the iMac desktop and iBook portable computer and the Power Macintosh G3 desktop and the PowerBook. The stylish-looking G3 was introduced in May of 1998, at a consumer-friendly price of $1,299, and was an immediate success. No more clunky boxes! Style had made a comeback at Apple. Jobs was making Apple cool again. In fewer than three years, Apple sold over five million iMacs.[65] They would continue to focus on the Macintosh line by making it more powerful and more consumer friendly for many years to come.

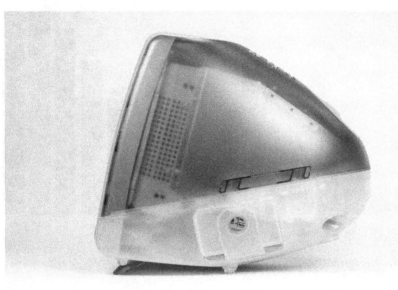

iMac G3
Source: Stephen Hackett, CC BY-SA 4.0 <https://creativecommons.org/licenses/by-sa/4.0>, via Wikimedia Commons

The company's recovery was well underway.

---

65   William Gallagher, "How Apple Went from Bust to Five Million Colorful iMacs Sold," AppleInsider, April 19, 2020, https://appleinsider.com/articles/20/04/19/how-apple-went-from-bust-to-five-million-colorful-imacs-sold. See also: Seán Moreau and Ken Mingis, "The Evolution of the Macintosh—and the iMac," *Computerworld*, April 28, 2021, https://www.computerworld.com/article/3025619/the-evolution-of-the-macintosh.html#slide4.

ANNUAL MAC SALES, 1998–2015

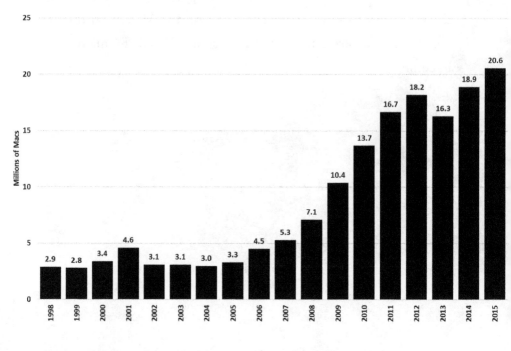

Source: SixColors.com

Over the next few years, Apple regained its financial footing and built momentum. Then came 2001, and the company was set to reshape itself and the entire industry. In March, it launched a powerful new operating system (built on the NeXT platform) called Mac OS X. It would serve as the heartbeat of future powerful Apple products.[66] In May, the company launched its first two retail stores in a space designed to highlight the stylish and cool nature of the Apple Computer experience and better control retail distribution. Then in

---

66   Brian X. Chen, "March 24, 2001: Apple Unleashes Mac OS X," *Wired*, March 24, 2010, https://www.wired.com/2010/03/macos-x-released/.

November, Apple Computer changed forever with the introduction of the iPod.[67]

Original iPod
Source: Blake Patterson from Alexandria, VA, USA, CC BY 2.0 <https://creative-commons.org/licenses/by/2.0>, via Wikimedia Commons

The iPod changed the face of Apple and sparked a run of cutting-edge innovations that the company still benefits from to this day. At the time, the digital music hardware business was both new and extremely fractured. There was no clear, easy-to-use consumer solution. There were limited flash players, which held around fifteen songs, and an MP3 CD format that held about 150 songs. Anyone who wanted anywhere near one thousand songs had to store them directly on their computer hard drive.

---

67   John Martellaro, "The Day Steve Jobs Launched the iPod and Changed Apple Forever," The Mac Observer, July 27, 2017, https://www.macobserver.com/columns-opinions/editorial/the-day-steve-jobs-launched-the-ipod-and-changed-apple-forever/.

"We lured you here today," Jobs announced to the crowd at the iPod launch event in October 2001, "with the promise of a breakthrough digital device that's not a Mac. And that's exactly what we're going to do … we love music, and it's always good to do something you love. More importantly, music is a part of everyone's life. But interestingly enough, in this whole new digital music revolution, there is no market leader."[68]

Jobs envisioned a simple, elegant, and small (!) device that would allow people to have "1,000 songs in your pocket." The iPod was an overnight phenomenon. Apple went on to sell over four hundred million iPods over the life of the product before its functionality was merged into other Apple devices. In 2003, Apple opened its iTunes store to complete the ecosystem by selling access to music that could be stored and played on the iPod.[69]

By being at the cutting edge of cool technology, Apple was back to being a leading innovator. So the company continued to create new products and push the envelope. In January 2007, Apple Computer, Inc. formally changed its name to Apple Inc. to reflect the fact that its focus had shifted from the narrow computer market to electronic consumer devices generally. At the same time, Apple Inc. and Steve Jobs announced both Apple TV and the revolutionary Apple iPhone. Apple TV never really moved the needle from a revenue standpoint, but it eventually allowed Apple to enter the fast-growing streaming video business, where it has about a 6 percent market share as of this writing.

---

68   "Apple's iPod Is the Other Device That Saved Apple, and Set the Table for the iPhone," AppleInsider, accessed March 11, 2023, https://appleinsider.com/articles/22/05/10/apples-ipod-is-the-other-device-that-saved-apple-and-set-the-table-for-the-iphone.

69   Sharon Pruitt-Young, "20 Years Ago, the iPod Was Born," NPR, October 23, 2021, https://www.npr.org/2021/10/23/1048706632/20-years-ago-the-ipod-was-born.

iPhone First Generation
Source: Carl Berkeley from Riverside California, CC BY-SA 2.0 <https://creative-commons.org/licenses/by-sa/2.0>, via Wikimedia Commons

The iPhone, however, was a game changer right from the beginning. In 2007, the cellular phone market was a very crowded space. Cell phone manufacturers primarily distinguished themselves from their competitors by having one or more different features. By contrast, the iPhone was designed to have maximum functionality along with a sleek and cool design. The original iPhone was a widescreen smartphone with touch controls, a built in iPod, and connectivity to the internet through Apple's web browser, Safari. The phone could also display visual voicemails and play video and included a two-megapixel camera. The device did not just feature a few new functions. Instead, it packed all the state-of-the-art features into one sleek device. Customers lined up overnight in front of Apple stores to get the first units, and that consumer excitement continued for years as crowds gathered for each successive version released. Sales took off like a rocket worldwide, and Apple Inc.'s market share of the smartphone industry exploded.[70]

iPHONE UNIT SALES

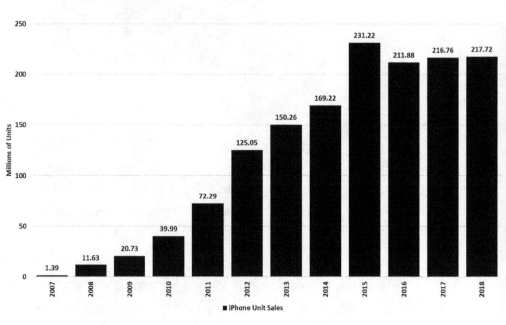

Source: Cult of Mac

70 Yuval Kossovsky and Ken Mingis, "Update: Jobs Touts iphone, 'AppleTV,'" *Computerworld*, January 9, 2007. https://www.computerworld.com/article/2549128/update--jobs-touts-iphone---appletv-.html.

GLOBAL PREMIUM SMARTPHONE (>$400) SALES MARKET SHARE, Q2 2020

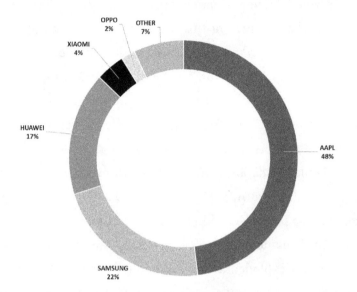

GLOBAL PREMIUM SMARTPHONE (>$400) SALES MARKET SHARE, Q2 2021

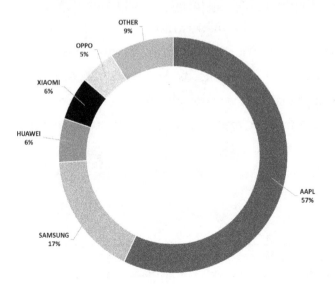

Source: Wake Phone

The iPhone had become a ubiquitous appendage to many people over the years since its launch as more and more functionality was added. It would come to dominate revenue drivers for the company in the years ahead. Much of this was due to the launch of the App Store in July 2008, where developers could provide an unlimited number of applications to run on the iPhone and at the same time pay Apple a fee for the privilege. It is important to note that Steve Jobs had fought since the beginning of Apple to keep the hardware and software systems at Apple as proprietary or closed-architecture systems. Apple had dabbled with opening its software to the industry just prior to Jobs's return, but he quickly used a loophole in the recent agreements the prior leadership team had created to shut that down. It took some convincing, but Jobs eventually agreed to the App Store concept, and it exploded as soon as it was launched. Five hundred third-party apps were available the first day, and there were over ten million downloads in the first seventy-two hours alone. Considering that Apple was taking 30 percent of the revenues generated by app developers just for allowing them on the platform (Apple reduced its cut to 15 percent in 2020 to try to avoid potential antitrust sanctions), the App Store was not an insignificant business line. By April 2009, there were one billion downloads. And as of 2020, there were over two million apps that had been downloaded more than two *billion* times, and the revenues had exploded over 3,500 percent since launch.[71]

---

71   Luke Dormehl, "Today in Apple History: App Store Opens Its Virtual Doors," Cult of Mac, July 10, 2022, https://www.cultofmac.com/491792/app-store-virtual-doors/#:~:text=App%20Store%20launch%20time&text=The%20App%20Store%20became%20an,day%20one%20reaped%20rich%20rewards.

APPLE APP STORE REVENUES

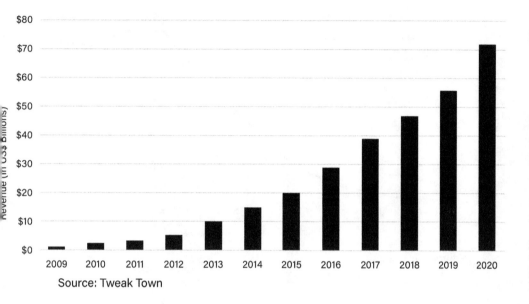

Source: Tweak Town

In the midst of all this explosive growth, Apple launched the iPad in January 2010, promoting the device as a highly portable hybrid combining a traditional laptop computer with the ease of use and functionality of the iPhone. Consumers loved the device, and it was another immediate success. Apple sold three hundred thousand iPads on the first day and sold 7.5 million iPads in the first year. Through 2020, Apple sold well over 350 million iPads.[72]

As of 2020, there were over two million apps that had been downloaded more than two *billion* times, and the revenues had exploded over 3,500 percent since launch.

72   Tom Warren, "Apple's iPad Changed the Tablet Game 10 Years Ago Today," The Verge, January 27, 2020, https://www.theverge.com/2020/1/27/21083369/apple-ipad-10-years-launch-steve-jobs-tablet-market.

APPLE UNIT SALES

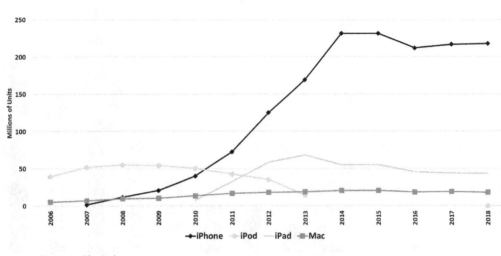

Source: Six Colors

Preparing for Succession and Continued Growth

Unfortunately, in the whirlwind of success, there was trouble in paradise. Steve Jobs was seriously ill and undergoing the fight of his life throughout much of this period of Apple's explosive growth. In October 2003, Jobs was diagnosed with pancreatic cancer, which generally has a very poor prognosis. Jobs finally agreed to have surgery in July 2004 after investigating homeopathic and other alternative forms of treatment. In his absence, he appointed Tim Cook, who was head of worldwide sales and operations, to run Apple. Jobs continued with a full work schedule after recovering from surgery but was forced to deal with ongoing speculation about his health when the cancer returned in 2006. He continued to deal with the matter privately, but there was rampant speculation about the ramifications for Apple, as Jobs's physical appearance continued to deteriorate markedly in the two years that followed. In January 2009, Jobs announced a six-month leave of absence to focus on his health. He received a liver transplant and returned as promised six months later. Then in January 2011, he announced another leave of absence to focus on his health, but this time offered no estimate of when he would return. In August 2011, Jobs resigned as CEO of Apple Inc., and he died on October 5 that same year. Rarely has one man been so closely identified with a company as successful as Apple Inc. And now he was gone.

Throughout Jobs's long period of decline, Tim Cook had always been there to assume temporary control of the company. The two worked extremely closely together, and Cook was immediately installed as CEO after Jobs's passing. Many were not sure that Tim Cook—or anyone—could step into Steve Jobs's shoes. But Cook excelled as CEO and continued Jobs's legacy of innovation and success.

Under Tim Cook, in May of 2014, Apple acquired headphone trendsetter Beats Electronics from Jimmy Iovine and Dr. Dre. Later that same year, Apple introduced the Apple Watch as a standalone and complement to the iPhone, opening up a new product sector and reenvisioning what watches might do. Revenues recovered across the company began to explode after Steve Jobs returned, as you can see from the table on the following page, reaching over $365 billion by 2021. By January 2022, Apple Inc. became the first publicly traded company with a market cap of more than $3 trillion.[73]

---

73 "How Apple Became One of the Largest Companies in the World," Yahoo! Finance, accessed March 11, 2023, https://finance.yahoo.com/news/how-apple-became-one-of-the-largest-companies-in-the-world-191110244.html#:~:text=The%20trillion%20dollar%20company&text=After%2042%20years%20in%20business,of%20more%20than%20%243%20trillion.

Revenue Growth

Establishing clear and strong succession may have been Steve Jobs's final gift to Apple Inc. and its millions of fans and shareholders. Under Tim Cook, Apple Inc. has continued to innovate and thrive. And as of this writing, Apple is still cool.

Apple Computer went public in December 1980 and can conceptually be divided into three separate companies over time: Apple with Steve Jobs, Apple without Steve Jobs, and Apple with Steve Jobs again. There were periods of rapid innovation, periods of stagnation and incredibly poor management, periods of serious infighting and dysfunction, and periods of serious financial danger. What follows is the consolidated table of annual revenues and net earnings for AAPL going back to the date of the IPO in 1980.

AAPL REVENUE AND NET INCOME HISTORY, 1980 TO 2022 ($ IN MILLIONS)

Fiscal Year	Revenue	Net Income
1980	$ 117.13	$ 11.70
1981	$ 335.00	$ 39.42
1982	$ 583.00	$ 61.00
1983	$ 983.00	$ 77.00
1984	$ 1,516.00	$ 64.00
1985	$ 1,918.00	$ 61.00
1986	$ 1,902.00	$ 154.00
1987	$ 2,661.07	$ 217.50
1988	$ 4,071.37	$ 400.26
1989	$ 5,284.01	$ 454.03
1990	$ 5,558.44	$ 474.89
1991	$ 6,308.85	$ 309.84
1992	$ 7,086.54	$ 530.37
1993	$ 7,976.95	$ 86.59
1994	$ 9,188.75	$ 310.18

1995	$	11,062.00	$	424.00
1996	$	9,833.00	$	(816.00)
1997	$	7,081.00	$	(1,045.00)
1998	$	5,941.00	$	309.00
1999	$	6,134.00	$	601.00
2000	$	7,983.00	$	786.00
2001	$	5,363.00	$	(25.00)
2002	$	5,742.00	$	65.00
2003	$	6,207.00	$	69.00
2004	$	8,279.00	$	276.00
2005	$	13,931.00	$	1,328.00
2006	$	19,315.00	$	1,989.00
2007	$	24,578.00	$	3,495.00
2008	$	37,491.00	$	6,119.00
2009	$	42,905.00	$	8,235.00
2010	$	65,225.00	$	14,013.00
2011	$	108,249.00	$	25,922.00
2012	$	156,508.00	$	41,733.00
2013	$	170,910.00	$	37,037.00
2014	$	182,795.00	$	39,510.00
2015	$	233,715.00	$	53,394.00
2016	$	215,639.00	$	45,687.00
2017	$	229,234.00	$	48,351.00
2018	$	265,595.00	$	59,531.00
2019	$	260,174.00	$	55,256.00
2020	$	274,515.00	$	57,411.00
2021	$	365,817.00	$	94,680.00
2022	$	394,328.00	$	99,803.00

Source: Bloomberg Finance L.P.

As you can see in the table above, after about 1987, growth at Apple stagnated. It is not a surprise that AAPL stock was moving closely with the overall market around this time. AAPL was not the standout growth company that investors thought they had purchased at the IPO. But then in the early to mid-1990s, the situation started to get downright ugly. Net income essentially evaporated, and any investors doing their fundamental homework would have seen clear signs to consider selling the stock. Once Steve Jobs came back in 1997, we start to see the ship recovering; earnings, slowly at first, start to move in the right direction. Then in the 2000s, we see an explosion in earnings as the different new products that Jobs introduced combined to propel AAPL stock into one of the most valuable companies ever. It would have been difficult for any investor to just hold this stock through all of the different phases since AAPL stock went public. Let's see if our three-step process can help an investor through *all* of the different phases of AAPL.

Applying the Three-Step Process

STEP 1: FUNDAMENTAL ANALYSIS / EARNINGS

AAPL FISCAL YEAR QUARTERLY EARNINGS HISTORY, 1980 TO 2022 (PER SHARE)

Fiscal Year	Q1	Q2	Q3	Q4	Annual
1981	$0.0000	$0.0000	$0.0000	$0.0000	$0.0000
1982	$0.0000	$0.0000	$0.0000	$0.0000	$0.0000
1983	$0.0000	$0.0000	$0.0000	$0.0000	$0.0000
1984	$0.0000	$0.0000	$0.0000	$0.0000	$0.0000
1985	$0.0000	$0.0000	$0.0000	$0.0000	$0.0000
1986	$0.0000	$0.0000	$0.0000	$0.0000	$0.0000
1987	$0.0000	$0.0000	$0.0000	$0.0000	$0.0000
1988	$0.0000	$0.0000	$0.0000	$0.0000	$0.0000
1989	$0.0000	$0.0000	$0.0000	$0.0000	$0.0000
1990	$0.0086	$0.0093	$0.0086	$0.0072	$0.0337
1991	$0.0114	$0.0096	-$0.0039	$0.0060	$0.0231
1992	$0.0121	$0.0097	$0.0096	$0.0072	$0.0386
1993	$0.0119	$0.0082	-$0.0146	$0.0002	$0.0057
1994	$0.0030	$0.0013	$0.0104	$0.0085	$0.0232
1995	$0.0138	$0.0053	$0.0075	$0.0043	$0.0309

1996	-$0.0050	-$0.0535	-$0.0023	$0.0018	-$0.0590
1997	-$0.0086	-$0.0504	-$0.0039	-$0.0113	-$0.0742
1998	$0.0033	$0.0037	$0.0068	$0.0071	$0.0209
1999	$0.0100	$0.0088	$0.0126	$0.0062	$0.0376
2000	$0.0101	$0.0129	$0.0111	$0.0093	$0.0434
2001	-$0.0104	$0.0021	$0.0030	$0.0034	-$0.0019
2002	$0.0020	$0.0020	$0.0016	-$0.0023	$0.0033
2003	-$0.0004	$0.0007	$0.0009	$0.0021	$0.0033
2004	$0.0030	$0.0023	$0.0029	$0.0050	$0.0132
2005	$0.0134	$0.0129	$0.0139	$0.0186	$0.0588
2006	$0.0243	$0.0175	$0.0196	$0.0225	$0.0839
2007	$0.0421	$0.0321	$0.0346	$0.0357	$0.1445
2008	$0.0646	$0.0446	$0.0457	$0.0904	$0.2453
2009	$0.0907	$0.0650	$0.0732	$0.1007	$0.3296
2010	$0.1336	$0.1211	$0.1275	$0.1682	$0.5504
2011	$0.2332	$0.2318	$0.2818	$0.2546	$1.0014
2012	$0.5011	$0.4446	$0.3364	$0.3129	$1.5950
2013	$0.4975	$0.3629	$0.2682	$0.2968	$1.4254
2014	$0.5211	$0.4175	$0.3225	$0.3575	$1.6186
2015	$0.7700	$0.5850	$0.4650	$0.4925	$2.3125
2016	$0.8250	$0.4775	$0.3575	$0.4200	$2.0800
2017	$0.8450	$0.5275	$0.4200	$0.5200	$2.3125
2018	$0.9800	$0.6875	$0.5900	$0.7350	$2.9925
2019	$1.0550	$0.6175	$0.5500	$0.7600	$2.9825
2020	$1.2591	$0.6400	$0.6525	$0.7400	$3.2916
2021	$1.7000	$1.4100	$1.3100	$1.2500	$5.6700
2022	$2.1100	$1.5400	$1.2000	$1.2900	$6.1400
2023	$1.8900				$1.8900
Key:	Positive	Negative			

Source: Bloomberg Finance L.P.

The quarterly earnings table above shows all the earnings announcements from Apple since the IPO through fiscal year-end 2022. Using our earlier methodology of looking for earnings surprises, either up or down, the quarterly earnings table above shows "surprise earnings," with black shaded boxes (positive) and gray shaded boxes (negative) marking instances where the stock moved up or down by 10 percent or more immediately after the earnings announcement. These events show up as clusters during the difficult period in the 1990s and then return a few quarters after Steve Jobs came back and got the innovation train rolling again. We will see later how this could have informed the management of a hypothetical position in AAPL over the years as we apply our hypothetical algorithm later in this chapter.

STEP 2: TECHNICAL ANALYSIS

Let's go all the way back to the AAPL IPO in December 1980 and take a long-term look at how some of the technical indicators we discussed earlier (the twenty-one-period EMA, RSI, momentum, money flows, and stochastics) behaved. The chart on page 154 illustrates the choppy first ten-plus years of trading in AAPL stock.

You can see from these next two charts that the first ten years of trading in AAPL stock were volatile. If you compare AAPL's stock chart to the chart of the overall S&P 500 for the same period on page 155, you can see that there are a lot of similarities; it seems AAPL was often trading in conjunction with the overall stock market during its first ten years. It traded a little worse during the first six years, as it took until 1987 for AAPL stock to finally get over (and stay over) the high prices hit in the very first month of trading. The prices are split adjusted, but the trajectory was sideways for a long time. Relative strength (RSI) didn't go and stay positive on a monthly basis until 1986, signaling a very significant run-up over the next few years. The same is true of the twenty-one-period EMA (gray and black arrows). Both RSI and EMA signaled a round trip in and out, up, and down from 1982 to 1983, but then EMA signaled another buy in 1986 shortly after RSI. With just a little more noise in the indicators, momentum, money flows, and stochastics generally reflected the same point: AAPL stock was nothing spectacular during the first six years on the market and then kicked into gear in early 1986 (along with the general stock market). Clearly, this would not have been an "easy" stock to hold over the first ten years, from an emotional but also a technical standpoint.

AAPL, DECEMBER 1980 TO DECEMBER 1989

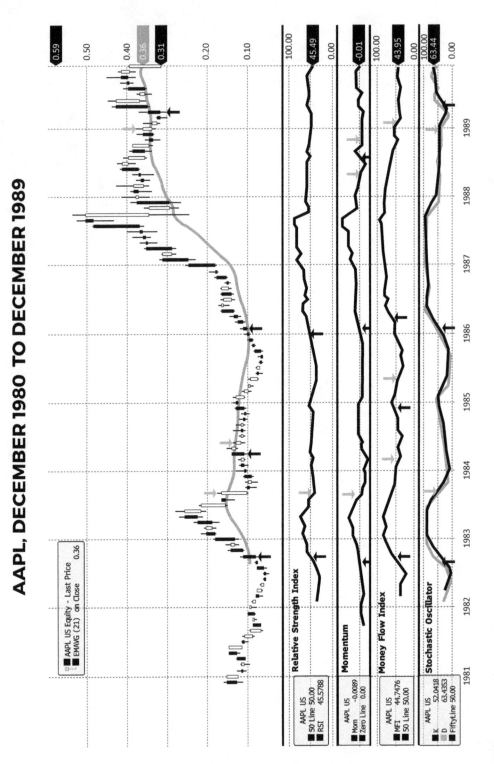

S&P 500 FROM DECEMBER 1980 TO DECEMBER 1989

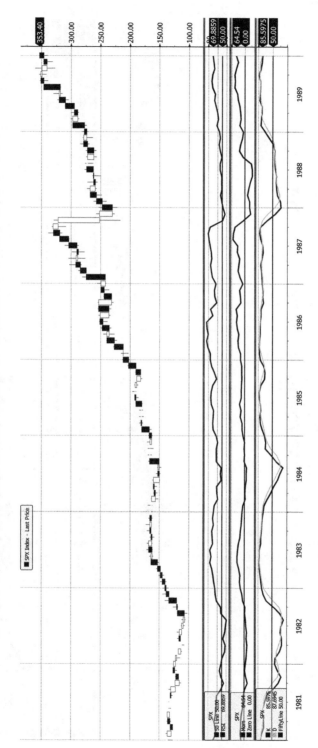

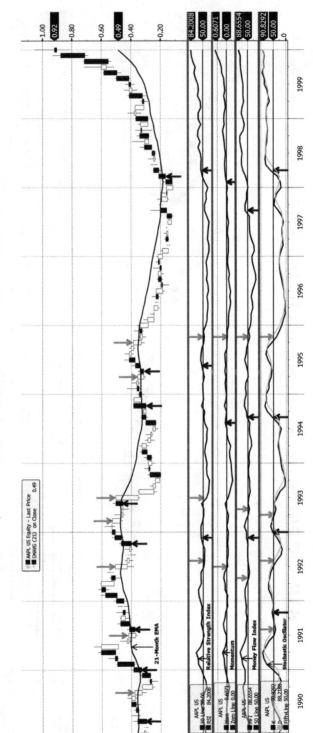

AAPL, JANUARY 1990 TO DECEMBER 1999

As Apple Computer floundered during the early 1990s, so, too, did the technicals. They all gave multiple buy and sell signals throughout the first years of the 1990s. The stock went nowhere again, and then in late 1995, you can see that all the technical indicators gave a unanimous sell signal. This is significant, because when all the technical indicators go off at once, it is a good indication that something significant may be happening. This signal corresponded to the near-death rattle that Apple Computer experienced right before Steve Jobs was brought back in 1997. In fact, AAPL stock lost over 50 percent of its value in that short time frame from 1995 to 1997. Remember, of course, that it was ninety days from insolvency at one point during that time. Then, and not coincidentally, all the indicators flipped back to positive in early 1998. This signal was right at the beginning of AAPL stock's historic comeback and emergence as a market leader.

The scale appears to change dramatically as we move to the next decade from January 2000 to December 2009 on page 160. Of course, this was an incredibly innovative decade for Apple, when it launched many of the successful products that would transform the company. It was also an extremely tumultuous time for the US economy and stock market—this period encompasses the dot-com bust of the early 2000s and the GFC of 2008. Interestingly, several of the technical indicators triggered a sell signal in late 2000 (EMA, RSI, momentum, and stochastics). And all of them reversed and triggered a buy signal after mid-2003 through 2004. That was right before another huge run in AAPL stock that saw about a tenfold increase by late 2007. Of course, that was right before the GFC debacle where, again, all the technical indicators triggered a sell signal in 2008 and then a buy signal the following year. Viewed simplistically, the technical indicators generally could have helped an investor to make relatively few trades during this extremely volatile and downright scary decade.

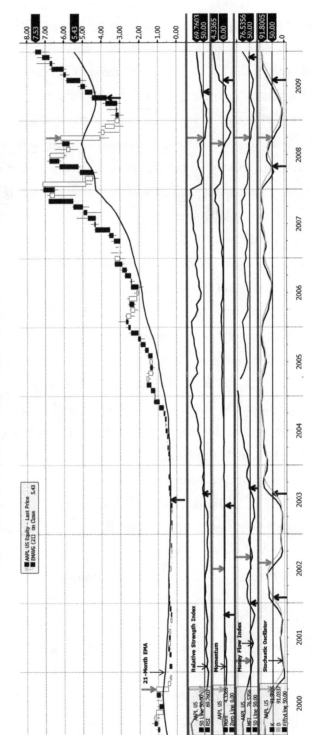

AAPL, JANUARY 2000 TO DECEMBER 2009

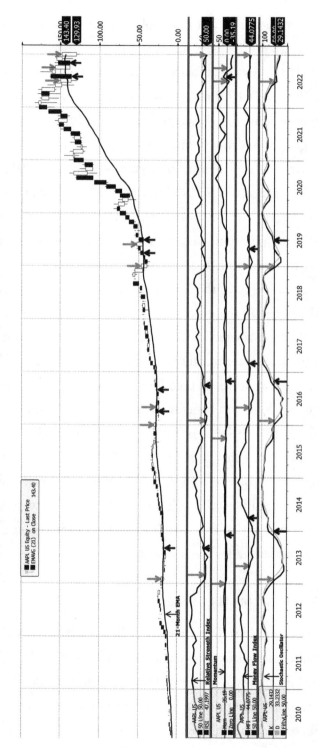

AAPL JANUARY 2010 TO DECEMBER 2022

We see a similar uniformity of technical signals from 2010 to the end of 2022 on the previous page. They all triggered a sell signal by April 2013 and were all back in buy mode by early 2014. The same is true in late 2015 through 2016 (money flows lagged a bit here). There were some sell signals in late 2018 with buy signals in 2019, although RSI and momentum never gave a clear sell signal during this period. Once the last buy signal was given in 2019, the stock advanced aggressively and did not generate any technical sell signals during the panic selling of the early COVID-19 pandemic in March 2020. That's important, because at the beginning of the pandemic, the market was dropping at a rate not seen since the Great Depression. Within a few weeks, the S&P had dropped about 35 percent from the highs. To say there was fear in the air is a wild understatement, but as the monthly technical readings show, AAPL stock theoretically never triggered a technical sell signal. So by the time the Fed stepped in with its "whatever it takes" monetary policy, an investor could have stayed long and benefited from the massive stimulus programs that drove the market quickly to new all-time highs. Technically, it would have been easy to hold the stock through 2021, as there were no technical sells generated through this period. Once the pandemic hangover and inflation watch started in 2022, we begin to see deterioration in some of the technical metrics, although not universally for this market leader.

STEP 3: RISK MANAGEMENT

The following chart illustrates when the stock price of AAPL dropped below the rolling fifty-two-week high. The top dotted black line is the rolling fifty-two-week high, and the lower dotted black line illustrates where a 20 percent price drop would be. There are many other signals, but these two examples help illustrate how this indicator could be

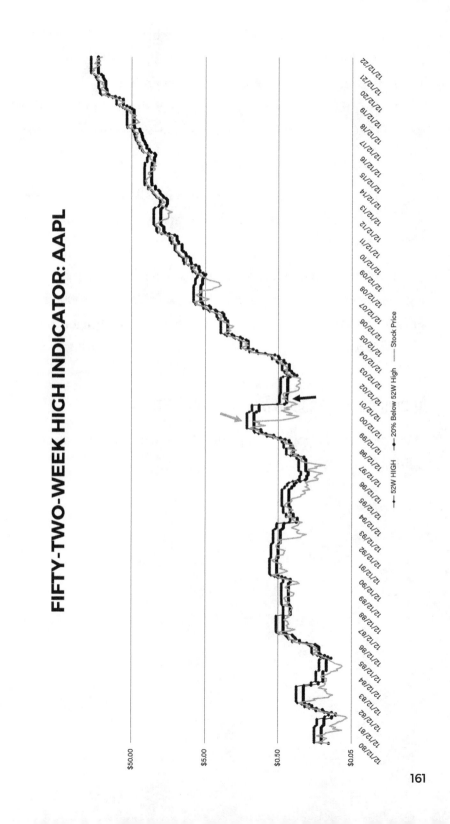

FIFTY-TWO-WEEK HIGH INDICATOR: AAPL

APPLE

161

used. The gray down arrow in 1999 and the black up arrow in 2001 are inserted for illustration purposes. If we look at the fifty-two-week high indicator, a few things are immediately noticeable:

- The stock was extremely choppy from the IPO in December 1980 all the way through the dot-com bust in the early 2000s.

- After about 2004, the stock mostly went straight up.

- There were a large number of buy/sell signals given over the decades, which would have caused a lot of hypothetical activity managing the stock.

Through the end of 2022, AAPL was generally still a very strong and consistent company, just as it had been since the early 2000s. Now let's add all of these details into our hypothetical scoring algorithm to see how it pans out.

Applying a Process to Manage AAPL Stock

Our hypothetical algorithm looks like this by comparison with a buy-and-hold approach:

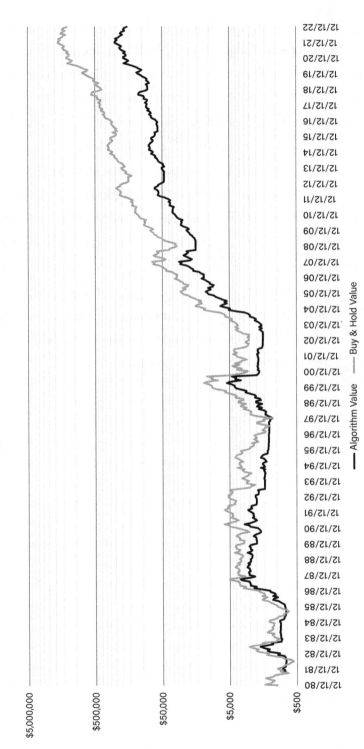

ALGORITHM VALUE VS. BUY & HOLD VALUE: AAPL

When you look at the long-term buy-and-hold results (gray line) and the hypothetical algorithm results (black line), APPL looks like a tale of two stocks. From the IPO in December 1980 through to nearly twenty years later, the stock went up and down and even had some crossovers between the different approaches. This largely reflected Apple's inability to execute until Steve Jobs's historic and triumphant return. After navigating the dot-com bust that affected all the markets generally, and beginning in about 2004, APPL stock began a relentless march higher. The algorithm we created never stood a chance once the company started executing and the stock started going almost straight up! The hypothetical algorithm could have provided some insurance against Apple ultimately failing to execute, but after Steve Jobs made his triumphant return, failure to execute no longer occurred. It is hard to imagine any trading system that would outperform one of the greatest comeback and success stories of all time.

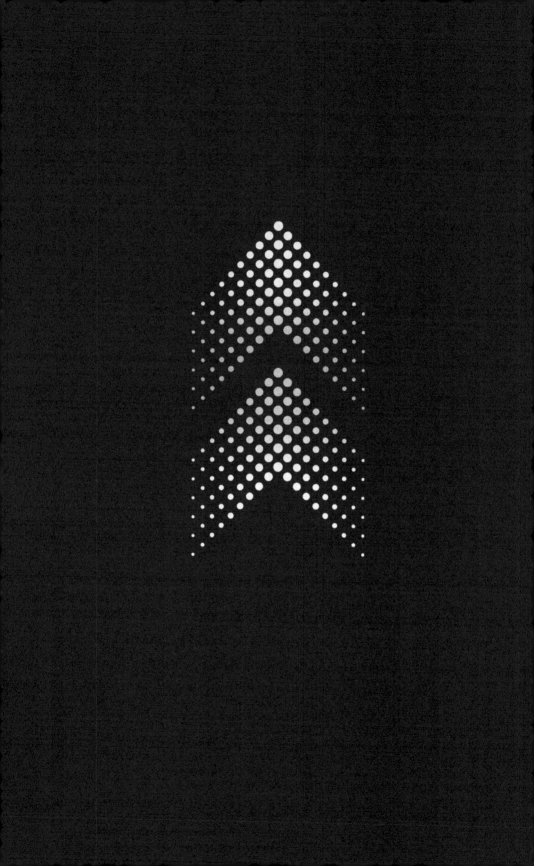

CHAPTER FIVE

GOOGLE (ALPHABET)

A total of $1,000 invested in Google stock the day it came public on August 19, 2004, at the IPO price of $85 was worth $41,520 on December 31, 2022, for a compounded return of 4,052 percent.

If you're changing the world, you're working on important things. You're excited to get up in the morning.

—LARRY PAGE

We want Google to be the third half of your brain.

—SERGEY BRIN

Timeline from Formation through Initial Public Offering

- 1996: Stanford students Larry Page and Sergey Brin write a search engine algorithm called BackRub. They quickly changed the name to Google.

- 1997: The domain name www.google.com is registered.

- 1998: Andy Bechtolsheim, cofounder of Sun Microsystems and also a Stanford alumnus, invests $100,000 in Google, and the company is officially incorporated. Google moves into its first office, the garage of one of Andy's friends.

- 1999: Google moves into an actual office space, attracts large private equity investors, and is processing five hundred thousand queries a day.

- 2000: Google becomes the search engine for Yahoo.com, launches AdWords, and revolutionizes advertising.

- 2001: Eric Schmidt, former CEO of Novell and former VP at Sun Microsystems, joins Google as CEO.

- 2004: Google launches Gmail and goes public later that same year on August 19, 2004, at $85 per share.

Origin Story

The story of Google has some familiar themes including Stanford University, a garage in Silicon Valley, and some really smart people. Sergei Brin met Larry Page at Stanford University in 1995. Both were twenty-two years old and taking graduate courses in computer science, and both came from academic households.

Page's parents were computer science and computer programming academics at Michigan State University. The apple doesn't fall far from the tree, as they say. Young Larry Page was surrounded by computers and computer culture at home, and he excelled at their use from an early age. He received a bachelor of science in computer engineering with honors from the University of Michigan in 1995 and an MS in computer science from Stanford University in 1998.

Sergei Brin's family was also focused on math and computer science. But he had a more complicated early life: he was born in Moscow, but his parents decided to emigrate from the USSR in 1978 during the height of the cold war. Their exit visas were approved in 1979, they made their way to the United States, and Sergei's father took a position teaching mathematics at the University of Maryland. Sergei excelled in school and received his BS from the Department of Computer Science at the University of Maryland in 1993 with honors in computer science and mathematics. He was only nineteen when he graduated. He earned his MS in computer science on a graduate fellowship at Stanford University in 1995.

Right Place, Right Time

After Page and Brin met at Stanford, they quickly joined forces to develop an internet search engine algorithm that they called "BackRub," which was a reference to how many "backlinks" (or inbound links) a website had. The algorithm would help the search engine prioritize and sort websites by relevance and popularity. At the time, most search engines—like Lycos and Ask Jeeves—would produce random results based on keywords. The world was rapidly moving from classified ads and print advertising to digital media and there was no clear leader or ubiquitous solution. Page and Brin's research led them to develop the trademarked PageRank™ link analysis algorithm that is the backbone of Google's search engine. By prioritizing popularity and relevance through backlinks, their search engine was much more efficient and user friendly. They had built a better mousetrap, one that led to the creation of one of the world's largest and fastest-growing companies. BackRub ran on the Stanford servers in 1996 for about a year before overwhelming those servers and being forced to move into the real world. The name was changed to "Google," and Google.com was officially registered in September 1997 and left Stanford in 1998. Google, of course, is a play on the mathematical term *googol*, which represents a 1 followed by 100 zeros, reflecting the almost infinite size of the internet.

> They had built a better mousetrap, one that led to the creation of one of the world's largest and fastest-growing companies.

Brin, Page, and Google were getting a lot of high-powered attention almost right from the beginning. That's most likely the result of several factors, including their association with Stanford University, the success of the algorithm driving Google.com, and their location in Silicon Valley.

In mid-1998, their first significant investor was Andy Bechtolsheim, a cofounder of Sun Microsystems, who invested $100,000 after seeing a demo on the porch of a Stanford faculty member's home in Palo Alto. This was followed by an investment of $250,000 by none other than Jeff Bezos of Amazon fame. Google was surrounded by heavy hitters from almost the very beginning and by 1999 was processing over five hundred thousand searches a day. The company raised another $25 million in funding from two more heavyweight firms, Sequoia Capital and Kleiner Perkins, adding both of these investors' influential general partners, Michael Moritz of Sequoia and John Doerr of Kleiner Perkins, to the board of directors.

SEARCH ENGINE MARKET SHARE, Q4 1999

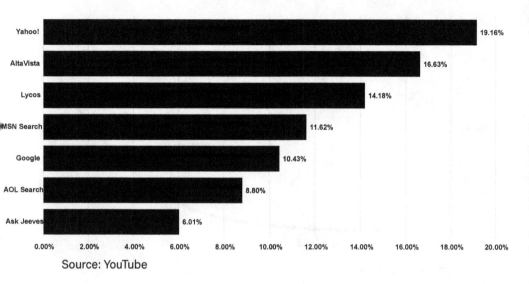

Source: YouTube

In 2000, Yahoo!, one of the internet's most popular sites at that time, chose Google as its internal search engine, and activity exploded. By the end of 2000, Google had achieved approximately a 35 percent market share including both its stand-alone site and the queries searched for Yahoo! The number of search queries only went up from there.

SEARCH QUERIES PER DAY (MILLIONS)

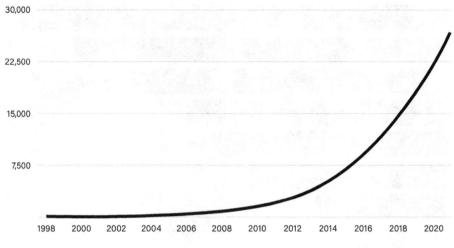

Source: RocketBlocks

In a move reminiscent of the early days of Apple, many of the experienced and influential people involved with Google felt that Page and Brin were too young and inexperienced to manage a company growing at this lightning pace. In 2001, Page and Brin were convinced to bring in Eric Schmidt as CEO. However, unlike at Apple, where they brought in a consumer-products-veteran soft drink executive to run things, Schmidt came from the technology world. He was familiar to most of the powerful players, had a doctorate in computer science, and had previously been the CEO of Novell. The "triumvirate" of Brin, Page, and Schmidt would endure successfully for many years.

State of the Industry

Brin and Page both hated the way other search engines were monetizing their sites. At the time, most were using tacky banner ads that were distracting and took too much time to load (slowing down the search experience). In fact, their original academic paper at Stanford describing the Google algorithm criticized search engines that were funded by advertising. But that was before there were millions of dollars invested by Silicon Valley heavy hitters focused on monetization. At some point, Google needed to make real money. AdWords was launched in 2000, allowing businesses to buy text ads that came up on the right-hand side of the screen along with normal search results. This pay-per-impression version generated significant revenue right from the beginning: Google made over $70 million from AdWords that first year. The company did not rest on its laurels but immediately worked to improve the approach. By 2002, Google released AdWords Select, which rewarded advertiser positions based on a combination of relevance and higher bids placed by advertisers for keywords. This was a revolutionary approach to selling ad space on the internet. Revenues exploded, allowing Google to report its first annual profit by the end of that same year. AdWords expanded into AdSense in 2003, allowing it to sell targeted ads on third-party websites.[74]

> This pay-per-impression version generated significant revenue right from the beginning: Google made over $70 million from AdWords that first year.

74 "The Evolution of Google AdWords—a $38 Billion Advertising Platform," WordStream, November 19, 2021, https://www.wordstream.com/blog/ws/2012/06/05/evolution-of-adwords. See also: Will Oremus, "The Forgotten Startup That Inspired Google's Brilliant Business Model," *Slate*, October 14, 2013, https://slate.com/business/2013/10/googles-big-break-how-bill-gross-goto-com-inspired-the-adwords-business-model.html.

Going Public

In 2004, the Boston Red Sox won their first World Series in eighty-six years. Facebook was launched, initially only for Harvard students. US swimmer Michael Phelps won his first six gold medals and set the record for most medals won at a single Olympic Games with eight in total. Bird flu plagued ten countries and regions in Asia. The average price of a new car in the US was about $24,600.

Overall stock market conditions in 2004 were somewhat shaky. The dot-com crash from 2000 to 2003 had just ended. But at the time no one could be certain the carnage was really over. During the dot-com bust, the NASDAQ stock exchange, where Google was to be listed, had dropped over 75 percent (!) from the peak. Investors were mortally wounded and not in an aggressive risk-taking mood. On top of that, the market in 2004 had gone literally nowhere by August of that year—the very month that the Google IPO was launched. Neither Google nor the overall stock market were considered "sure things" at that point in time.

Despite challenging market conditions, the Google stock offering (GOOG) IPO generated a lot of interest at the time due to its rapid earnings growth.

S&P 500, JANUARY 2004 TO DECEMBER 2004

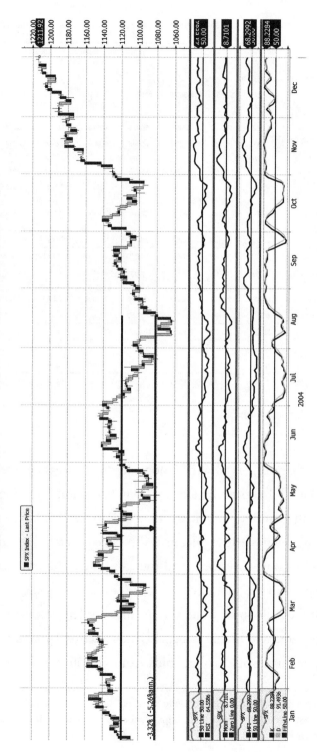

■ SPX Index - Last Price

	Mar 31, 2002	Jun 30, 2002	Sep 30, 2002	Dec 31, 2002	Mar 31,2003	Jun 30, 2003	Sep 30, 2003	Dec 31, 2003	Mar 31, 2004	Jun 30, 2004
				(in thousands, except per share amounts) (unaudited)						
Consolidated Statements of Income Data:										
Revenues	$42,285	$78,525	$130,787	$187,911	$248,618	$311,199	$393,942	$512,175	$651,623	$700,212
Costs and expenses:										
Cost of revenues	5,692	20,407	39,622	65,789	87,195	117,401	170,390	250,868	315,398	326,377
Research and development (1)	6,183	6,457	9,053	10,055	2,505	17,492	32,774	28,457	35,019	45,762
Sales and marketing	7,294	11,176	11,704	13,675	17,767	24,822	36,575	41,164	47,904	56,777
General and administrative	4,135	5,653	7,313	7,199	10,027	12,535	13,853	20,284	21,506	25,577
Stock-based compensation (2)	3,774	3,735	6,182	7,944	36,418	34,165	73,794	84,984	76,473	74,761
Total costs and expenses	27,078	47,428	73,874	104,662	163,912	206,415	327,386	425,757	496,300	529,254
Income from operations	15,207	31,097	56,913	83,249	84,706	104,784	66,556	86,418	155,323	170,958
Interest income, expense and other, net	(501)	(310)	(677)	(63)	(47)	766	464	3,007	300	(1,498)
Income before income taxes	14,706	30,787	56,236	83,186	84,659	105,550	67,020	89,425	155,623	169,460
Provisions for income taxes	6,780	14,194	25,929	38,356	58,859	73,382	46,594	62,171	91,650	90,397
Net income	$7,926	$16,593	$30,307	$44,830	$25,800	$32,168	$20,426	$27,254	$63,973	$79,063
Net income per share										
Basic	$0.07	$0.15	$0.26	$0.37	$0.20	$0.24	$0.14	$0.19	$0.42	$0.51
Diluted	$0.04	$0.08	$0.13	$0.19	$0.10	$0.12	$0.08	$0.10	$0.24	$0.30

Source: Tech Crunch

Perhaps that is why the Google leadership team elected to use an unusual IPO approach called a "Dutch auction."[75] Being a team of primarily computer scientists, they did not really like the traditional IPO approach where regular investors were generally excluded in favor of institutional investors. And they also didn't like the concept of a huge pop-up the first day of trading, followed by the air getting let out of the balloon with the average investor left holding the bag. The complicated and highly unusual Dutch auction approach meant that the company would collect bids from all interested investors, then

---

75 James Chen, "Dutch Auction: Understanding How It's Used in Public Offerings," Investopedia, January 15, 2023, https://www.investopedia.com/terms/d/dutchauction.asp.

group them by how much each investor was willing to pay and use that approximate price to go public. No company of this size had ever gone this route before.

In the aftermath of the dot-com bubble, the Dutch auction didn't go particularly well for Google. The company ended up cutting its planned IPO price from an original range of between $108 and $135 to a target range of between $85 and $95 before finally settling on the low end of the reduced range. IPO shares were priced at $85 per share on August 19, 2004, for a total market capitalization value of $23 billion.[76]

Whether it was the Dutch auction approach or the general hangover from the dot-com bust, shares of the new GOOGL IPO did not have the traditional huge run-up on their first day of trading. They closed higher—by about 18 percent—so still not too bad. As you can see from the chart of that first year on the following page, GOOG had the traditional chart pattern of receding from the early first few days' highs and then retesting the opening price. After that, the stock took out the original high price set in those first few days of trading and began to advance aggressively. By the end of the year, investors in GOOG had achieved over a 90 percent return relative to the IPO price. It didn't hurt that the overall market as measured by the S&P 500 was very favorable in that time frame and advanced over 20 percent from the GOOG IPO date through the end of the year.[77]

76   "How I Did It: Google's CEO on the Enduring Lessons of a Quirky IPO," *Harvard Business Review*, August 1, 2014, https://hbr.org/2010/05/how-i-did-it-googles-ceo-on-the-enduring-lessons-of-a-quirky-ipo. See also: Wayne Duggan, "This Day in Market History, August 19: The Google IPO—Alphabet (Nasdaq:Goog), Alphabet (Nasdaq:GOOGL)," Benzinga, August 19, 2022, https://www.benzinga.com/general/education/21/08/14291439/this-day-in-market-history-the-google-ipo-1.

77   John Shinal and Verne Kopytoff. "Google Finds Success on First Day of Trading / Stock: Search Engine Company Worth More Than Ford after Going Public," *San Francisco Chronicle*, January 26, 2012, https://www.sfgate.com/news/article/Google-finds-success-on-first-day-of-trading-2732254.php.

GOOGL, AUGUST 2004 TO AUGUST 2005

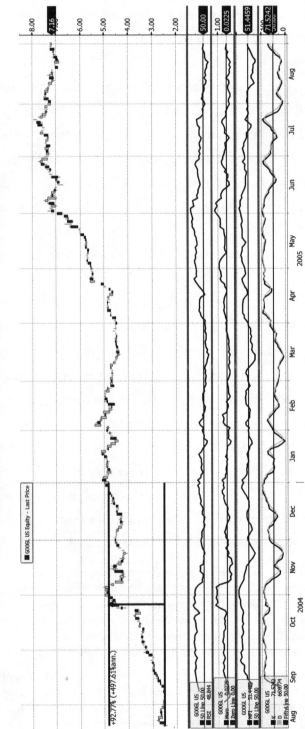

Achievements and Milestones

As a company, Google has an innovative soul. And under the triumvirate of Brin, Page, and Schmidt, innovation, development of existing businesses, and acquisitions accelerated. The same year as the IPO, Google launched Gmail, which would eventually become one of the dominant email services. Gmail was different from many other email providers at the time in that it wasn't associated with an ISP (internet service provider), it had robust search capabilities, and it came with an unprecedented one gigabyte of storage.

They leveraged off this platform to expand the Google footprint by adding features and apps to the site over the years, including Google Docs (a direct attempt to compete with Microsoft Office), video conferencing, calendars, news, cloud storage, photos, shopping, maps, and much, much more. Gmail took off and ultimately went on to become one of the dominant providers.[78]

---

78 Harry McCracken, "How Gmail Happened: The Inside Story of Its Launch 10 Years Ago Today," *TIME*, April 1, 2014, https://time.com/43263/gmail-10th-anniversary/. See also: Jordan Valinsky and Ivory Sherman, "Google's Incredible Growth: A Timeline," CNN, accessed March 12, 2023, https://www.cnn.com/interactive/2018/12/business/google-history-timeline/index.html.

ESTIMATED GMAIL USERS (MILLIONS)

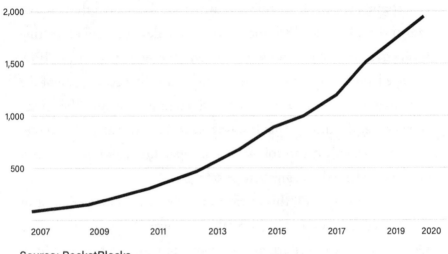

Source: RocketBlocks

MARKET SHARE OF THE MOST USED EMAIL CLIENTS IN 2021

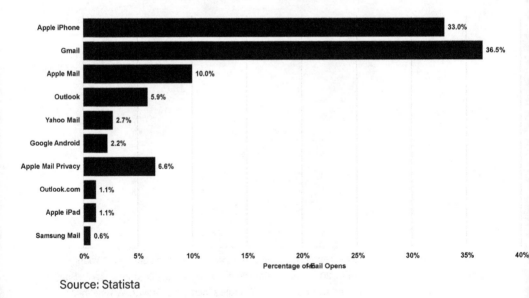

Source: Statista

Google Maps, launched in April 2005, was an ambitious project that would feed into numerous other projects in the future (for example, you can't make successfully autonomous-driving cars without good digital maps, can you?). The utility of having a web-based map for directions continued to drive traffic to Google. The product was quickly upgraded to Google Earth, which allowed users to see high-definition satellite images of almost everywhere in the world. This undercut the paid GPS navigation market that existed at the time and drove even more traffic to Google. Then, in 2008, Google integrated all of its functionality into a powerful web browser called Chrome, which drove even more traffic to the company.

ANDROID

In July 2005, Google acquired a small mobile phone software company called Android for $50 million. The original iPhone would not be launched by Apple until two years later, but this relatively small acquisition would prove to be extremely important to Google as it expanded its product lines into what would become a huge smartphone market. The Android OS was designed to enable "smarter mobile devices that are more aware of [their] owner's location and preferences" according to one of the original founders, Andy Rubin. The Android OS was intentionally designed as an open-source operating system that could be offered for free to third-party phone manufacturers. Google integrated its apps and functionality (and eventually its app store, Google Play) into the operating system, with the goal of profiting from providing these other services.

Google launched its original beta version of the Android operating system to developers in November 2007, shortly after the huge success of the Apple iPhone. The company publicly announced its intention to become a dominant player in the smartphone market; CEO Eric

Schmidt remarked, "Today's announcement is more ambitious than any single 'Google Phone' that the press has been speculating about over the past few weeks. Our vision is that the powerful platform we're unveiling will power thousands of different phone models."[79]

Early Android Phone
Source: Fumquat, CC BY-SA 4.0 <https://creativecommons.org/licenses/by-sa/4.0>, via Wikimedia Commons

The decision to give the operating system away for free and make it open-source catapulted Android into the dominant mobile OS provider within just a few years. It ultimately became one of the larger revenue drivers for Google. Then, in May 2012, Google

---

79   "The History of Android: The Evolution of the Biggest Mobile OS in the World," Android Authority, August 16, 2022, https://www.androidauthority.com/history-android-os-name-789433/.

acquired Motorola Mobility for $12.5 billion to further strengthen its dominant position in the global smartphone market.[80]

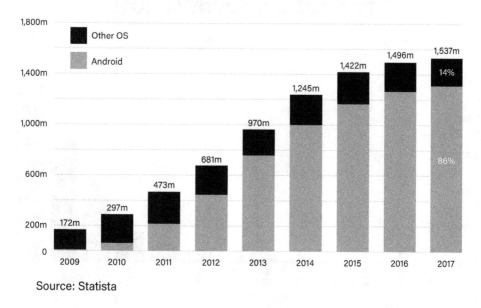

ESTIMATED WORLDWIDE SMARTPHONE SALES BY OPERATING SYSTEM (IN MILLION UNITS)

Source: Statista

YOUTUBE

In January 2005, Google launched Google Video to allow users to upload and share video content. Just one month later, YouTube.com launched with the same goal. The YouTube platform was growing at such a fast rate that Google Video could not compete with it, so in October 2006, Google bought YouTube outright for $1.65 billion. YouTube was becoming a phenomenon and was even included in a

---

80   "Let's Face It, the Android Brand Refresh Was Long Overdue," Android
      Authority, August 22, 2019, https://www.androidauthority.com/
      android-brand-refresh-overdue-1021462/.

roundabout way as person of the year by *TIME* magazine in 2006, reflecting user-generated contributions to internet sites. YouTube continued to grow at a meteoric pace, and Google was able to monetize the new acquisition.

HOURS OF CONTENT UPLOADED TO YOUTUBE EVERY MINUTE

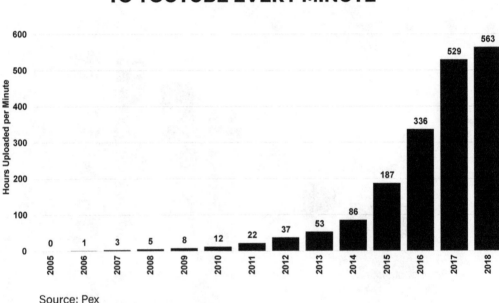

Source: Pex

Through 2007, Google focused on growing the number of users on the YouTube platform globally. That same year, it laid the foundation to supercharge its overall advertising business and to monetize YouTube by acquiring DoubleClick for $3.1 billion. The Double-Click acquisition allowed Google to build an advertising ecosystem on YouTube and its other platforms that collectively made sense for users, partners, and advertisers. YouTube is now running more monetized views than any other video site has total views, while also displaying ads against over a billion video views a week. YouTube is another of several Google products and applications with over one billion users and another huge revenue stream for the company.[81]

GOOGLE PRODUCTS WITH ONE BILLION OR MORE USERS

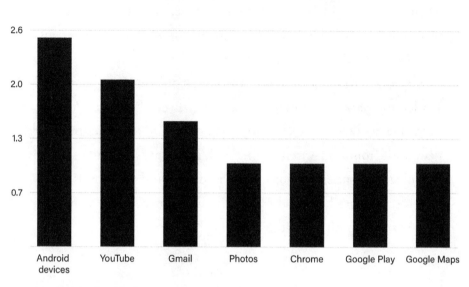

Source: RocketBlocks

Preparing for Succession and Continued Growth

With the launch of Google Drive in 2012, Google entered the cloud storage business to compete with companies like Dropbox. The market for cloud storage and services has exploded and continues to grow as I write this book. The race for dominance also continues, with Amazon

---

81   "History of Monetization at YouTube—YouTube5Year," Google Sites, accessed March 12, 2023. https://sites.google.com/a/pressatgoogle.com/youtube5year/home/history-of-monetization-at-youtube. See also: Tony Yiu, "Why Did Google Buy Doubleclick?," Towards Data Science, May 6, 2020, https://towardsdatascience.com/why-did-google-buy-doubleclick-22e706e1fb07.

AWS and Microsoft Azure leading the way. Google currently has about a 10 percent market share of this fast-growing sector but may have a demographic advantage that will benefit it over time. According to a survey conducted by Creative Strategies in 2016, when students write papers by themselves, only 12 percent use Google Docs.[82] But when students write papers in groups—when they collaborate—78 percent use Google Docs. On the other hand, 80 percent of students use Microsoft Word for individual work, and 13 percent use it for group work. The dynamic is the same for all millennials, regardless of gender, the phone they use, or where they live: Microsoft Word for individual work, Google Docs for collaborative work.[83] Combine the new work-from-home trend along with millennials favoring Google for collaboration, and Google may have the wind at its back for its cloud services products in the years ahead. You can see the company's already strong position in the following graphic:

82   Sean Chan, "Report: Students Prefer Google Docs over Microsoft Word for Collaborative Work," MSPoweruser.com, July 29, 2016, https://mspoweruser.com/report-students-prefer-google-docs-microsoft-word-collaborative-work/.

83   Matt Richman, "Millennials Prefer Microsoft Word for Individual Work, Google Docs for Collaborative Work," Vox, July 29, 2016, https://www.vox.com/2016/7/29/12312086/millenials-microsoft-word-google-docs-collaboration-study.

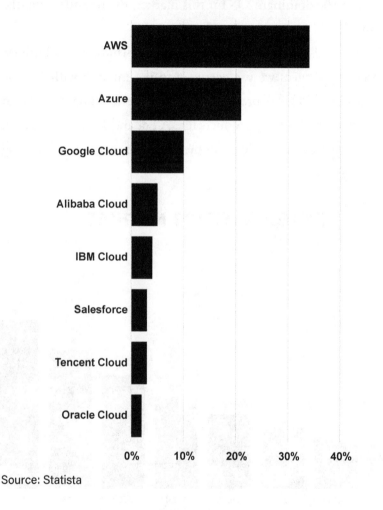

WORLDWIDE MARKET SHARE OF LEADING CLOUD INFRASTRUCTURE SERVICE PROVIDERS IN Q2 2022

Source: Statista

Google is also a leader in the nascent self-driving car business through its ownership of Waymo (along with Google Maps and the Waze navigation app acquisition for $1.2 billion in 2013). It is likely that at some point in the future, we won't be jumping into the back of a stranger's car (like Uber) to get a ride. As self-driving technology continues to improve (through companies like Tesla and Waymo/ Google), it is likely that the car will just come get us and we won't have to come up with things to talk about with the driver. If Google can become the dominant OS for this market, the revenue potential is massive.

Google is also pushing into the Internet of Things (IoT) business of connecting devices we use everyday to the internet with Google Nest and Google Home products. Amazon has a strong position in this new market also with products like Alexa and Ring. The market is expected to grow dramatically in the decade ahead, as the following graphic illustrates.

ENTERPRISE IOT MARKET

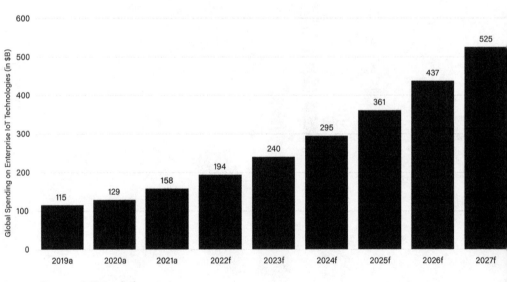

Source: IoT Analytics

Finally, artificial intelligence, or AI, may be the next gold rush for companies like Google. Google acquired London-based DeepMind back in 2014 for about $600 million. This division of Google has continued generating losses, but Google remains committed to funding the AI think tank because of the massive long-term revenue opportunities that could be created. "I'm very happy with the pace at which our R&D on AI is progressing," Alphabet CEO Sundar Pichai said on the company's second-quarter 2020 earnings call. "And for me, it's important that we are state-of-the-art as a company, and we are leading. And to me, I'm excited at the pace at which our engineering and R&D teams are working both across Google and DeepMind."[84]

After a decade of success as Google CEO, Eric Schmidt stepped down from that role in 2011, at which point Larry Page assumed CEO responsibilities. By 2015, Google reorganized under the name Alphabet to accommodate the diverse businesses and projects the company was working on. Google became the largest subsidiary of Alphabet. After the reorganization, Sundar Pichai was named CEO of Google, while Larry Page and Sergei Brin would run the parent company Alphabet as CEO and president, respectively. Then, in December 2019, Page and Brin announced that they were stepping down, and Pichai would become CEO of Alphabet. Sundar Pichai had been with Google since 2004 and had enjoyed a meteoric rise inside the company. He was instrumental in the development of the Chrome browser, and was eventually put in charge of Android, Chrome, and Google Play/Apps, as well as leading the Nest acquisition at $3.2 billion in 2014. Pichai is considered a true "Googler." Having helped build the company over many years, he is in a great position to take Google/Alphabet into its next chapters.

84   Sam Shead, "DeepMind A.I. Unit Lost $649 Million Last Year and Had a $1.5 Billion Debt Waived by Alphabet," CNBC, December 17, 2020, https://www.cnbc.com/2020/12/17/deepmind-lost-649-million-and-alphabet-waived-a-1point5-billion-debt-.html.

Dealing with Adversity

In addition to managing one of the fastest-growing companies in the history of the world, Pichai will have his hands full dealing with regulators. Companies that get as big as Google and that dominate their markets get a lot of antitrust scrutiny. In 2017, the European Union fined Google $2.42 billion (euros) for violating EU antitrust rules.[85] In 2021, seventeen US states brought a massive antitrust case against Google, and at the start of 2023, the US Department of Justice sued Google for illegally dominating the digital advertising market.[86] Google controlled about 28.6 percent of the $211.2 billion in US digital ad spending in 2021, according to Statista, while Facebook made up 23.8 percent and Amazon 11.6 percent.[87] Regulatory scrutiny will likely intensify, and how Pichai navigates these challenges will be a large part of his legacy when the next chapter for Google/Alphabet gets written.

Revenue Growth

Revenue growth for Google has been nothing short of astronomical. The table and graphic that follow illustrate an almost relentless upward trajectory as Google entered and dominated new markets.

85 "Press Corner," European Commission, accessed March 12, 2023, https://ec.europa.eu/commission/presscorner/detail/es/MEMO_17_1785.

86 "Justice Department Sues Google for Monopolizing Digital Advertising Technologies," US Department of Justice, January 26, 2023, https://www.justice.gov/opa/video/justice-department-sues-google-monopolizing-digital-advertising-technologies.

87 "Ad-Selling Companies U.S. Digital Ad Revenue Shares 2020-2025," Statista.com, May 17, 2023, https://www.statista.com/statistics/242549/digital-ad-market-share-of-major-ad-selling-companies-in-the-us-by-revenue/.

GOOGL REVENUE AND NET INCOME HISTORY, 2004 TO 2022 ($ IN MILLIONS)

Fiscal Year	Revenue	Net Income
2004	$ 3,189.22	$ 399.12
2005	$ 6,138.56	$ 1,465.40
2006	$ 10,604.92	$ 3,077.45
2007	$ 16,593.99	$ 4,203.72
2008	$ 21,795.55	$ 4,226.86
2009	$ 23,650.56	$ 6,520.45
2010	$ 29,321.00	$ 8,505.00
2011	$ 37,905.00	$ 9,737.00
2012	$ 46,039.00	$ 10,737.00
2013	$ 55,519.00	$ 12,733.00
2014	$ 66,001.00	$ 14,136.00
2015	$ 74,989.00	$ 16,348.00
2016	$ 90,272.00	$ 19,478.00
2017	$ 110,855.00	$ 12,662.00
2018	$ 136,819.00	$ 30,736.00
2019	$ 161,857.00	$ 34,343.00
2020	$ 182,527.00	$ 40,269.00
2021	$ 257,637.00	$ 76,033.00
2022	$ 282,836.00	$ 59,972.00

Source: Bloomberg Finance L.P.

The chart below provides a dramatic illustration of the revenue growth rate over the years.

ANNUAL REVENUE OF ALPHABET

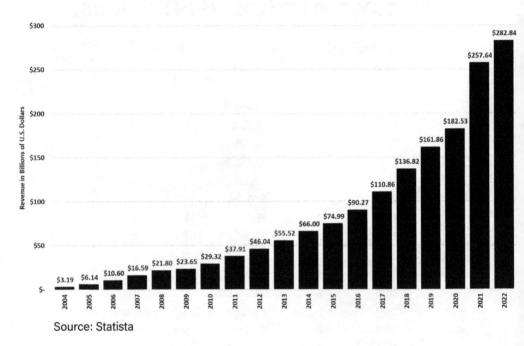

Source: Statista

The next table gives us a deeper look into how and where those revenues have been generated. You can see that advertising across all Google properties represented about 80 percent of total revenues in 2021. You can also see Google Cloud and other services, while still a small portion of overall revenues, are growing rapidly.

ANNUAL REVENUES OF ALPHABET, 2017 TO 2021, BY SEGMENT

Segment	2017	2018	2019	2020	2021
Google Search & Other	$69,811.00	$85,296.00	$98,115.00	$104,062.00	$148,951.00
YouTube Ads	$8,150.00	$11,155.00	$15,149.00	$19,772.00	$28,845.00
[TOTAL] Google Properties	$77,961.00	$96,451.00	$113,264.00	$123,834.00	$177,796.00
Google Network Members' Properties	$17,616.00	$20,010.00	$21,547.00	$23,090.00	$31,701.00
[TOTAL] Google Advertising	$95,577.00	$116,461.00	$134,811.00	$146,924.00	$209,497.00
Google Cloud	$4,056.00	$5,838.00	$8,918.00	$13,059.00	$19,206.00
Google Other	$10,914.00	$14,063.00	$17,014.00	$21,711.00	$28,032.00
[TOTAL] Google Revenues	$110,547.00	$136,362.00	$160,743.00	$181,694.00	$256,735.00
Other Bets Revenues	$477.00	$595.00	$659.00	$657.00	$753.00

Source: Statista

Applying the Three-Step Process

STEP 1: FUNDAMENTAL ANALYSIS / EARNINGS

Google demonstrated almost nonstop aggressive revenue growth since going public in 2004. It had to endure its share of challenges like the Global Financial Crisis and legal issues. It is hard to remember, but even GOOGL, one of the greatest stocks of all time, dropped by as much as 66 percent during that GFC. What was the average investor to do in the middle of such carnage? Hold one's nose, stay long, and hope? Let's see what sort of help the three-step process and our hypothetical technical algorithm could have provided.

GOOGL FISCAL YEAR QUARTERLY EARNINGS HISTORY, 2004 TO 2022 (PER SHARE)

Fiscal Year	Q1	Q2	Q3	Q4	Annual
2004	$0.0060	$0.0075	$0.0048	$0.0177	$0.0360
2005	$0.0323	$0.0298	$0.0330	$0.0305	$0.1256
2006	$0.0488	$0.0583	$0.0590	$0.0823	$0.2484
2007	$0.0795	$0.0733	$0.0845	$0.0948	$0.3321
2008	$0.1030	$0.0980	$0.1015	$0.0303	$0.3328
2009	$0.1123	$0.1165	$0.1283	$0.1533	$0.5104
2010	$0.1515	$0.1427	$0.1680	$0.1952	$0.6574
2011	$0.1377	$0.1920	$0.2083	$0.2055	$0.7435
2012	$0.2188	$0.2105	$0.1633	$0.2155	$0.8081
2013	$0.2485	$0.2425	$0.2190	$0.2475	$0.9575
2014	$0.2520	$0.2440	$0.1844	$0.3395	$1.0199
2015	$0.2550	$0.2465	$0.2865	$0.3531	$1.1411
2016	$0.3010	$0.3500	$0.3625	$0.3780	$1.3915
2017	$0.3865	$0.2505	$0.4785	-$0.2175	$0.8980
2018	$0.6245	$0.2270	$0.6530	$0.6385	$2.1430
2019	$0.4750	$0.7105	$0.5060	$0.7675	$2.4590
2020	$0.4935	$0.5065	$0.8200	$1.1150	$2.9350
2021	$1.3145	$1.3630	$1.3995	$1.5345	$5.6115
2022	$1.2300	$1.2100	$1.0600	$1.0500	$4.5500
Key:	Positive	Negative			

Source: Bloomberg Finance L.P.

The black (positive surprise) and gray (negative surprise) boxes in the quarterly earnings table indicate the market reaction to the earnings announcement. A "surprise" announcement that moved the stock up more that 10 percent is coded with black box and a 10 percent drop based on a negative surprise is coded with a gray box. The first thing you notice is that there are no gray or "negative surprise" boxes in the table. Google's earnings were consistently in line with expectations or viewed as positive surprises by the market.

We will look into the quarterly earnings and apply our hypothetical scoring approach later to see if that can help manage all the volatility.

STEP 2: TECHNICAL ANALYSIS

Let's go back to the IPO in August 2004 and take a long-term look at how some of the technical indicators we discussed earlier (the twenty-one-period EMA, RSI, momentum, money flows, and stochastics) behaved. The following chart illustrates the choppy first several years of trading in GOOGL stock—its launch out of the destruction of the dot-com bust and its progress through the chaos of the GFC.

The monthly chart tracking August 2004 to December 2011 shows that GOOGL stock was a huge winner, gaining up to 900 percent (!) by late 2007. None of the technical indicators we have been looking at went negative during that time, allowing a hypothetical investor to hold on to the stock for the entire early run. But then things got ugly. The GFC broke out, and GOOGL stock was not immune to the volatility. All of the technical indicators were firing off buy and sell triggers. It was truly a choppy period. Having a technically based algorithm would certainly have helped take the emotion out of the equation. The year 2011 ended with almost all of the technical indicators suggesting that the hypothetical investor should stay long in the stock.

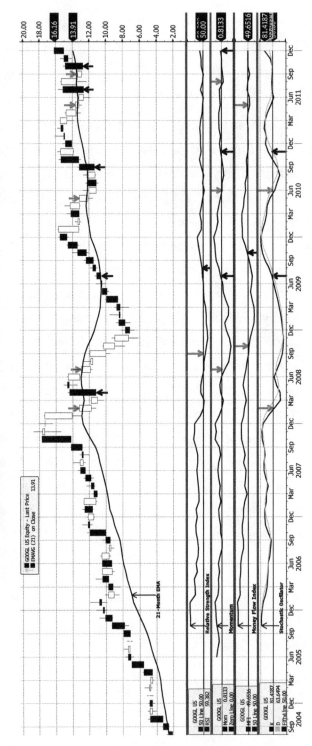

GOOGL, AUGUST 2004 TO DECEMBER 2011

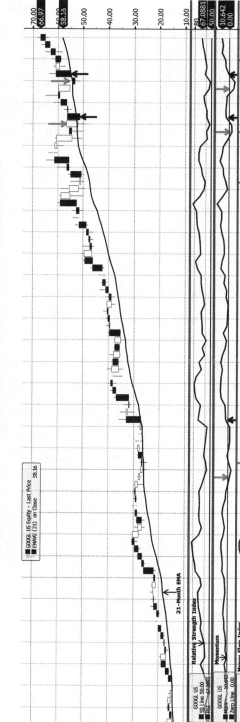

GOOGL, JANUARY 2012 TO DECEMBER 2019

The chart tracking January 2012 to December 2019 shows that GOOGL stock rose about 400-plus percent and was the opposite of choppy. RSI never gave a sell signal the entire time. And the sell signals generated by the other indicators were relatively few and short in duration. This was a great period to hold GOOGL stock.

I selected this shorter time period of 2020 to 2022 on the following page for two reasons:

1. It is easier to see because of the scale.

2. It includes the pandemic panic period, recovery, and inflation shock, which had as much volatility and emotion tied to it as just about any period in history.

The amazing thing about this period is that there was only one very short sell/buy signal given by any of the technical indicators until 2022. Only the twenty-one-period EMA triggered a sell signal during the pandemic and then quickly reversed to a buy. The stock moved up as much as ~100 percent during this short period, and the technical indicators supported generally holding the stock. As inflation took hold in 2022, red flags appeared, suggesting some caution might be appropriate around GOOGL for the speculative trader.

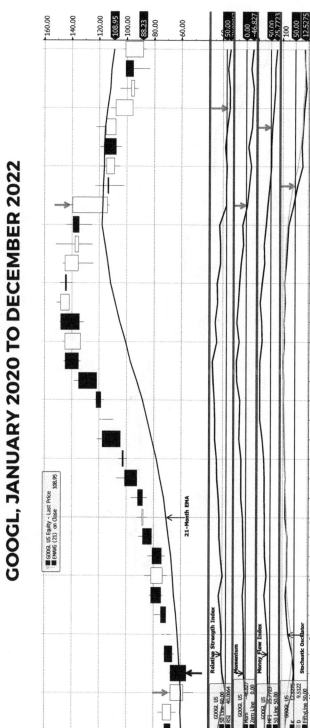

GOOGL, JANUARY 2020 TO DECEMBER 2022

FIFTY-TWO-WEEK HIGH INDICATOR: GOOGL

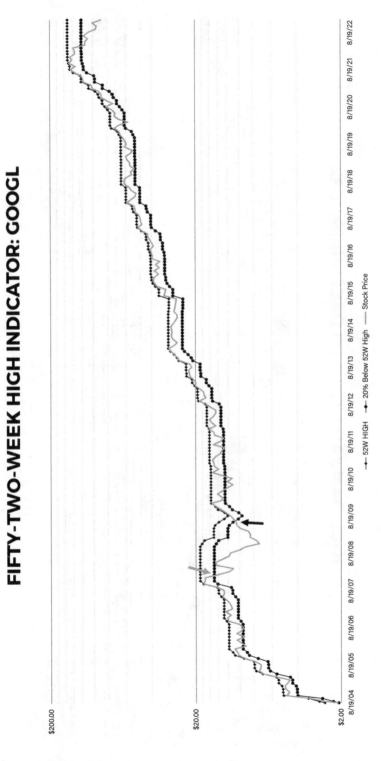

STEP 3: RISK MANAGEMENT

This chart illustrates when the stock price of GOOGL dropped below the rolling fifty-two-week high. The top black dotted line is the rolling fifty-two-week high, and the lower black dotted line illustrates where a 20 percent price drop would be (along with a down gray arrow and a black up arrow for illustration purposes only). If we look at the fifty-two-week high indicator, we immediately notice a few things:

- There were not many signals given by this indicator over the years.

- The stock enjoyed long periods of moving mostly up.

From the IPO through the end of 2021, most of the signals given by this indicator for GOOGL were quickly reversed. It remains to be seen if they can continue to execute and perform at their historical level.

Let's plug all this data into our scoring algorithm.

Applying a Process to Manage GOOGL Stock

Bringing it all together in our hypothetical algorithm looks like this compared to a buy-and-hold approach (with the gray line representing the buy-and-hold investor):

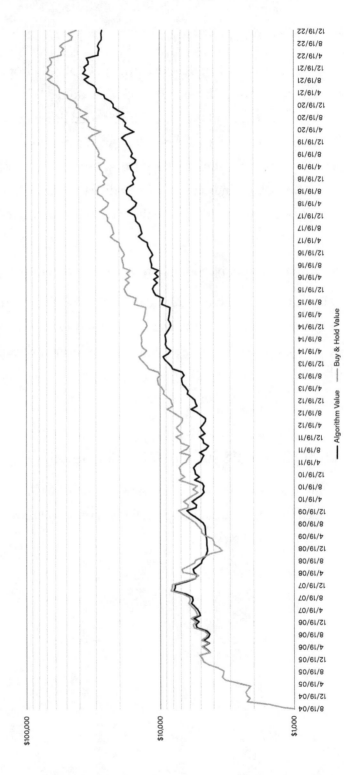

ALGORITHM VALUE VS. BUY & HOLD VALUE: GOOGL

—— Algorithm Value   —— Buy & Hold Value

With a powerhouse like GOOGL, it would be hard to expect any approach other than buy-and-hold to generate superior results. In fact, the only time the hypothetical algorithm exceeded buy-and-hold was during the GFC crash of 2008 and 2009. And that was temporary, as GOOGL was off to the races thereafter. The buy-and-hold investor saw $1,000 become $41,520 through the end of 2022 while the hypothetical algorithm investor might have realized $26,790.71.

There was a price to be paid for risk management around this monster winning stock. That's to be expected when a stock goes almost straight up over time. With the exception of the Global Financial Crisis and 2022, GOOGL has been a relatively consistent winner year in and year out. Trading around an almost perfect stock like GOOGL would make it almost impossible to beat a buy-and-hold approach. But maybe having a plan to protect against calamity is worth the cost of the insurance.

CHAPTER SIX

TESLA

A total of $1,000 invested in TSLA stock the day it came public on June 29, 2010, at the IPO price of $17 was worth $108,688.24 on December 31, 2022, for a compounded return of 10,769 percent.

---

*When something is important enough, you do
it even if the odds are not in your favor.*

—ELON MUSK

Timeline from Formation through Initial Public Offering

- 2003: Tesla is founded by Martin Eberhard and Marc Tarpenning in July 2003.

- 2004: Elon Musk invests $6.4 million as majority shareholder and chairman of the board.

- 2008: Tesla's first vehicle, the Roadster, begins production in March 2008.

- 2008: Elon Musk assumes the role of CEO in October 2008.

- 2010: Chief executive Elon Musk and team ring the NASDAQ opening bell on June 29, 2010, as Tesla becomes the first car company to go public in the United States since Ford Motor Company in 1956. On June 29, 2010, TSLA goes public at $17 per share.

Origin Story

The story of Tesla is a bit different than the other companies we are profiling in this book, because Tesla primarily manufactures cars and is not necessarily a pure technology company (although they might disagree). But this book is primarily about finding and managing winners, and there is no doubt that long-term holders of TSLA stock have achieved incredible returns. So let's dig into this story and see how Tesla went from a company few thought would survive to being one of the largest companies in the S&P 500 in a little over a decade.

As many people know, Tesla was named after Nikola Tesla, who did pioneering work on electromagnetic fields. Along with Thomas Edison, Nikola Tesla is considered one of the two great electricity pioneer inventors of the late nineteenth century. Notably, Nikola Tesla championed the alternating current (AC) form of electricity, while Edison promoted direct current (DC). It is AC that we use in our homes every day, and both AC and DC power Tesla vehicles (AC for the drive motors and DC for everything else).

A few years prior to Tesla Motors, General Motors had demonstrated that the electric vehicle concept could work through its 1996 experimental model called the EV1. GM never released any of these cars for public purchase, and even though they shuttered the program in 1999 and eventually destroyed all the cars (!), the program was generally considered successful from an engineering standpoint. Two Silicon Valley friends, Martin Eberhard and Marc Tarpenning, both engineers, were inspired by the possibilities of an all-electric vehicle as demonstrated by the EV1 and decided to start a company to build their vision of an entirely electric car. They named the company Tesla Motors. The goal was to build affordable mass-market electric vehicles to prove that people didn't need to compromise performance to drive electric cars.[88]

Eberhard initially served as CEO and Tarpenning as CFO. One of the first orders of business for the fledgling company was to raise money. And so goes the story of how Elon Musk first became involved with Tesla Motors. In early 2004, Musk led the initial round of venture capital funding, investing $6.5 million of the $7.5 million total. He then joined Tesla Motors as the head of the board of directors.[89] We can't talk about Tesla from that point forward without talking about Elon Musk, so let's take a look at how he led Tesla to become one of the greatest-performing stocks of the last few decades.

Elon Musk was born on June 28, 1971, in Pretoria, South Africa. Like many of the other leaders we've discussed in prior chapters, he had an early interest in computers and programming. Musk launched his first business venture at the age of twelve when he created a video game for PCs called Blastar. His parents were successful and considered wealthy, but his childhood had some unique ups and downs. For one, he grew up while the apartheid system was still firmly in place in South Africa. There are reports that he was bullied at times and was

---

88   "About," Tesla, accessed March 12, 2023, https://www.tesla.com/about#:~:text=Tesla%20was%20founded%20in%202003,to%20drive%20than%20gasoline%20cars.

89   "History of Tesla: Timeline and Facts," TheStreet, accessed March 12, 2023, https://www.thestreet.com/technology/history-of-tesla-15088992.

hospitalized after one particular beating that may have been driven by his dislike of apartheid and his being seen as an introverted loner.[90] His parents also divorced when he was about nine years old. Over the years, he split time with one parent, then another, but friction with his father caused them to become and stay estranged as time went on. After graduating high school in South Africa, Musk moved to Canada, where he studied for two years at Queen's University in Kingston, Ontario. In 1992, he left for the University of Pennsylvania, where he earned his bachelor of science degree in physics from Penn's College of Arts and Sciences and his bachelor of arts degree in economics from the Wharton School of the University of Pennsylvania. At the age of twenty-four in 1995, Musk moved to California to get his PhD in physics from Stanford University but left the university after just two days to launch a business tied to the fast-growing phenomenon called the internet. (Yes, another Stanford dropout ...)[91]

ZIP2

The new venture was originally called Global Link Information Network. Musk started it along with his brother Kimball with the goal of creating online city guides for consumers to find local small businesses. With limited funds, they rented a small office in Palo Alto, California, and basically lived in the office while working twenty-four

90   Jon Christian, "Why Elon Musk Got Bullied in High School," Futurism.com, May 6, 2022, https://futurism.com/elon-musk-bullied-high-school.

91   Pascale Daives, "The Highs and Lows of Elon Musk," Euronews, April 15, 2022, https://www.euronews.com/next/2022/04/14/elon-musk-s-life-story-the-highs-and-lows-of-the-tesla-and-spacex-boss. See also: Avery Hartmans, "Elon Musk Regained the Title of 'World's Richest Man.' Here's How the Billionaire Went from Getting Bullied as a Child to Becoming One of the Most Successful and Controversial Men in Tech," Business Insider, accessed March 12, 2023, https://www.businessinsider.com/the-rise-of-elon-musk-2016-7#after-graduating-from-high-school-musk-moved-to-canada-with-his-mother-maye-his-sister-tosca-and-his-brother-kimbal-and-spent-two-years-studying-at-queens-university-in-kingston-ontario-6.

seven. In the daytime, they kept the website up and running, and then they coded updates to the site all night. They even showered at the YMCA for the first few months until things got going. Musk was hardly living the billionaire's life back then.

Global Link Information Network was not an overnight success, but the online product kept improving, and word about what they were doing got out around Silicon Valley. By 1996, a venture capital firm offered the brothers a $3 million investment, and they formally changed the name of the company to Zip2. They hired real engineers, moved to a better office, and changed their business model from door-to-door sales to creating a software package to sell to newspapers that would allow them to build their own online directories to businesses and classified listings. This transformed the young company from a very slow grower to a very successful enterprise. With the involvement of a venture capital team, Musk was moved to chief technology officer, and a new CEO took his place. The new business plan worked, and revenues took off.

In April of 1998, Zip2 announced a merger with CitySearch, valued at over $300 million. Unfortunately, the deal was scuttled over multiple disagreements among all the parties. Pressures were running high at Zip2 after the failed merger and in light of ongoing internal personality conflicts—not the least of which was driven by Musk's belief that he would have served better as CEO. But just as internal conflict and outside competition were building around the company, Compaq made an offer to purchase Zip2 for $307 million in 1999. Without hesitation, the board said yes, and the company sold. This early experience of being forced to report to and cooperate with others who he felt were not of his same caliber may have gone a long way toward helping define Musk's future management style … which could be referred to as a "beneficent dictatorship." Musk walked away from the Zip2 sale with $22 million and was ready for the next chapter.[92]

PAYPAL

In 1999, Musk launched X.com, an online banking company. Then in March 2000, X.com merged with the Peter Thiel–founded financial start-up called Confinity. Musk was initially named CEO of the newly combined venture. But after several months of ongoing disagreements over software platforms, branding, and micromanagement issues, Musk was fired. That was in September 2000 and happened while Musk was on holiday in Australia. Years later, he told *Fortune*, "That's the problem with vacations."[93]

Things moved quickly after that. The name of the company was changed to PayPal in early 2001 and went public in 2002. At the time, PayPal was used in about 70 percent of all transactions for the popular auction site eBay, so eBay acquired PayPal later that year at a total value of $1.5 billion. Despite his unceremonious removal as CEO, Musk was the largest shareholder of PayPal and left that deal with $165 million. Musk departed with more money and a deeper sense of dissatisfaction at coming out on the short end of the stick from the rough and tumble of corporate politics.[94]

92 Tom Huddleston Jr., "Elon Musk Slept on His Office Couch and 'Showered at the YMCA' While Starting His First Company," CNBC, June 19, 2018, https://www. cnbc.com/2018/06/19/how-elon-musk-founded-zip2-with-his-brother-kimbal. html. See also: Tanner Papy, "The Unknown Story of Elon Musk's First Company," Medium, Level Up Coding, March 8, 2021, https://levelup.gitconnected.com/ the-unknown-story-of-elon-musks-first-company-7481ef7867a3.

93 Chris Anderson, "The Shared Genius of Elon Musk and Steve Jobs," Fortune.com, November 21, 2013, https://fortune.com/2013/11/21/the-shared-genius-of-elon-musk-and-steve-jobs/.

94 "PayPal Launches IPO and Is Now Worth More than eBay," Proactive Investors, July 20, 2015, https://www.proactiveinvestors.com/companies/news/117397/paypal-launches-ipo-and-is-now-worth-more-than-ebay-117397.html.

SPACEX

Colonizing the planet Mars has long been the exclusive purview of science fiction. But in 2001, Elon Musk came up with the concept of "Mars Oasis" as an actual business plan. I'm not sure if this qualified him as a visionary or something more questionable from a mental health standpoint. The concept was to have experimental greenhouses land on Mars to generate public interest with the hope of eventually setting up an international space station. Sounds pretty reasonable (tongue firmly in cheek). In October 2001, Musk traveled to Moscow to purchase old ICBMs to launch to Mars. Legend has it that he and his team were viewed by their Russian hosts as neophytes and essentially rejected on that first trip. The group persisted but never made any acquisitions. So, fresh off his ouster from PayPal, Musk resolved to do it himself.

He invested $100 million and launched SpaceX in 2002 to fund the development of its first rockets. SpaceX launched the first *Falcon 1* rocket in 2006. The rocket failed to reach orbit, but the company was awarded a contract by NASA, which allowed it to continue development. After two more failures, the situation was getting desperate at SpaceX.[95] Finally, in 2008, SpaceX succeeded in launching the *Falcon 1* rocket into orbit. It became the first commercial company to accomplish this historic feat. The successful launch could not have come at a better time for SpaceX, as it was close to having to declare bankruptcy. However, on the heels of the company's recent success, SpaceX received a new contract from NASA for a total of twelve flights to the International Space Station valued at $1.6 billion. SpaceX has gone on to become a leader in private spaceflight, reusable rocket

95 Eric Berger, "Inside the Eight Desperate Weeks That Saved Spacex from Ruin," arstechnica.com, September 21, 2018, https://arstechnica.com/science/2018/09/inside-the-eight-desperate-weeks-that-saved-spacex-from-ruin/.

technology, and private space transportation. The company was valued as high as $127 billion in May 2022. The company sent its first two astronauts to the International Space Station in May 2020 and has made multiple trips since. As of mid-2022, it was the only commercial spaceflight company capable of sending astronauts to space.

In 2008, SpaceX succeeded in launching the *Falcon 1* rocket into orbit. It became the first commercial company to accomplish this historic feat.

Colonizing Mars is still on the drawing board. As of the start of 2023, Musk was both CEO and CTO of SpaceX. As we move forward, there's a story to tell about how Musk's relationship with SpaceX affected Tesla. You may be sensing a little bit of frenetic chaos around all the success Elon Musk was enjoying. That would only intensify in the years ahead.[96]

It was in the midst of all this activity around SpaceX that Elon Musk joined Tesla. As in all his projects, Musk took an active role in Tesla right from the beginning. In 2004, Tesla contracted with Lotus to provide the chassis of its first model, a premium sports car that was to be called the Roadster. Building mass production cars is an extremely cost-intensive endeavor, and Tesla needed money. So in 2006, the company launched another fundraising round (which coincidentally included our friends Sergey Brin and Larry Page from Google), raising $13 million. This was quickly followed by a fourth round of fundraising in 2007, yielding $45 million. Financing would continue to be an issue for the company as it moved to execute what Musk called his "secret plan": "Build a sports car. Use that money to

---

96   "SpaceX Raises Another $250 Million in Equity, Lifts Total to $2 Billion in 2022,"
      CNBC, August 5, 2022, https://www.cnbc.com/2022/08/05/elon-musks-spacex-
      raises-250-million-in-equity.html#:~:text=The%20equity%20raising%20lifts%20
      the,round%20in%20May%2C%20CNBC%20reported.

build an affordable car. Use that money to build an even more afford-able car. While doing the above, also provide zero-emission electric power generation options."[97]

Tesla Roadster
Source: IFCAR, Public domain, via Wikimedia Commons

The Roadster was originally unveiled to the public in 2006. As a fully electric vehicle, it was revolutionary for its time. The cutting-edge battery technology used in the Roadster was rechargeable and would allow users to travel relatively large distances at high speeds without needing to be recharged. In short, it could be used as a daily driver. Development of the Roadster continued until the official pro-duction launch to the public in 2008. Early Roadster models could travel a total of up to 250 miles on a single charge, could accelerate from 0 to 60 miles per hour in just 4.6 seconds, and could reach a top speed of 125 miles per hour. The base model price was $109,000—a reasonable base price for a cutting-edge, state-of-the-art, all-electric

---

97 Christopher McFadden, "The Short but Fascinating History of Tesla," Interesting Engineering, July 5, 2020, https://interestingengineering.com/transportation/the-short-but-fascinating-history-of-tesla.

vehicle but too high for the mass market. Also, recharging the battery required twenty-four to forty-eight hours. Development continued, and so did the improvements in horsepower, speed, and other features. Ultimately, only 2,450 Roadsters were ever built, but the proof of concept had been achieved, and Tesla was on its way to bigger things.[98]

State of the Industry

It is important to remember that none of the major car manufacturers were building electric vehicles for the masses, and Tesla was effectively building out that sector of the industry from scratch. Mass-producing a revolutionary automobile was not only extremely expensive but also involved a lot of stress (just ask John DeLorean). The intense corporate management friction surrounding Elon Musk in his earlier endeavors continued to follow him at Tesla. During the development of the Roadster, both original cofounders were essentially shown the door. The board of directors asked Martin Eberhard to resign from the position of CEO in 2007. He was moved to another position but left the company in January 2008. Marc Tarpenning also left that same month. Eberhard would later sue Musk for allegedly forcing him out of the company. The CEO role was then held by Michael Marks, a Tesla investor who served as temporary CEO. Ze'ev Drori took over as Eberhard's permanent replacement, but less than a year later, in October 2008,

> None of the major car manufacturers were building electric vehicles for the masses, and Tesla was effectively building out that sector of the industry from scratch.

---

98   Jay Ramey, "The First Tesla Roadster: A Look Back at the Early Adopter's Electric Car," *Autoweek*, September 6, 2020, https://www.autoweek.com/news/green-cars/a1835876/first-tesla-roadster-look-back-early-adopters-electric-car/.

Elon Musk took over the role of CEO and at the same time fired about 25 percent of the company. Always starved for cash in the early years, Tesla found itself down to less than $10 million in cash on hand by 2009. But on the strength of the relative success of the Roadster, Daimler AG bought a 10 percent stake in Tesla for $50 million in May of that year, and Tesla received a $465 million loan from the US Department of Energy in June. The company had dodged a financial bullet and Tesla was now poised to attempt a mass production electric vehicle for consumer sale.[99]

Let's pause here to reflect on Musk's management style, which has been described as direct and highly opposed to the chain of command. "Communication should travel via the shortest path necessary to get the job done, not through the 'chain of command.' Any manager who attempts to enforce chain of command communication will soon find themself working elsewhere," Musk wrote in a 2018 email to employees.[100] As a driven executive who believes in hard work (remember, he slept in his first office and showered at the YMCA), precision, and who thinks everything can be done better, Musk can come off as abrasive and demanding. But turning rolled sheets of raw aluminum into a mass produced vehicle was definitely going to take a leader with exceptional focus and motivational skills. And besides, corporate chaos had always surrounded Musk and he always overcame it.[101] Would that continue to be the case with so much on the line?

99 "History of Tesla: Timeline and Facts," TheStreet, accessed March 12, 2023, https://www.thestreet.com/technology/history-of-tesla-15088992.

100 Evannex, "Elon Musk's Management Style Is Definitely Direct," InsideEVs, June 13, 2022, https://insideevs.com/news/591766/elon-musk-tesla-spacex-direct-management-style/#:~:text=Musk's%20management%20style%20can%20be,a%20report%20from%20Inc.com.

101 "Elon Musk Leadership Style," Financhill, February 28, 2021, https://financhill.com/blog/investing/elon-musk-leadership-style.

Going Public

In 2010, the US economy was just starting to recover from the Global Financial Crisis. The British Petroleum offshore drilling megarig, the Deepwater Horizon, exploded, killing eleven workers and spilling up to 260 million gallons of raw crude oil into the Gulf of Mexico. A 7.0 earthquake leveled Haiti and killed over 230,000 people. Wikileaks released hundreds of thousands of top secret documents relating to the war in Afghanistan, US operations in Iraq, and US State Department diplomatic cables. The average price of a new car was about $24,300.[102]

Overall stock market conditions in 2010 were encouraging but still tenuous, to put it mildly. The market had gone up nicely during the first quarter of 2010 but by June had settled at a new low for the year. This would not normally be too much of a cause for concern, but it is important to remember that investors were still recovering from the shock of the GFC, and many investors were waiting for more shoes to drop. The market hadn't gone anywhere in over a decade, and investors had suffered through massive volatility with the S&P 500 dropping over 50 percent twice during that period (see chart on the next page). It was a wild ride, and the choppy start to 2010 had investors holding on to their hats.[103]

---

102 "Top 10 World Events in 2010: Year in Review," *Long Island Press*, accessed March 12, 2023, https://archive.longislandpress.com/2010/12/24/top-10-world-events-in-2010-year-in-review/.

103 "Update 4: Tesla Prices at $17 in Upsized IPO-Source," Reuters, June 29, 2010, https://www.reuters.com/article/tesla-ipo-idAFN2724387520100629.

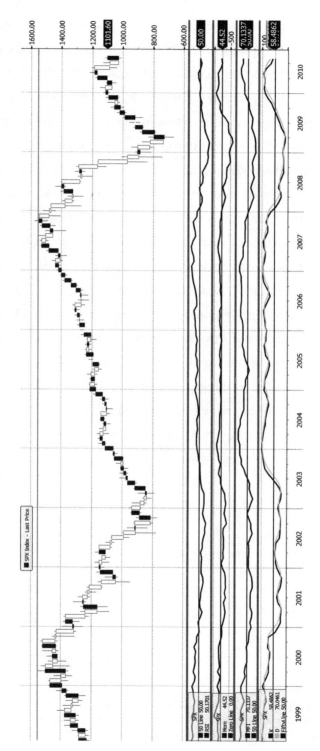

MONTHLY S&P 500, JANUARY 1999 TO JULY 2010

Adding to the general sense of uncertainty was the now-infamous "flash-crash" on May 6, 2010 (circled on the chart on the next page). Just before noon on that day, the stock market literally "broke" for about thirty-six minutes. Out of nowhere, the Dow Jones Industrial Average dropped about 1,000 points and then quickly recovered most of that loss. The 9 percent drop was the second-largest intraday point decline in history. Approximately $1 trillion in market value evaporated in thirty-six minutes. Trust in the markets was already low, and this market meltdown with no reasonable explanation only added to the general fears of the day. Initial investigations into the matter pointed to a small trader who was actively "spoofing" the markets (creating multiple false sell orders to trick the institutional automated computer trading systems into driving prices down so he could then flip the orders and buy them cheaper). Further study revealed that serious flaws in the way institutional automated computer trading algorithms were running contributed to the breakdown.[104] I was there that day, and I can remember how unsettling it was to see everything collapse for no apparent reason.

---

104 Mark Melin, "Here's What Actually Caused the 2010 'Flash Crash,'" Business Insider, accessed March 12, 2023, https://www.businessinsider.com/what-actually-caused-2010-flash-crash-2016-1.

S&P 500, JANUARY 2010 TO DECEMBER 2010

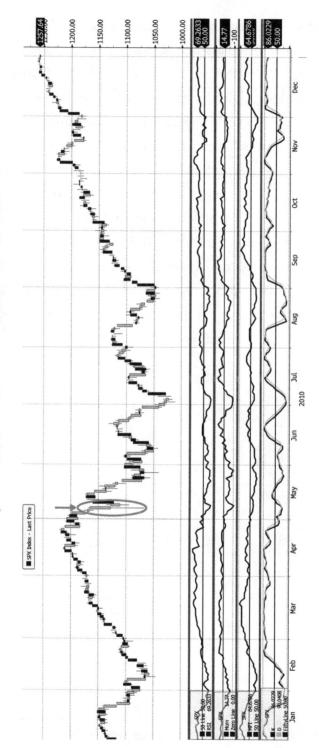

Despite challenging market conditions, and despite being highly unprofitable, the Tesla stock offering (under the symbol TSLA) was considered a hot IPO because of the "cool factor" around building a sleek-looking, fully electric car. As I mentioned earlier, Tesla was also the first US car company to go public since the Ford Motor Company went public in 1956. On June 29, 2010, the company sold 13.3 million shares for $17 per share (after increasing from the initial $14–$16 per share range) raising about $226 million (valuing the company at an ~$1.6 billion market cap). Despite years of operating losses, despite losing $29.5 million for the quarter ended March 31, 2010, and with its next-generation Model S not due to be released until 2012, Tesla stock struck a chord with investors and had a great first day. Shares closed at the high of the day, $23.89, for a greater-than-40-percent one-day gain.[105]

---

105   Chuck Squatriglia, "Tesla IPO Raises $226.1m, Stock Surges 41 Percent," *Wired*, June 29, 2010, https://www.wired.com/2010/06/tesla-ipo-raises-226-1-million/.

Summary Consolidated Financial Data

The following summary consolidated financial data for the years ended December 31, 2006, 2007 and 2008 are derived from our audited consolidated financial statements that are included elsewhere in this prospectus. The summary unaudited consolidated financial data for the nine months ended September 30, 2008 and 2009 and as of September 30, 2009 are derived from our unaudited consolidated financial statements for such periods and dates, which are included elsewhere in this prospectus. The unaudited consolidated financial statements were prepared on a basis consistent with our audited consolidated financial statements and include, in the opinion of management, all adjustments necessary for the fair presentation of the financial information contained in those statements. The historical results presented below are not necessarily indicative of financial results to be achieved in future periods.

Prospective investors should read these summary consolidated financial data together with "Management's Discussion and Analysis of Financial Condition and Results of Operations" and our consolidated financial statements and the related notes included elsewhere in this prospectus.

	Years Ended December 31,			Nine Months Ended September 30,	
	2006	2007	2008	2008	2009
	(in thousands, except per share amounts)				
Consolidated Statements of Operations Data:					
Automotive sales (including zero emission vehicle credit sales of $3,458, $495 and $7,645, for the periods ended December 31, 2008, September 30, 2008 and 2009, respectively)	$ —	$73	$14,742	$580	$93,358
Cost of sales (1)	—	9	15,883	19	85,604
Gross profit (loss)	—	64	(1,141)	561	7,754
Operating expenses (1):					
Research and development (net of development compensation of $17,170 for the period ended September 30, 2009)	24,995	62,753	53,714	41,888	11,139
Selling, general and administrative	5,436	17,244	23,649	13,935	25,587
Total operating expenses	30,431	79,997	77,363	55,841	36,726
Loss from operations	(30,431),	(79,933)	(78,504)	(55,280)	(28,972)
Interest income	938	1,749	529	486	97
Interest expense	(423)	—	(3,747)	(2,648)	(2,506)
Other income (expense), net (2)	59	137	(963)	231	(320)
Loss before income taxes	(29,857)	(78,047)	(82,685)	(57,211)	(31,701)
Provisions (benefit) for income taxes	100	110	97	73	(203)
Net loss	$(29,957)	$(78,157)	$(82,782)	$(57,284)	$(31,498)
Net loss per share of common stock, basic and diluted (3)	$(3.93)	$(7.56)	$(4.15)	$(2.88)	$(1.51)
Shares used in computing net loss per share of common stock, basic and diluted (3)	8,824,264	10,331,420	19,929,512	19,872,823	20,928,840
Pro forma net loss per share of common stock, basic and diluted (2) (4) (unaudited)					
Shares used in computing the pro forma net loss per share of common stock, basic and diluted (2) (4) (unaudited)					

Source: SEC

TSLA stock followed a familiar pattern for many hot IPOs: A fast start, a pause and drop as the initial excitement fades, a consolidation period, and then a recovery to or above the initial first few days' high price. That's the exact pattern TSLA stock followed, as you can see in the split-adjusted chart on the next page). The highest early closing price was achieved on the first day of trading. An intraday higher high was achieved on both of the next two days, but the actual close never exceeded the high set on the first day. On the sixth day of trading, the stock actually sank as low as $15, $2 below the IPO price of $17. But that was it for the downside; the stock then entered a three-month-plus trading range as it consolidated the initial offering excitement between prices of $17.50 and about $22.50. In November, the stock abruptly broke out of that range and flew up as high as about $35 before ending the year at $26.65 for an approximate 56 percent gain through the end of 2010. Not a bad start! However, the company had a major challenge ahead as it attempted to be the first company to launch the successful mass-market fully electric automobile ever: the Model S.

Achievements and Milestones

Tesla needed to execute its business plan fast. Just prior to the IPO, Tesla entered into an agreement to purchase a huge 270-acre production facility in Fremont, California, from Toyota for $42 million. As part of the agreement, Toyota would also purchase $50 million of common stock when Tesla went public shortly thereafter. The deal included facilities to house a massive 5.5 million square foot assembly plant where development and production of the mass-market Model S could begin immediately (although at first most of the site went unused because of its massive size).

THE MODEL S

The Model S had been on the drawing board since 2007 but was now on track for prototype production and eventually to take Tesla

TSLA, JUNE 29, 2010, TO DECEMBER 31, 2010

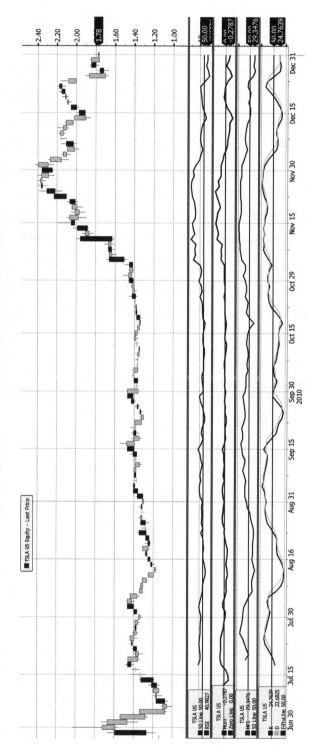

to the mass-market sales goals it had envisioned. Musk publicly stated that the goal was to launch the Model S in 2012. Tesla had a major challenge ahead and if it did not execute, it would become just another start-up car company that ended up in the dustbin of history.

This execute or fail theme existed for each of the companies we have profiled so far. Many executed elegantly right from the beginning. Apple was a glaring exception, foundering for years before almost going bankrupt. Tesla faced similar challenges. Its goal was to produce an all-electric vehicle for daily use with a range of around two hundred miles and a purchase price below $70,000 (depending on options and before federal tax credits were applied—about $7,500 in 2012). Many inside Tesla felt that the original drive train technology licensed from AC Propulsion for the Roadster was ultimately unusable, so the company brought almost the entire manufacturing process in-house for better quality control. That early speedbump with the Roadster gave Tesla a massive head start on the production of the Model S.[106]

106 Damon Lavrinc, "Tesla Lets Us Peek in on Model S Development," Autoblog, March 21, 2011, https://www.autoblog.com/2011/03/21/tesla-lets-us-peek-in-on-model-s-development/. See also: Bob Sorokanich, "Elon Musk Admits to Shareholders That the Tesla Roadster Was a Disaster," *Road & Track*, August 17, 2020, https://www.roadandtrack.com/new-cars/news/a29378/elon-musk-admits-to-shareholders-that-the-tesla-roadster-was-a-disaster/.

Tesla Model S
Source: Kowloonese, CC BY-SA 3.0 <https://creativecommons.org/licenses/by-sa/3.0>, via Wikimedia Commons

The Model S was a completely different design from the Roadster. The goal was to create a sleek four-door, multipassenger sedan designed from the ground up to be an electric vehicle (EV) and not an internal combustion engine vehicle converted into an EV. Long-range-driving capability was paramount (by 2011 Tesla's three prototype options could travel between 160 and 300 miles on a full charge), along with style innovations like sleek flush-mount external door handles and the first-ever in-car touch-sensitive, internet-capable, seventeen-inch infotainment screen in the middle of the instrument panel. All the batteries were to be mounted underneath the body of the vehicle, allowing for front and rear trunks and larger safety crumple zones. Tesla wanted the Model S to have excellent zero-to-sixty performance and to be easily recharged overnight at home. Tesla was also determined to earn the US government's highest five-star safety rating.

To complement the launch, Tesla announced that it was building Tesla Supercharger stations (the first six of which would be located in California) to charge Tesla cars for free. By 2020 there were over one thousand stations around the world. The company also expanded its pioneering retail stores. These had typically been located in shopping malls as opposed to the sprawling car lots used by other car companies in every city across the US. Tesla's first standalone location, opened in May 2008, was a sleek storefront at the intersection of Santa Monica Boulevard and the 405 Freeway in Los Angeles. Tesla was making a bold statement for the world to see.

Tesla Model S Digital Panels
Source: jurvetson (Steve Jurvetson), CC BY 2.0 <https://creativecommons.org/licenses/by/2.0>, via Wikimedia Commons

By October 2011, Tesla already had six thousand reservations for the still-unavailable Model S. The vehicle officially launched in June 2012 and was hailed as a triumph both in design and sales success. There was real excitement and buzz around the launch and celebration of the "cool factor" of the Model S. Innovation and some sort of cool factor have been qualities of all the companies we have profiled, and Tesla was no different. Lucky early customers were able to make a pilgrimage to the huge Fremont, California, plant to take delivery of their new, cool Tesla Model S and drive it home. I actually accompanied a client on his factory tour and delivery when I was living most of the week in San Jose, California, while building Alpha Cubed Investments. I remember being impressed by the huge rolls of raw aluminum sheets at the front of the plant and watching finished Model S cars rolling out from the production line. The base model available for order was rated at 160 miles of range and sold for $57,400, but the first ones actually delivered were the high-end Signature series. The Model S Signature series was rated at 265 miles of driving between charges with a 416 horsepower rear-wheel-drive system and a starting price of $87,900. Certainly not cheap by any standard at that time, but the vehicle was truly revolutionary.

The company announced that it intended to build five thousand cars by year-end 2012 and added that it had orders for ten thousand cars at the time of the launch. The Model S was an instant hit, and sales took off from there, but Tesla struggled with production delays to meet the ever-growing demand while maintaining its high standards for quality. The following chart illustrates the relatively slow start of production deliveries. That noted, the Model S went on to win several automotive awards and was eventually crowned with the prestigious Motor Trend Car of the Year award in 2013. When I was on the factory tour, I saw the award displayed on Musk's desk—located in the center of the room right on the production floor.[107]

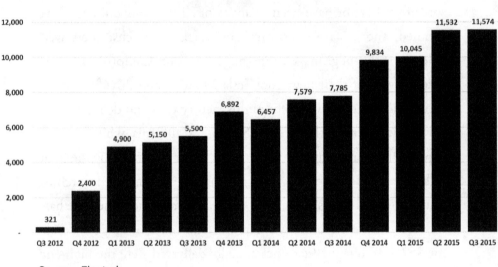

GLOBAL TESLA MODEL S DELIVERIES BY QUARTER

Source: Electrek

Let's not forget the "secret plan" I mentioned earlier (which, given that it was a public comment made by Musk, wasn't so secret): the race was to "Build a sports car. Use that money to build an affordable car. Use that money to build an even more affordable car."[108] This all sounds good, but in the extremely capital-intensive world of manu-

107   Gary Gastelu, "The Tesla Model S Turned 10 Today, but Where Is the First One?," Fox Business, June 27, 2022, https://www.foxbusiness.com/lifestyle/tesla-model-s-where-first-one. See also: "Tesla Motors to Begin Customer Deliveries of Model S on June 22nd," Tesla, accessed March 12, 2023, https://www.tesla.com/blog/tesla-motors-begin-customer-deliveries-model-s-june-22nd.

108   "The Secret Tesla Motors Master Plan (Just Between You and Me)," Tesla, accessed March 12, 2023. https://www.tesla.com/blog/secret-tesla-motors-master-plan-just-between-you-and-me.

facturing cars, a lot can go wrong if the cash flows aren't what they need to be at every point along the way.

In September 2012, Tesla cut its forecast for 2012 revenue because of a slower-than-expected rollout of its Model S sedan. That move sent its shares down almost 10 percent. Analysts were getting worried by the end of 2012, when fewer than three thousand Model S cars had been delivered. MarketWatch financial analyst Jon Shinal suggested early in 2013 that Tesla was "among the top candidates in Silicon Valley for a 2013 stock collapse" unless it secured additional funds. Shinal noted that Tesla spent down its cash through the third quarter of 2012 and would have been essentially out of money had it not drawn on the last of its $465 million in low-interest loans from the US Department of Energy. He also noted that Tesla had to lower its 2012 revenue forecasts in September, had less than six months of cash on hand at the end of *that* month, and had assets of $809 million versus liabilities of $837 million. Tesla had just spent two years completing development of the 2012 Model S, along with equipping its Fremont assembly plant—which was itself a very capital-intensive endeavor. The same analyst went on to say that Tesla's stock was "in worse shape even than such high-profile Internet IPO flameouts as [online game developer] Zynga and [social group-couponing company] Groupon." Tesla would run this same gauntlet of pessimism between missed sales goals and cash burn rates for many years to come.[109]

Tesla shocked the market when it announced its first-quarter 2013 earnings (fiscal year) in May 2013. On the heels of increased

---

109 "Tesla Now Delivering Model S, but Cash Crunch Judgment Waits for Financials," Business Insider, accessed March 12, 2023, https://www.businessinsider.com/tesla-now-delivering-model-s-but-cash-crunch-judgment-waits-for-financials-2013-1. See also: Ben Klayman, "Tesla Cuts Revenue Forecast Due to Slow Model S Rollout," Reuters, September 25, 2012, https://www.reuters.com/article/us-tesla-outlook/tesla-cuts-revenue-forecast-due-to-slow-model-s-rollout-idUSBRE88O0JN20120925.

deliveries of the Model S, the company announced its first-ever profit of $15 million. "We are pleased with the strong global demand for Model S and are currently receiving orders at a rate greater than 20,000 per year worldwide," Musk wrote in the letter to shareholders. "We are seeing orders in a particular region increase proportionate to the number of deliveries, which means that customers are selling other customers on the car." Tesla stock jumped 31 percent after recording $562 million in sales and first-ever quarterly profit. The company had escaped the fire of potential financial ruin again but would see this cycle repeat in the years ahead.[110]

Overcoming Adversity I

As if skimming just above financial insolvency was not enough stress for the young company, another new and potentially crippling problem arose seemingly out of nowhere. In October 2013, a Tesla Model S caught fire near Seattle after the car collided with a large piece of metal debris on the road that punched a hole through the protective armor plating. The driver was not injured, but the event generated an ever-growing media interest in the safety of the lithium-ion batteries in electric vehicles generally, and in Tesla vehicles specifically, since Tesla was the industry leader. By November, there were reports of at least three Tesla Model S fires. There were no fatalities yet, but the images of burning cars were graphic, and the media was fanning the flames, so to speak.

Although most fires can be put out with relatively small amounts of water, fires caused by lithium-ion batteries burn at 3,632 degrees Fahrenheit and typically will burn a car to the ground in a spectacular,

110   John Koetsier, "Tesla Stock Jumps 31% after Record $562m in Sales and First-Ever Quarterly Profit," Reuters, May 9, 2013, https://www.reuters.com/article/idUS360742956120130509.

out-of-control blaze. This was not an image that Tesla wanted associated with its beautiful new environmentally friendly vehicles. Elon Musk himself took to the official Tesla blog to defend the Model S, pointing out that these crashes occurred after the vehicles came into contact with metal objects that punctured the metal firewall. "For consumers concerned about fire risk, there should be absolutely zero doubt that it is safer to power a car with a battery than a large tank of highly flammable liquid," Musk wrote. And in many ways, he was right. Dangerous accidents come with the territory when you are making cars. But the spectacular fires were not something the public was used to seeing. And Tesla was fully aware of the risks around lithium-ion batteries; they acknowledged in their 10-Q that the lithium-ion battery cells "have been observed to catch fire or vent smoke and flame, and such events have raised concerns, and future events may lead to additional concerns, about the batteries used in automotive applications." At the time, the public was generally assuaged by these arguments, but the issue with fires and other accidents would be an ongoing theme for Tesla for years to come.[111]

THE GIGAFACTORY

Powering electric cars requires batteries—lots of batteries. Panasonic had supplied Tesla the batteries for the Model S at an estimated cost of over 20 percent of the total manufacturing costs, so Tesla needed to ensure the control of supply, cost, and quality if it was going to hit its lofty production numbers. In 2014, Tesla announced a partnership with Panasonic to build a massive battery manufacturing plant for an estimated $5 billion with the goal of producing five hundred

---

111   Mamta Badkar, "Tesla Stock Is Tanking after a Third Model S in Two Months Catches Fire," Business Insider, accessed March 12, 2023, https://www.businessinsider.com/third-tesla-model-s-catches-fire-2013-11.

thousand lithium-ion batteries per year by 2020. An industrial site outside of Sparks, Nevada, won the competition to host the massive factory, which would be called the Gigafactory.

Tesla Gigafactory
Source: Smnt, CC BY-SA 4.0 <https://creativecommons.org/licenses/by-sa/4.0>, via Wikimedia Commons

The Gigafactory was designed to be built in phases and to be entirely powered by renewable energy sources. On its company blog, Tesla noted that the Gigafactory was "designed to be a net zero energy factory upon completion, primarily powered by solar, wind and geothermal sources." The original Gigafactory ended up covering about five million square feet or about 126 acres (making it one of the largest factories in the world). And by 2022, the Nevada factory had produced its one-millionth battery pack. By the end of 2022, there were six huge Gigafactories either in operation or under construction around the world, with Giga Texas and Giga Shanghai boasting even larger facilities than the original. More Gigafactories are planned for different parts of the world, including India and the UK, as Tesla prepares to execute on its lofty growth goals.[112]

Tesla Model X
Source: Turnstange, CC BY-SA 4.0 <https://creativecommons.org/licenses/by-sa/4.0>, via Wikimedia Commons

THE MODEL X

Back in 2012, the company announced it would expand its product line with the Model X, a crossover SUV that featured gull-wing doors and definitely kept the Tesla "cool factor" in place. Chief designer Franz Von Holzhausen explained that the Model X "has the functionality and roominess of a minivan, the style of an SUV, and the performance of a sportscar." The goal was to deliver the Model X in 2013; however, production delays (many related to the fancy gull-wing doors) delayed delivery until September 2015. Production delays and concerns would continue to be a cause for concern for Tesla for years

---

112 "How Many Gigafactories Does Tesla Have? Tesla Factory Locations," Licarco, March 2, 2023, https://www.licarco.com/news/how-many-tesla-gigafactories.

to come. According to Tesla, the Model X was the "safest, quickest and most capable sport utility vehicle in history that holds 5-star safety ratings across every category from the National Highway Traffic Safety Administration." The luxury SUV started at about $89,000 but regularly sold for more than $100,000 with options included. Although the car was well received by the public, Tesla was only able to deliver 206 units by the end of 2015. Eventually Tesla mostly ironed out its supply chain issues (which were primarily driven by outside vendors) and went on to ship over one hundred thousand units before terminating production of the Model X in 2020 (and then reintroducing it for potential delivery in 2023). In 2017, the Tesla Model X officially became the highest-safety-rated SUV with five-star ratings in every safety category in the National Highway Traffic Safety Administration's (NHTSA) tests.[113]

---

113   Christopher McFadden, "The Short but Fascinating History of Tesla," Interesting Engineering, July 5, 2020, https://interestingengineering.com/transportation/the-short-but-fascinating-history-of-tesla.

GLOBAL TESLA MODEL X
DELIVERIES BY QUARTER

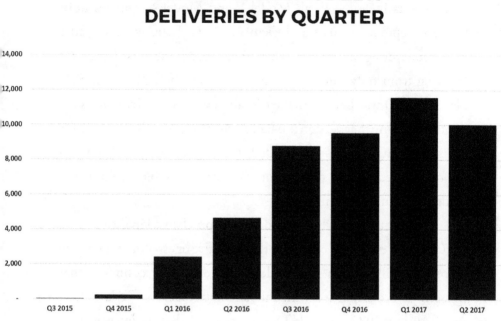

Source: Insider

Autopilot

In 2014, while all this was happening, Tesla began rolling out its controversial semiautonomous driving feature, called "autopilot." The first version was a little bit misleading, because drivers would still need to keep their hands on the wheel and stay alert. The ongoing saga around the promises and goals of full self-driving capability illustrates a company culture at Tesla that makes bold promises, then has to delay delivery, and then eventually meets some or most of the promises. Obviously, the technological challenges of creating a truly self-driving vehicle are enormous, and there is massive life-and-death risk around the project.

Through the end of 2021, there were at least ten deaths and 33 crashes in the United States involving Tesla vehicles where Autopilot was suspected to be a factor.[114] Autopilot Hardware 1.0, the first version, was included in all Model S and Model X vehicles built between September 2014 and October 2016. There were upgrades to versions designed after 2016 that included additional cameras (shifting from only one camera to eight), and by 2019, Autopilot Hardware 3.0 was being installed in all new Tesla vehicles. Musk is quoted as saying that version 3.0 had all the components necessary for full self-driving features. As of 2022, Musk's statement and the corresponding technology remain controversial and subject to ongoing regulatory and legal scrutiny.

Musk remains his überassured self and proclaimed in the summer of 2020, "I'm extremely confident that level five or essentially complete autonomy will happen." He added, "I'm extremely confident that this can be accomplished with the hardware that is in Tesla today." As of August 2022, the NHTSA announced that its investigation was widened to cover an estimated 830,000 Tesla Model Y, X, S, and 3 vehicles from the 2014 model year onward. The regulator has the power to deem cars defective and order recalls, so this story will continue to evolve. As this component of the overall Tesla story evolves, there is increasing competition to accomplish autonomous driving from all corners, including Waymo (part of Alphabet/Google), Nvidia, and many others.[115]

---

114   Keith Barry, "Big Bets and Broken Promises: A Timeline of Tesla's Self-Driving Aspirations," Consumer Reports, November 11, 2021, https://www.consumerreports.org/autonomous-driving/timeline-of-tesla-self-driving-aspirations-a9686689375/.

115   "Tesla Autopilot Scrutiny Grows as Federal Inquiry Gets Upgraded," Los Angeles Times, June 9, 2022, https://www.latimes.com/business/technology/story/2022-06-09/tesla-autopilot-scrutiny-grows-as-federal-probe-gets-upgraded#:~:text=U.S.%20authorities%20have%20expanded%20an,of%20the%20automated%20driving%20features.

MODEL 3

By 2016, there was no question that Tesla was terraforming the new electric vehicle market with cutting-edge cars that the public wanted. What had not yet been proven was that Tesla could make and sell a mass-market car at a low enough price for the average consumer. The Tesla Model 3 was announced in March 2016 as the next step of the "secret" or "master plan": a lower-priced, mass-market sedan. The announced pricing goal was a very affordable $35,000. Consumers loved the idea, and preorders and deposits flowed in. One month later, there were already 276,000 preorders worldwide. But—and we almost know to expect this by now—there would be massive production delays. Musk tweeted in July 2017 that Model 3 production could reach up to twenty thousand units by December.

Production costs were huge, so Tesla sold $1.46 billion of stock in a secondary offering in May 2016 attempting to meet its stated goal of selling five hundred thousand vehicles by the end of 2018. That same month, Musk also announced that Tesla would produce one hundred thousand to two hundred thousand of those vehicles by the end of 2017. In the end, the company managed to make a mere 1,550 Model 3s by the end of 2017—while there were about four hundred thousand preorders waiting to be filled. Continued delays put significant stress on the company.

You can fault Musk for being overly optimistic, but at least he is consistently overly optimistic. And Tesla fans seem willing to accept the constancy of his overeager production promises, perhaps because eventually, he delivers. And who doesn't appreciate a positive person? (Tongue firmly planted in cheek, again). During an interview with *Axios* on HBO in late 2018, Musk explained: "Tesla faced a severe threat of death due to the Model 3 production ramp. Essentially, the company was bleeding money like crazy and if we didn't solve these problems over a short period of time we would die. It was extremely difficult." Musk revealed that the company was "within single-digit weeks" of going under. Just another day in the manic-depressive wild ride at Tesla, right? To top it off, Musk added that earlier in 2018, he had taken to sleeping on the floor at the Tesla Fremont factory and working over one hundred hours per week. Another consistency identified: Musk has never been known as someone who isn't willing to personally sacrifice to succeed.[116]

That said, the delays continued. The promised price of $35,000 had not been achieved, though initial Model 3 cars sold for as low as $36,200, with additional features (including some "basic" features like electric seat adjustments) boosting the car's price to about $55,000. Although Tesla had not met its price goal, the price was more affordable. Consumers flocked to the Model 3, and by the second half of 2018, Tesla was able to make significant strides toward hitting its production delivery goals. By August 2018, the Model 3 surpassed the Nissan Leaf as the world's best-selling plug-in car. Tesla sold more than fifty-nine thousand units for that year, while Nissan sold about fifty-seven thousand. You can see from the next chart that Model 3 sales began to explode in 2018. By 2021, the Model 3 became the eighth-best-selling electric car in the world, with over one million units sold worldwide.[117]

Musk has never been known as someone who isn't willing to personally sacrifice to succeed.

116   Mike Allen and Jim VandeHei, "Elon Musk Says Tesla Came 'within Single-Digit Weeks' of Death," *Axios*, November 26, 2018, https://www.axios.com/2018/11/26/elon-musk-tesla-death-bleeding-cash.

117   Zachary Shahan, "Tesla Model 3 Has Passed 1 Million Sales," CleanTechnica, August 26, 2021, https://cleantechnica.com/2021/08/26/tesla-model-3-has-passed-1-million-sales/.

TESLA MODEL 3 SALES

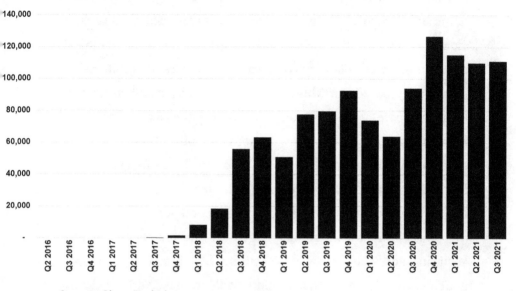

Source: Clean Technica

SOLARCITY

Meanwhile, and in keeping with the frenetic pace of seemingly disparate but possibly related activities, in August 2016, Tesla entered into a controversial agreement to acquire SolarCity for $2.6 billion. The acquisition was controversial because SolarCity was alleged to be having financial trouble at the time, and Elon Musk and his cousins were running SolarCity. Many felt that the acquisition was really nothing more than the bailout of a troubled asset that personally benefited Elon Musk. SolarCity was founded in 2006 by Musk's cousins, Peter and Lyndon Rive. It was backed by Musk, who also served as chairman of the board. Musk's spaceflight and transport company, SpaceX, had also purchased tens of millions of dollars' worth of bonds from SolarCity.

However, over a year earlier, in April 2015, Tesla founded a subsidiary called Tesla Energy to broaden its product offering with Powerwall home and Powerpack industrial battery packs (designed to power individual homes and offer photovoltaic [solar] cells). On the one hand, the acquisition of SolarCity could easily be seen as self-dealing since it essentially bailed out Musk, some of his family members, and his company SpaceX. That position is bolstered by the fact that there were no other bidders for the acquisition. On the other hand, there were obvious synergies between SolarCity, Tesla, and Tesla Energy. Tesla had long been committed to developing solar technology as a means of powering its facilities and meeting its production goals.

Musk himself believed the merger was a no-brainer and that the acquisition of SolarCity would transform Tesla into a vertically integrated energy company that would be able to make and sell electric cars, make and sell energy storage for buildings and the grid, and make and install solar panels, all under one roof. In the end, more than 85 percent of the nonaffiliated shareholders of Tesla (shareholders who do not hold executive positions at either company) approved the acquisition. The shareholder lawsuit that followed was decided in Musk's favor and in favor of the transaction in general. Tesla remains in the solar business and committed to clean energy solutions to this day. In fact, in November 2016, just a handful of months after acquisition of SolarCity, Tesla took over the American Samoan island of Ta'u, which has a population of about six hundred, and converted it to a solar and battery microgrid to test the ability to provide 100 percent renewable energy.[118]

---

118 Brian Deagon, "Tesla's Risky SolarCity Acquisition Wins Shareholder Approval," *Investor's Business Daily*, November 17, 2016, https://www.investors.com/news/technology/teslas-risky-acquisition-of-solarcity-gets-shareholder-approval/.

Overcoming Adversity II, or "Just Another Day at Tesla"

Given that there has been so much turmoil throughout the history of Tesla, you may wonder if we could title nearly every other section of this chapter "Creating and Overcoming Adversity." Overcoming production delays and concerns about financial viability were certainly ongoing issues over the years.

In August 2018, Musk made a series of tweets about taking Tesla private, claiming that he had secured funding. Then, in September 2018, the SEC charged Musk with securities fraud, alleging that his tweets were both "false and misleading." Later that same month, Tesla's board rejected a proposed settlement from the SEC that would have barred Musk as chairman for two years and would require Tesla to appoint two new independent directors. News of the rejected deal sent Tesla's stock plummeting, and the board quickly accepted a less generous settlement, the terms of which included Musk stepping down as chairman for at least three years and having his tweets pre-approved by Tesla's lawyers. In addition, both Tesla and Musk were fined $20 million. But Musk was allowed to remain as CEO.

Musk continued making provocative tweets on multiple subjects thereafter and became an even more controversial figure over time. And in keeping with the chaotic energy surrounding him, Musk went on to tweet in February 2019 that "Tesla made 0 cars in 2011, but will make around 500k in 2019." Hours later, Musk sent a follow-up tweet indicating that the company would actually deliver just four hundred thousand cars that year. The tweets about production appeared to the SEC to violate the 2018 agreement to have all of Musk's company communications vetted. The SEC asked a judge to hold Musk in contempt, but the settlement that followed ended up amending the original agreement outlining topics Musk cannot tweet about until he obtains preapproval from an "experienced securities lawyer." As we all know, there would be more controversy and even more about Twitter later.[119]

MODEL Y

In March 2019, Tesla unveiled the Model Y and began deliveries just a year later, in March 2020. The Model Y, with a starting base price of about $50,000, was designed to be a compact crossover filling a segment between the smaller Model 3 and less expensive than the Model X.

Tesla Model Y
Source: Alexander Migl, CC BY-SA 4.0 <https://creativecommons.org/licenses/by-sa/4.0>, via Wikimedia Commons

The following chart makes it clear that the Model Y was almost an instant success and further solidified Tesla as the world leader in electric vehicles.

---

119   Jackie Wattles, "Elon Musk and SEC Reach an Agreement over Tweeting," CNN Business, April 27, 2019, https://www.cnn.com/2019/04/26/tech/elon-musk-sec-settlement.

TESLA QUARTERLY DELIVERIES

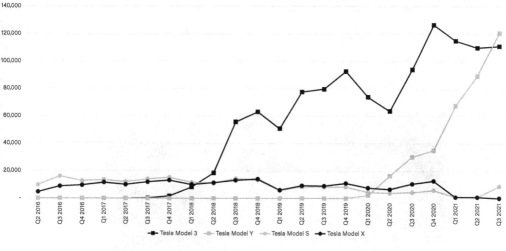

Source: Clean Technica

Speaking at Tesla's annual shareholder's meeting in August 2022, Musk claimed that, from a revenue perspective, the Model Y would be the world's best-selling vehicle that year. He went on to predict that it will be the world's number-one vehicle when it came to overall sales volume in 2023, thereby surpassing the Toyota Corolla (which had over 1.15 million units sold in 2021).[120]

Preparing for Succession and Continued Growth

Never letting too much grass grow under his feet, Musk has myriad projects under development for Tesla as I write this book. As usual, some of these projects are momentous in size and scope. Tesla brought

---

120   Fred Lambert, "Tesla Reduces Model Y Prices, Now Starts below $50,000," Electrek, July 12, 2020. https://electrek.co/2020/07/11/tesla-model-y-price-drop/. See also: Ben O'Hare, "Tesla Model Y Expected to Become World's Best-Selling Car," InsideEVs, August 6, 2022, https://insideevs.com/news/602829/tesla-modely-best-selling/.

back the discontinued Model S in 2021. Tesla's bid to revolutionize the trucking industry, the Tesla Semi, was scheduled to start shipping in 2022. Then, it announced the futuristic Cybertruck at the bargain-basement target price of just $39,900 set for delivery some time in 2023. And the company announced that the Roadster was coming back for delivery in 2023 at a price as high as $250,000.

Tesla Cybertruck
Source: u/Kruzat, modified by Smnt, CC BY-SA 4.0 <https://creativecommons.org/licenses/by-sa/4.0>, via Wikimedia Commons

Tesla Semi
Source: Korbitr, Public domain, via Wikimedia Commons

Along the way, Musk founded additional companies with incredibly lofty goals. Neuralink was founded in 2016 to create devices that could be embedded in the brain for integration with a computer or mobile device. (Just your run-of-the-mill, easy idea!) The Neuralink project remains ongoing. In 2017, Musk launched the Boring Company to build underground transportation tunnel systems to circumvent above-ground traffic in major cities. The Boring Company completed its first tunnel underneath the Las Vegas Convention Center in early 2021. Obviously, this project required an extensive amount of extremely precise and careful engineering, along with moving untold tons of rocks and earth.

In his spare time, Musk has been lobbying different locations around the United States for the development of a high-speed vacuum tube train, or a hyperloop, and has mentioned that it would be interesting to build "a supersonic vertical-takeoff-and-landing electric jet." Oh, and in April 2022, Musk made a $43 billion offer to buy Twitter at $54.20 per share. After threatening to pull the deal over controversy surrounding the number of fake or "bot" Twitter accounts, the acquisition finally closed in October 2022. Musk seemed intent on ramping up his controversial image by turning Twitter upside down and sending controversial tweets out from day one. Finally, in March 2022, Musk announced that the "Master Plan Part 3" was to scale Tesla to "extreme size" around the themes of shifting humanity away from fossil fuels and toward AI.[121]

What we see, in review, are more lofty goals that may seem questionably attainable in huge markets. The Tesla story is still unfolding around its polarizing leader and his ever-optimistic goals to create

---

121 Jaclyn Trop, "Musk Reveals Plan to Scale Tesla to 'Extreme Size,'" *TechCrunch*, March 21, 2022, https://techcrunch.com/2022/03/21/musk-reveals-plan-to-scale-tesla-to-extreme-size/.

dramatic change. As of this writing, Musk has made hints about succession but, as usual, we will have to wait to see what actually happens at Tesla.

By September 2021, Elon Musk bypassed Jeff Bezos to become the richest person in the world at an approximate net worth of $185 billion and was also named *TIME* magazine's Person of the Year. But for investors, the frenetic pace of activity by Musk—with dozens of technologically challenging and demanding projects, controversies, and huge financial takeover propositions all going on at once—there's good reason to be exhausted. This book is designed to give investors a process to identify and manage future huge winners in the stock market, but the other news I am breaking here is that there are definitely five or six Elons, probably clones. (If you're wondering, I've carefully calculated that it would take at least that many Elons to even come close to properly managing all the existing companies, be present at the celebrity sightings and the Joe Rogan media appearances, and to generate all the tweets.) I'm kidding, of course, but I can't really think of anyone in history who has worked at such an ultrahigh level of both productivity and controversy. And that includes Thomas Edison, who, in his pursuit to maximize the productive hours in his day, famously would sleep sitting up in a chair, with his arms draped over the sides and a steel ball in each hand, to minimize time wasted sleeping. Of course, Edison only *"invented"* electricity (once again, tongue firmly implanted in cheek).[122]

---

122 Alejandro de la Garza, "Elon Musk Net Worth: How the Person of the Year Built His Fortune," *TIME*, December 13, 2021, https://time.com/6127754/elon-musk-net-worth-person-of-the-year/.

Valuation Issues

Tesla has been controversial from the beginning as it entered the highly competitive, capital-intensive, low-margin automobile manufacturing business. There has been near-constant discussion about valuation. As of December 31, 2021, Tesla has a market capitalization greater than Toyota, Ford, Volkswagen, and GM combined. So what was going on here?

Tesla, which delivered approximately five hundred thousand units in 2020, was valued at over $1 trillion as of December 31, 2021. Toyota, which sold nearly ten million units in the same period, was valued at only $300 billion on the same date. It's true that many factors go into determining company valuation, including profitability and growth potential, but this extreme divergence is worth examining. Even if we assume the success of the company is a foregone conclusion, it could potentially be decades until Tesla grows into its 2021 valuation, and it may yet be a bumpy ride. Obviously, there is a lot of excitement around Tesla. And Musk may continue to deliver and help Tesla evolve beyond simply being an electric vehicle manufacturer and into being, for example, a clean energy solution provider. So far, those who have bet against Elon Musk have generally not fared very well.

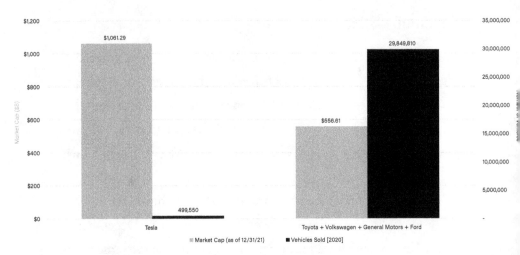

Source: Bloomberg Finance L.P., December 31, 2021

Remember, history may not repeat itself, but it often rhymes. We have seen similar valuation behavior before, most notably in the dot-com bubble of the late 1990s. During that period, companies were awarded lofty valuations in anticipation of how they would revolutionize society, and many of those companies eventually completely failed. Given that we want to focus on the ones that succeeded, we need look no further than one of the largest and most successful companies of all time that we profiled earlier: Microsoft (MSFT). As the developer of the most ubiquitous business productivity software on the planet, Microsoft is a household name and valued at almost $1.8 trillion as of December 31, 2022. Additionally, the company is now a leader in cloud computing and other emerging technologies, including a splashy entry into AI with the $10 billion investment in ChatGPT maker OpenAI.[123] Investors betting on the future success of

123 Ashley Capoot, "Microsoft Announces New Multibillion-Dollar Investment in CHATGPT-Maker Openai," CNBC.com, January 23, 2023, https://www.cnbc.com/2023/01/23/microsoft-announces-multibillion-dollar-investment-in-chatgpt-maker-openai.html.

the company have been proven correct; however, that does not mean that investments in the company have always been immediately profitable. In fact, as the following chart illustrates, investors who bought shares of MSFT at the top of the tech bubble in late 1999 would not break even on their investment for nearly seventeen years (assuming they actually held the stock for the duration of that period). And we're talking here about a company that has proven to be one of the best and most innovative companies in the history of the stock market. Caveat emptor, or let the buyer beware.

MSFT

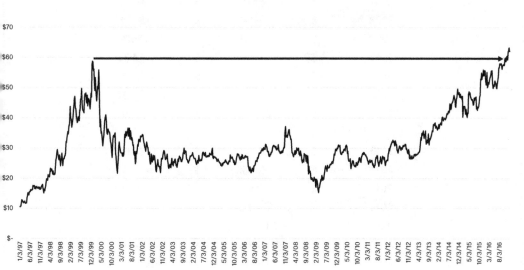

Revenue Growth

The constant chaos, potential financial ruin, and ongoing production delays over the years along with valuation concerns and media controversies at Tesla would have made the average investor's head spin. Let's see if we can get some help managing this monster winner using our hypothetical three-step process. Tesla wasn't making money when it went public in June 2010. After the dot-com era, this was not unusual, but companies do eventually need to make money. For Tesla, it was really quite a high-wire act before the success of the Model 3. As you can see from the table that follows, Tesla didn't become profitable on an annual basis until 2020.

TSLA REVENUE AND NET INCOME HISTORY, 2007 TO 2022 ($ IN MILLIONS)

Fiscal Year	Revenue	Net Income
2007	$ 0.07	$ (78.16)
2008	$ 14.74	$ (82.78)
2009	$ 111.94	$ (55.74)
2010	$ 116.74	$ (154.33)
2011	$ 204.24	$ (254.41)
2012	$ 413.26	$ (396.21)
2013	$ 2,013.50	$ (74.01)
2014	$ 3,198.36	$ (294.04)
2015	$ 4,046.03	$ (888.66)
2016	$ 7,000.13	$ (674.91)
2017	$ 11,758.75	$ (1,961.40)
2018	$ 21,461.27	$ (976.09)
2019	$ 24,578.00	$ (862.00)
2020	$ 31,536.00	$ 721.00
2021	$ 53,823.00	$ 5,519.00
2022	$ 81,462.00	$ 12,556.00

Source: Bloomberg Finance L.P.

What we *can* see from this table is a steady trend in revenues and then a huge jump in 2013. Remember, Tesla recorded its first profitable quarter ever in May 2013. Tesla's fortunes really started to turn once it proved it could create large amounts of profitable revenue. The "secret plan" had started working, and eventually the company started producing massive net profits.

Applying the Three-Step Process

STEP 1: FUNDAMENTAL ANALYSIS / EARNINGS

TSLA FISCAL YEAR QUARTERLY EARNINGS HISTORY 2010 TO 2022 (PER SHARE)

Fiscal Year	Q1	Q2	Q3	Q4	Annual
2010	-$0.2693	-$0.3360	-$0.0253	-$0.0360	-$0.6666
2011	-$0.0340	-$0.0400	-$0.0420	-$0.0520	-$0.1680
2012	-$0.0573	-$0.0667	-$0.0700	-$0.0527	-$0.2467
2013	$0.0002	-$0.0173	-$0.0213	-$0.0087	-$0.0471
2014	-$0.0267	-$0.0333	-$0.0400	-$0.0573	-$0.1573
2015	-$0.0813	-$0.0967	-$0.1187	-$0.1627	-$0.4594
2016	-$0.1420	-$0.1393	$0.0093	-$0.0520	-$0.3240
2017	-$0.1360	-$0.1360	-$0.2467	-$0.2673	-$0.7860
2018	-$0.2793	-$0.2813	$0.1167	$0.0520	-$0.3919
2019	-$0.2706	-$0.1540	$0.0520	$0.0373	-$0.3353
2020	$0.0053	$0.0333	$0.0998	$0.0800	$0.2184
2021	$0.1300	$0.3400	$0.4800	$0.6833	$1.6333
2022	$0.9533	$0.6824	$0.9500	$1.0777	$3.6634
Key:	Positive	Negative			

Source: Bloomberg Finance L.P.

The black and gray boxes on the quarterly earnings table above indicate large market reactions to the earnings announcements. A "surprise" announcement that moved the stock up more that 10 percent is coded with black box. A 10 percent drop based on a negative surprise is coded with a gray box. The first thing we notice here is that TSLA's earnings were full of surprises relative to the other companies we have been looking at. There's a lot of activity on this table! We will look into the quarterly earnings and apply our hypothetical scoring approach later to see if that can help manage around all the action.

TSLA, JUNE 2010 TO DECEMBER 2022

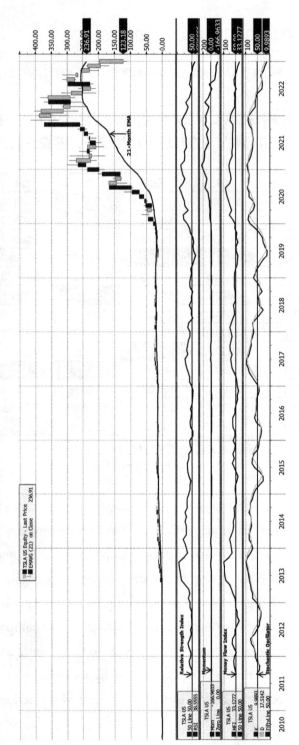

STEP 2: TECHNICAL ANALYSIS

When you step back and look all the way back to the beginning in one frame as we see in the chart on the left, it looks like TSLA had a pretty smooth ride until 2022. However, we know that there were multiple periods where the company faced financial ruin if it proved unable to execute. Let's look closer at how some of the technical indicators we discussed earlier (the twenty-one-period EMA, RSI, momentum, money flows, and stochastics) behaved for TSLA over the years to see what the average investor was facing in real time.

The following chart on page 254 illustrates the first few, relatively quiet, trading years as the markets were figuring out if Tesla could even survive.

From 2010 to 2013, the overall stock market was generally enjoying the beginning stages of recovering from the huge losses generated by the Global Financial Crisis. That provided a nice, generally supportive backdrop for a tender young company that was in survival mode and trying to prove its critics wrong. Momentum, money flows, and stochastics gave a couple of short sell and buy signals. But RSI stayed positive the entire time. Even the twenty-one-period exponential moving average (black arrow) never suffered a decisive break. Using this approach, there was a strong case to make for holding at least some portion of the stock throughout this period and for ending March 2013 holding a full position in TSLA.

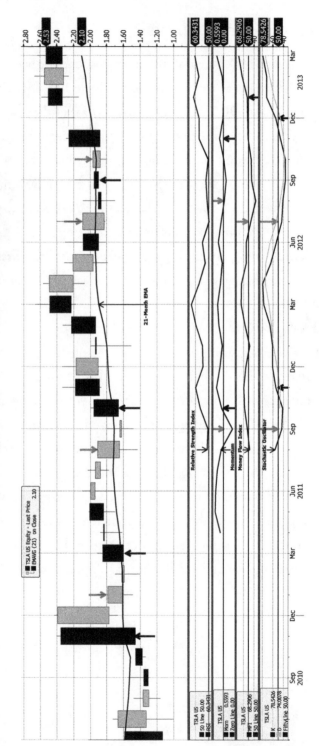

TSLA, JUNE 2010 TO MARCH 2013

TSLA, APRIL 2013 TO NOVEMBER 2019

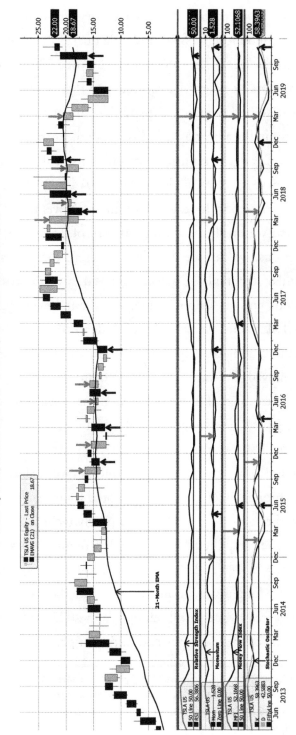

Then, as we know, the Tesla story started to improve. The company announced its first profitable quarter in May 2013, and it was off to the races. The stock moved up over 800 percent in fewer than two years. It essentially consolidated that move for another five years as it shifted from a company that might survive to a serious competitor in the automotive industry. All the technical metrics we've been looking at gave multiple buy and sell signals throughout those five choppy years of consolidation from 2014 to 2019. However, they were all turning positive toward the end of November 2019.

When we break the trading history of TSLA stock into these three periods, we can see that they represent three separate periods with similar activity: large moves, followed by consolidations as Tesla figured out how to keep growing. On the following page, you can see that TSLA stock weathered the pandemic drop in 2020 relatively well and then fully participated in the growth spurt the general stock market enjoyed afterward. On the back of massive Model 3 and Model Y sales and earnings, TSLA stock went up as much as tenfold over the next two years as the company established itself as a profitable world dominator! TSLA was also added to the S&P 500 in December 2020.

All of the hypothetical technical metrics we are looking at stayed positive through 2021, suggesting it could have been easy to hold the position through this period using a purely technical approach. The meteoric rise catapulted Musk above Jeff Bezos as the world's richest man in September 2021 at a personal net worth of about $203.4 billion.[124] Momentum, money flows, and the twenty-one-period EMA triggered hypothetical sell signals in 2022, so maybe we are in another one of those choppy consolidation periods. Or maybe Tesla

124 Kenrick Cai, "Elon Musk Eclipses $200 Billion to Become Richest Person in the World Again," *Forbes*, September 28, 2021, https://www.forbes.com/sites/kenrickcai/2021/09/27/elon-musk-200-billion-richest-person-in-the-world/?sh=16b76a283c3e.

TSLA, DECEMBER 2019 TO DECEMBER 2022

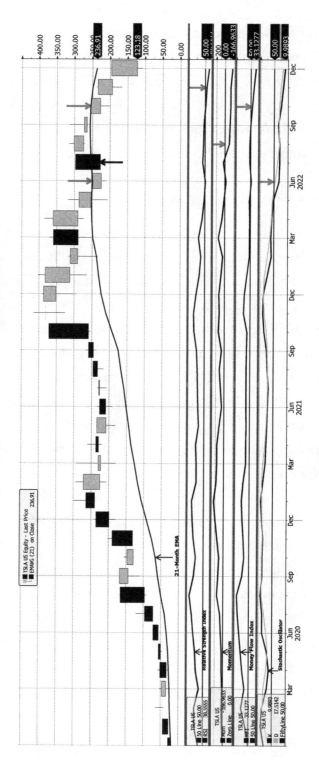

will not find a new way to keep the growth going and the technical metrics will suggest more sales. Or Elon Musk will continue to pull rabbit after rabbit out of the hat to achieve his extremely aggressive and lofty goals. Or ... maybe having an objective framework to evaluate Tesla's progress, like the one we have been contemplating, can take some of the guesswork and risk out of the process.

STEP 3: RISK MANAGEMENT

The next table shows large price movements, which we have been considering to help us sniff out any underlying issues that may exist within the company. This indicator reminds me of what I call the "Don King theory" (after the famous fight promoter) that everything is probably fixed (no disrespect intended to Mr. King). Although there are laws against inside information, it is likely that there is some level of "smart money" trading around every stock. By that I mean people who are actually in the know and taking action because of it. At a minimum, I mean people who know more than me or you about what's happening inside the company. The stock price represents all the known information available (whether public or not) at a given time, so it is important to pay attention to price. There may be things we don't know that show up in the price action before those things become common knowledge.

The fifty-two-week high indicator for TSLA is illustrated below, with black dotted lines to illustrate the rolling high price and then 20 percent below that level (along with a gray down arrow and a black up arrow to illustrate possible exit and entry points). Our two takeaways are these: choppy markets and a consolidating or sideways-moving stock can create a lot of false signals, but the two big thrusts up would do a pretty good job of getting you in on the stock at a pretty opportune time.

FIFTY-TWO-WEEK HIGH INDICATOR: TSLA

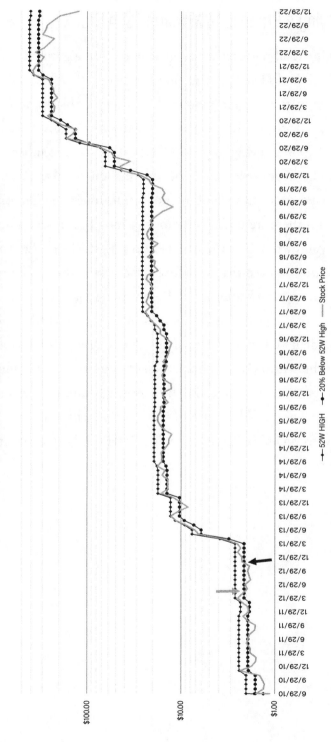

Legend: 52W HIGH — 20% Below 52W High — Stock Price

Applying a Process to Manage TSLA Stock

Bringing it all together with our hypothetical algorithm versus buy-and-hold looks like the chart on page 261.

Again, the gray line is buy-and-hold, and the black line is the hypothetical algorithm. The buy-and-hold investor clearly did a lot better with $1,000 growing to $108,688.24 through December 31, 2022, while the hypothetical investor only made it to about $28,553.05. You can expect this type of inferior result from a mechanical trading system if there are no serious drops or long bear markets during the time you own one of the best-performing stocks in the world. It is interesting to note that with Tesla, there were really only two huge moves in the stock after it had been trading for a while, then longer periods of choppy consolidation as investors weighed the evidence to decide if Tesla would actually be able to execute on its lofty goals. As of the writing of this book, Tesla has become the dominant EV automobile manufacturer in an increasingly competitive market, as almost all of the old line automobile manufacturers have entered the fray with prejudice. Time will tell if Tesla can keep executing on its huge plans.

ALGORITHM VALUE VS. BUY & HOLD VALUE: TSLA

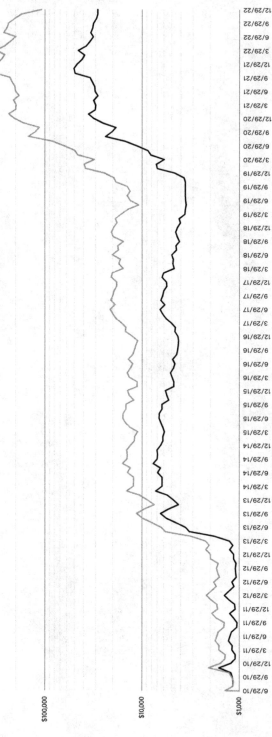

$100,000

$10,000

$1,000

—— Algorithm Value   —— Buy & Hold Value

6/29/10
9/29/10
12/29/10
3/29/11
6/29/11
9/29/11
12/29/11
3/29/12
6/29/12
9/29/12
12/29/12
3/29/13
6/29/13
9/29/13
12/29/13
3/29/14
6/29/14
9/29/14
12/29/14
3/29/15
6/29/15
9/29/15
12/29/15
3/29/16
6/29/16
9/29/16
12/29/16
3/29/17
6/29/17
9/29/17
12/29/17
3/29/18
6/29/18
9/29/18
12/29/18
3/29/19
6/29/19
9/29/19
12/29/19
3/29/20
6/29/20
9/29/20
12/29/20
3/29/21
6/29/21
9/29/21
12/29/21
3/29/22
6/29/22
9/29/22
12/29/22

CHAPTER SEVEN

WHERE TO FROM HERE?

Before we get into lessons learned from these great stocks, let's look quickly at a few companies that we omitted. *Kiplinger* ranks Facebook (now Meta Platforms) as the eighth-best stock over the last thirty years. It would have been fun to review Facebook's and Mark Zuckerberg's rise to success, given the company's antitrust issues with the government and involvement in ongoing free speech debates. However, after the success of the movie *The Social Network*, almost everyone knows the details of how the company evolved, and no one really needs an update. *Kiplinger* also lists Walmart as the number-seven most successful stock of the last thirty years. Johnson & Johnson is listed at number ten. Both of these companies have been considered blue-chip stocks for a long time. Walmart went public on the NYSE in 1972, duking it out in the low-margin retail business from day one and just simply doing a better job, year in and year out, than any of its competitors. Johnson & Johnson went public in 1944. It has been a blue-chip stock "forever" and, as of the writing of this book, remains one of only two companies with a AAA rating from both Moody's and S&P (the other company is Microsoft). Neither Johnson & Johnson nor Walmart fit our small start-up/highly speculative company profile. But they do prove that owning great blue-chip companies can have a strong impact on your overall portfolio. The other names in the *Kiplinger* top ten are the Chinese company Tencent and the South Korean company Samsung.[125] We have no special insight into these foreign companies, and many foreign companies, especially in China, have opaque accounting practices (at best), so they were omitted as well from our more thorough review.

Amazon, Microsoft, Apple, Google, and Tesla: What are the common characteristics of the great stocks we have covered in this book? The first (perhaps silly, perhaps not) is that most of them were founded by people who were academically gifted and who also either dropped out of Harvard or Stanford before graduating. All kidding about specific universities aside, there really is a lot of brainpower at the center of each of these companies. Another characteristic is that each of these companies was generally considered speculative for many of the first years that they were publicly traded. Moreover, each of our companies was involved in cutthroat competition as it began its journey; any serious misstep could have derailed its journey. Execution was a critical and almost unquantifiable component of their ultimate success. In other words, a failure to execute at key moments would have derailed each one of the companies we covered. If Barnes & Noble had succeeded at its online offering and expanded from there, it could have killed Amazon's early revenue streams, along with Amazon's chances of future retail domination. Microsoft and Apple were going head to head with IBM, one of the biggest companies in the world. If IBM had made better strategic and innovation decisions, it could have destroyed both companies. Google entered the internet advertising space and was essentially taking on the world in a land

---

125 Dan Burrows, "The 30 Best Stocks of the Past 30 Years," *Kiplinger,*
      November 19, 2021, https://www.kiplinger.com/investing/
      stocks/603777/30-best-stocks-of-the-past-30-years.

rush for dominance. If Google had not made good decisions around innovations like AdWords/AdSense and around acquisitions like DoubleClick, would it be the dominant player, or would it be just another company that didn't make it? And Tesla set its sights on terraforming the automobile industry, a low-margin, highly competitive industry in which there had been no new major successful players since the Ford Motor Company went public in 1956. All of these companies were considered risky, at best. But they all had the promise of a revolutionary product or service that could potentially reach a huge global market. All of our leaders could be, and have been, called excessively competitive. Many were seen as being very demanding, perfectionists, or at the very least difficult to work with. Steve Jobs and Elon Musk are the poster children for this character trait (with Bill Gates not far behind). It could be possible that being hypercompetitive and demanding are prerequisites for battling with other great business leaders at the frontiers of new and potentially huge markets. Future great companies also need rapidly increasing revenues and rapidly expanding market share if they hope to become huge winners. The stocks we've looked at were also generally considered "hot" IPOs and shares were generally difficult to get right out of the gate.

Let's build a simple checklist so we can start comparing the companies we reviewed against other companies and create at least a subjective process for moving forward:

- Academically highly accomplished leader
- Hypercompetitive leader
- Demanding, perfectionist leader
- Revolutionary product or service
- Huge or global market potential

- Rapidly growing revenues and market share

- "Hot" initial public offering (IPO)

You can make the case that all of our companies checked all of those boxes. The only exception might be Alphabet/Google, where Sergei Brin and Larry Page were not considered to be as ultracompetitive or demanding as the other leaders. Though they are both certainly highly competitive individuals, they also had a team of venture capital partners known for being hypercompetitive, so they could be said to satisfy our checklist by proxy.

These may be good preconditions for success when dealing with speculative stocks, but one could almost make the case that every new, hot IPO meets all or most of these criteria. In other words, there is way too much left for subjective interpretation when it comes to determining who is or is not genius or hypercompetitive enough. Elizabeth Holmes famously dropped out of Stanford to start Theranos, but that company was uncovered as a fraud.[126] So we definitely need more than just a highly subjective checklist.

We saw mixed results from the algorithm as we applied it to the stocks we reviewed. But the primary value of using a technically based algorithm is *not* to maximize profits on the perfect stock. We took some of the best-performing stocks in the world, in hindsight, and assumed an investor held them for the duration and throughout all the drama within and without. Then we applied our algorithm to see if it made any sense at all to *ever* consider selling what we already knew were some of the best-performing stocks in the last century. The fact that we got generally decent results is almost a minor miracle, since it is logical that just holding the best-performing stocks in the last

---

126 "Elizabeth Holmes and the Theranos Case: History of a Fraud Scandal," integrityline.com, April 17, 2023, https://www.integrityline.com/expertise/blog/elizabeth-holmes-theranos/.

century (with the benefit of hindsight) would logically make the most sense. If you pick the best stocks and hold them forever, obviously you will do great: they are some of the best-performing stocks of their era. The algorithm should have blown up our results no matter what in terms of real total return.

So the beauty of creating a technically based algorithmic approach is twofold:

1. If you pick one of the best-performing stocks in the future, you might do worse than buy-and-hold, except of course in a really bad bear market (like the dot-com bust) or if the company just completely fails to execute at some point.

2. If you pick the wrong stock (which you will at some point), it could get you out of a loser, so you don't just have to rely on your gut instincts, guesses, and hopes that things will actually work. In other words, it is giving you some insurance for when things go wrong (which they can and will).

Combining the checklist with an algorithm is like adding an insurance policy to your selection and management process. Using just your gut instincts with no process whatsoever starts to look and feel a lot like gambling. Let's take a look at a few companies using our checklist along with the algorithm we created to see what might have happened with some of the other most famous stocks of the past thirty years.

> Combining the checklist with an algorithm is like adding an insurance policy to your selection and management process. Using just your gut instincts with no process whatsoever starts to look and feel a lot like gambling.

Facebook (Meta)

Facebook/Meta has been big news since its early days, and it definitely checks all the boxes:

- Academically highly accomplished leader: Another Harvard dropout and academically gifted. Yes.

- Hypercompetitive leader: Zuckerberg cut his co-creating partner out of his share of the company (supposedly).[127] Yes.

- Demanding, perfectionist leader: Zuckerberg and his team were known for working twenty-four hours a day. Yes.

- Revolutionary product or service: Connecting the entire world socially was a big goal. Yes.

- Huge or global market potential: Facebook was global from almost the beginning. Yes.

- Rapidly growing revenues and market share: Facebook shot out of a cannon right from the beginning. Yes.

- Hot IPO: Check!

---

127   Nicholas Carlson, "Exclusive: How Mark Zuckerberg Booted His Co-Founder out of the Company," buisinessinsider.com, May 15, 2012, https://www.businessinsider.com/how-mark-zuckerberg-booted-his-co-founder-out-of-the-company-2012-5.

FACEBOOK (META), MAY 2012 TO DECEMBER 2022

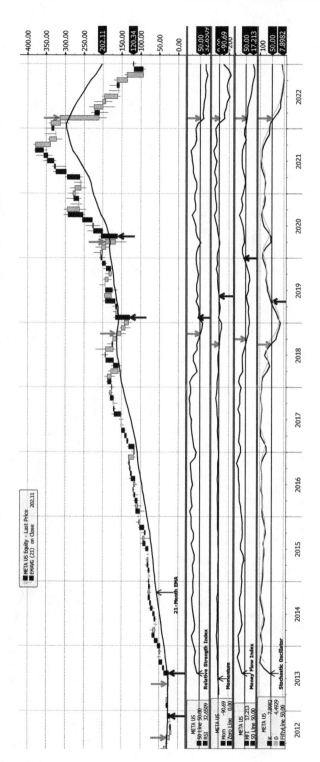

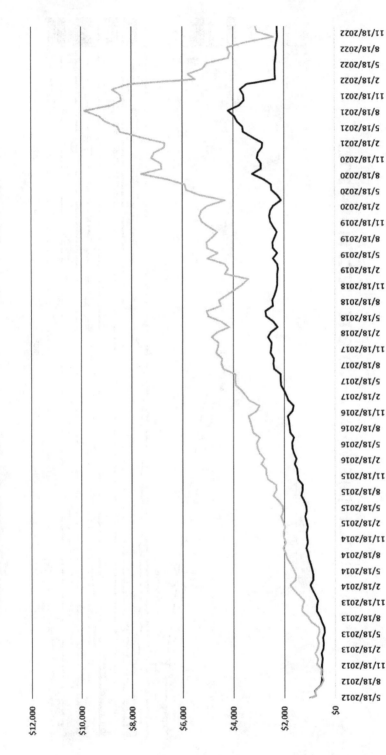

ALGORITHM VALUE VS. BUY & HOLD VALUE: META

Facebook was a highly anticipated IPO but struggled a bit at the beginning as investor excitement gave way to execution realities. The IPO price of $38 per share reflected a market capitalization of $16 billion, which was a record at the time. The stock floundered for almost a year after going public, until accelerating revenues demonstrated that the high IPO valuation was justified. Eventually, the stock started to crater as Facebook changed its name to Meta and aggressively pursued a strategy focused on virtual reality. As of December 31, 2022, this shift in strategy to virtual reality through the Metaverse was seen as a major failure, and the stock paid the price along with Facebook/Meta investors. Let's take a look at our algorithm to see if it could have potentially spared an investor some pain.

You can see from the graph that using a buy-and-hold approach would have been a better approach—until things started going bad with the company's commitment of resources to the Metaverse. The stock cratered as losses piled up with little market acceptance (at least so far). Our process-driven algorithm could have helped here—protecting our hypothetical investor from a company that makes a big execution mistake. At its lows in 2022, Meta had lost 80 percent of its value from the all-time high.[128] Time will tell whether they can regain traction and execute more consistently.

Uber (UBER)

In a lot of ways, Uber sounded like the idea of the century: take a lot of people with cars who also need extra revenue, and get them driving around transporting people everywhere in the world, all the while displacing a highly fragmented and non-technologically-coordinated

128 Elizabeth de Luna, "Zuckerberg Backtracks after Horizon Worlds Backlash, Claims Meta Is 'Capable of Much More,'" Mashable, August 19, 2022, https://mashable.com/article/mark-zuckerberg-horizon-worlds-backlash-meta.

worldwide taxi market. Talk about a huge opportunity! With GPS and the power of connectivity through the internet, Uber was likely to be an obvious winner.

Let's see how our checklist fared:

- Academically highly accomplished leader: Former CEO Travis Kalanick studied computer engineering and business economics at UCLA, then (unlike me—I went to UCLA) dropped out to pursue a search-engine-based business start-up. Cofounder Garret Camp also has a very strong academic pedigree. Yes.

- Hypercompetitive leader: Maybe too competitive? Yes.

- Demanding, perfectionist leader: Check!

- Revolutionary product or service: Check!

- Huge or global market potential: Double check.

- Rapidly growing revenues and market share: Check.

- Hot IPO: Check.

At first pass, Uber looks like it fits the model of another "greatest stock ever." But a funny thing happened on the way to limitless success. Let's see what happened with the stock, and then let's see what could have potentially happened using our algorithmic process. Uber was founded in 2009 and did not go public until 2019. During the time it was a private company, its valuation went through the roof. By the time of the IPO, Uber was valued at $75.5 billion, making it one of the largest public offerings of all time![129] Over the years, the private

---

129 "History of Uber: Timeline and Facts," TheStreet, accessed March 12, 2023, https://www.thestreet.com/technology/history-of-uber-15028611. See also: "Uber Valued at $82.4bn as It Prices IPO at $45 per Share," *The Guardian*, May 9, 2019, https://www.theguardian.com/business/2019/may/09/uber-value-wall-street-ipo-friday.

funding valuations had taken a lot of the potential short-term returns away from the average public investor. We can see the progression in private valuation (that includes some heavy hitters like Softbank, Google, and even Jeff Bezos, as part of the Benchmark funding) in the graph that follows (scale is billions of dollars).[130]

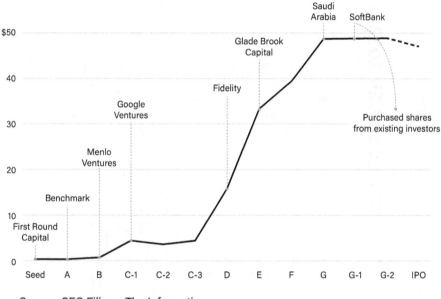

Source: SEC Filings, The Information

Now let's look at the stock chart.

---

130 Amir Efrati, "Uber's Biggest IPO Winners," The Information, December 21, 2020, https://www.theinformation.com/articles/ubers-biggest-ipo-winners.

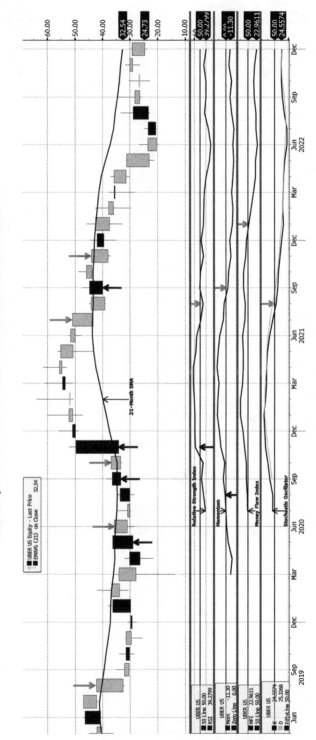

UBER, MAY 2019 TO DECEMBER 2022

We can see that while Uber sounded like a great idea (and might still be one) and checked all the boxes, the stock has gone almost nowhere. If we follow the metrics we have been covering, the stock was in a technical sell condition by late 2021 and into 2022. On the next page, we have the comparison between buy-and-hold and the algorithm. As you might expect, there is not much advantage versus buy-and-hold in a stock that has chopped around sideways and gone almost nowhere since the IPO.

The jury is definitely still out on whether or not this stock can deliver on the promise of changing the way the world travels (profitably).

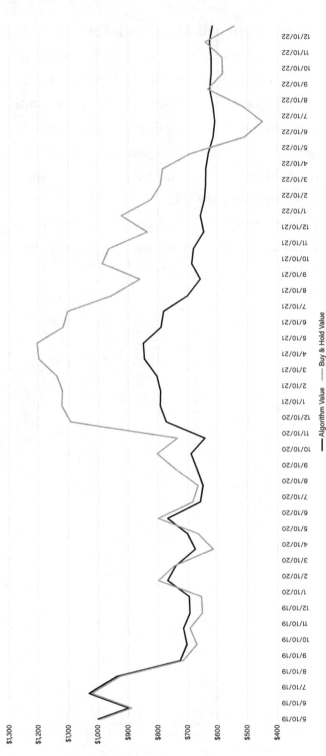

ALGORITHM VALUE VS. BUY & HOLD VALUE: UBER

Netflix (NFLX)

Netflix did not start out as the streaming behemoth that we all know today. At the beginning, the company mailed DVD copies to people's homes, and people had to mail them back. It was an extremely clunky operation, to say the least. Streaming was always the promise and hope, but technology had not caught up yet. Let's start with the basics and take a look at our subjective checklist:

- Academically highly accomplished leader: Cofounder, chairman, and co-CEO Reed Hasting graduated with a master's in computer science from Stanford but has a decidedly more eclectic past than most of the leaders we have profiled, including training with the US Marine Corps and then the Peace Corps. Maybe not Steve Jobs but reminiscent … Yes.

- Hypercompetitive leader: You have to be competitive to pioneer a brand-new industry. Yes.

- Demanding, perfectionist leader: No. Reed Hastings is famous for shifting his leadership style from autocratic to more laissez-faire.[131]

- Revolutionary product or service: Streaming media content was an industry that didn't exist when NFLX started. So yes.

- Huge or global market potential: Yes!

- Rapidly growing revenues and market share: Yes.

---

131 Nilesh Agarwal, "Leadership Lessons from Reed Hastings' No Rules Rule Book," Peak Performer, May 17, 2022, https://blog.peakperformer.io/reed-hastings-no-rules-rule-leadership/#:~:text=Reed%20Hastings%20Leadership%20Style%3A%20Laissez,company%20he%20ran%20before%20Netflix.

- Hot IPO: It was a good IPO but not necessarily considered "hot." It priced at $15 on May 23, 2002, and closed the first day up $1.20 at $16.20. Not bad, but not "hot."[132]

A lot of the boxes could be checked with Netflix right from the beginning, but that didn't make it a no-brainer. That was especially true if you could not look beyond the clunky early business model of mailing DVDs back and forth. The chart on page 279 takes a closer look at the monthly price chart of Netflix since inception.

You can see from this chart and the next that the stock initially went up but ultimately chopped around for almost the first ten years. After hiccups and sideways activity through about 2012, and as the streaming platform started to gain serious market share, the stock really got traction.

---

132 "Netflix's IPO Was 16 Years Ago Wednesday—Here's How Much You'd Have Made If You Invested $1,000 Back in the Day (NFLX)," Yahoo! News, accessed March 12, 2023, https://www.yahoo.com/news/netflix-apos-ipo-16-years-170300960. html?guccounter=1&guce_referrer=aHR0cHM6Ly93d3cuZ29vZ2xlLmNvbS8 &guce_referrer_sig=AQAAAGXHT4smxyVV5ulesKm4zdh7HT-HZDmcGqlq_ D8NF9-OS6o0GIL5IdAXipjKNYlXWs_uWCuK8dUP8p09GNQpFC0UycXDzg9mtJS- niqWu4woRwMC24mKqXdeXA4garCOU5PHDJF48HTUF0KERiUmfatbmYpmzok-ze- DK8WfgTQeI.

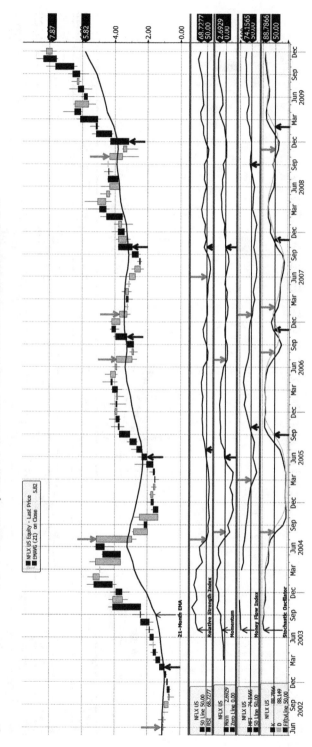

NFLX, MAY 2002 TO DECEMBER 2009

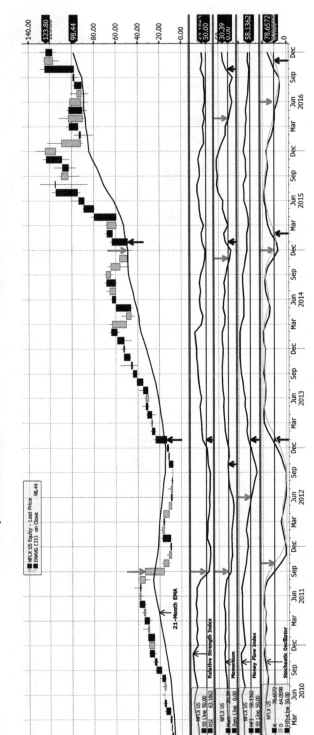

NFLX, JANUARY 2010 TO DECEMBER 2016

NFLX, JANUARY 2017 TO DECEMBER 2022

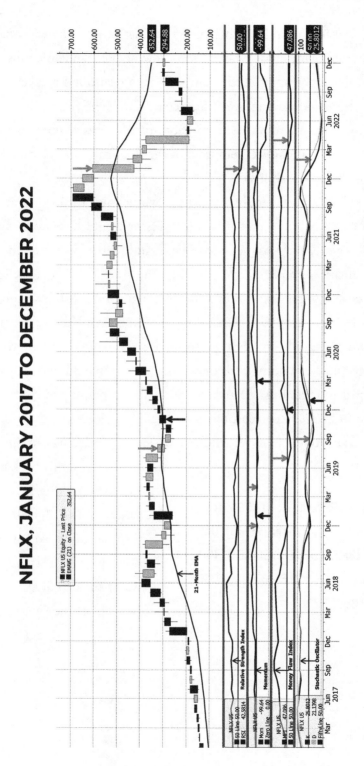

It wasn't until 2022, when the realities of intense new competition from many quarters along with slowing postpandemic subscriber growth caught up with the company. As a result, it got taken to the woodshed—dropping over 75 percent from its highs.

In sum, there was a lot of chop, then explosive growth, then a large drop in the stock. Let's see how the algorithm could have worked with all this variability.

NFLX has generally been a huge winner over the long term. This is a case where the buy-and-hold investor would have done significantly better most of the time, even including the large drop in 2022 as valuation concerns overwhelmed the stock. NFLX stock fell as much as ~75 percent from the all-time high, and the drops happened relatively fast around earnings dates. The smoother-riding algorithmic approach lagged behind the performance of this buy-and-hold winner. That said, a hypothetical algorithm process would certainly have helped an investor sleep at night with all the volatility in Netflix—at least in 2022. Reed Hastings is generally considered one of the best CEOs in America, so we will have to wait and see if he can right the ship and take Netflix back to the summit or even higher in the years ahead. As usual, it all comes down to execution, so having an objective process certainly can take some of the guesswork and emotion out of the equation.

It all comes down to execution, so having an objective process certainly can take some of the guesswork and emotion out of the equation.

ALGORITHM VALUE VS. BUY & HOLD VALUE: NFLX

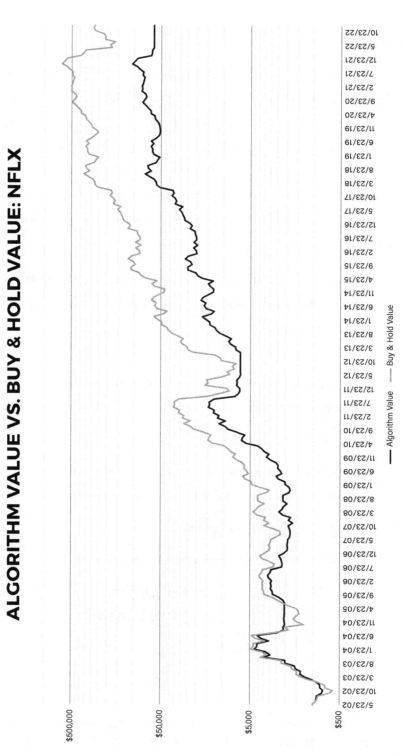

Algorithm Value ——— Buy & Hold Value

Zoom (ZM)

We talked earlier about the benefits of being in the right place at the right time and how that worked for companies like Amazon when it came to the global COVID-19 pandemic and the rise of stay-at-home and work-from-home trends. Well, Zoom might be the poster child for being in the right place at the right time. When nearly everyone was forced to stay at home, Zoom provided the perfect easy-to-use solution for ongoing face-to-face communication. Let's take a look at the checklist to begin our process.

- Academically highly accomplished leader: Founder and CEO Eric Yuan could be considered to check this box with a degree in applied mathematics and a minor in computer science from Shandong University of Science and Technology. Yes.

- Hypercompetitive leader: He could also be considered to check this box. Yes.

- Demanding, perfectionist leader: No.

- Revolutionary product or service: We cannot really call Zoom revolutionary, but it was a better/easier mousetrap. No.

- Huge or global market potential: Yes.

- Rapidly growing revenues and market share: Yes.

- Hot IPO: Zoom had a very strong IPO in April 2019 (up 72 percent on the first day of trading, then went sideways until the pandemic hit).[133] Yes.

---

133 Jordan Novet, "Zoom Rocketed 72% on First Day of Trading," CNBC, April 18, 2019, https://www.cnbc.com/2019/04/18/zoom-ipo-stock-begins-trading-on-nasdaq.html.

ZOOM REVENUE

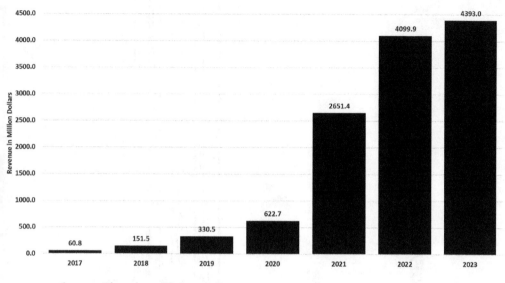

Source: Bloomberg Finance L.P.

Zoom checked almost all the boxes on the checklist we created, and make no mistake, this was a "hot" stock because of the pandemic. The stock exploded. Unfortunately, Webex, by Cisco; Teams, by Microsoft; and others were in the competitive mix. As usual, Microsoft was competing by giving Teams away for free as a built-in feature (they've never made that move before, right?). So Zoom stock (ZM) has had quite a round trip, going up almost 1,000 percent and then retreating almost all the way back.

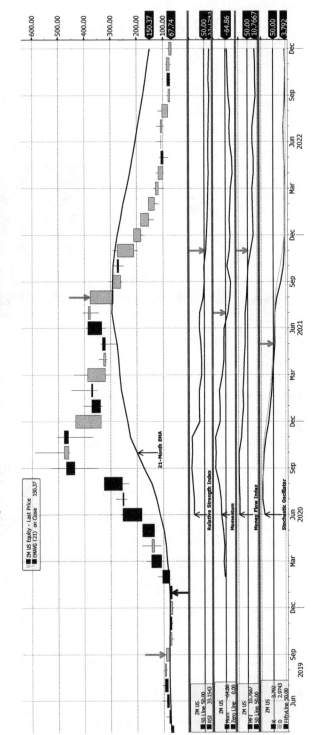

ZM, APRIL 2019 TO DECEMBER 2022

ALGORITHM VALUE VS. BUY & HOLD VALUE: ZM

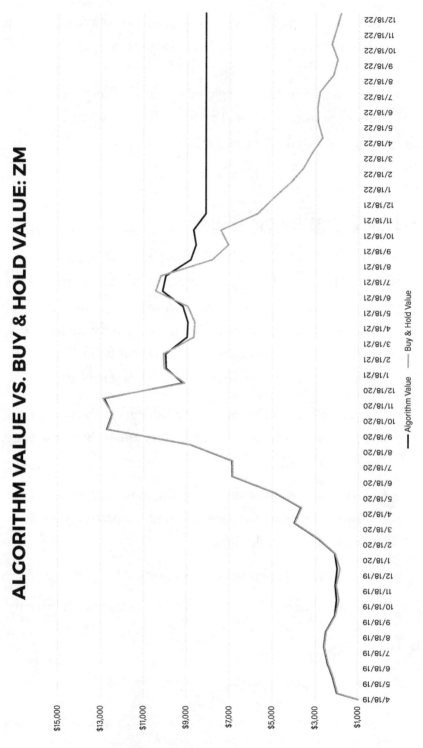

The chart on page 287 shows the comparison between the actual buy-and-hold stock performance and our algorithm applied after the fact.

The hypothetical algorithm picked up the breakdown of the stock and could have taken you out. This is another case where a process-driven approach could have potentially saved investors from some big losses.

Peloton Interactive, Inc. (PTON)

Like Zoom, Peloton (PTON) stock was red hot because of the pandemic. Having a full spin/cycling experience, complete with internet/video access to other riders and instructors right in one's home, amounted to the very definition of being in the right place at the right time. The perfect solution for the stay-at-home fitness buff. Nevertheless, a quick look at our checklist shows some deficiencies.

- Academically highly accomplished leader: Founders John Foley and Tom Cortese may be very smart, but they don't check this box.

- Hypercompetitive leader: While this innovative and entrepreneurial company was aggressive and resourceful, I wouldn't necessarily check this box.

- Demanding, perfectionist leader: Same.

- Revolutionary product or service: Connecting stationary cyclers through the internet was new and could be considered revolutionary. Maybe.

- Huge or global market potential: Yes.

- Rapidly growing revenues and market share: You could argue yes, until the COVID-19 pandemic when it became a huge *yes*.

- Hot IPO: No.

This company does not really hit all the boxes in our checklist of subjective criteria. But once the pandemic hit, investors flooded into this name. However, the stock performed almost exactly the same as Zoom, going up about 800 percent and then giving all of it back, and then some.

Again, the hypothetical algorithm on the next page picked up the breakdown in the stock. It was a wild ride up and down with Peloton, but our algorithmic approach could have resulted in a profit instead of a loss for the dates covered in this example.

PTON, SEPTEMBER 2019 TO DECEMBER 2022

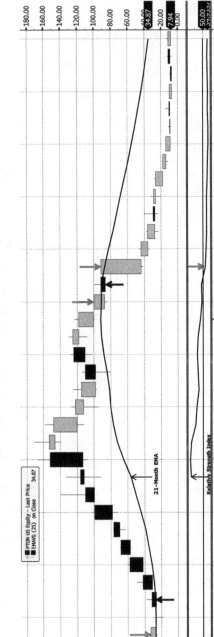

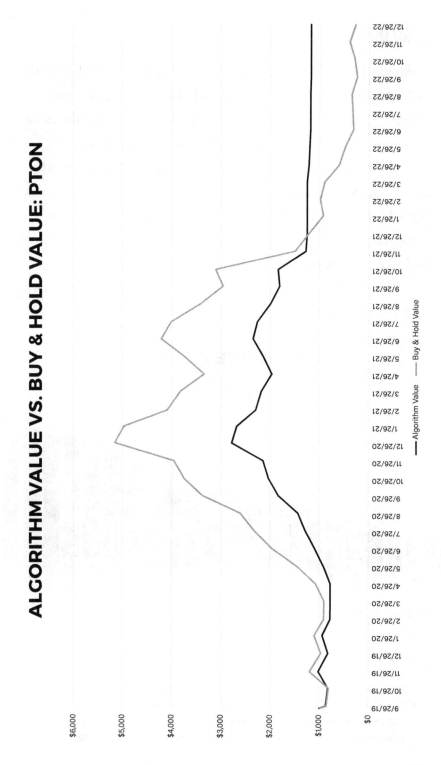

ALGORITHM VALUE VS. BUY & HOLD VALUE: PTON

Buy & Hold Value

Algorithm Value

Roku (ROKU)

Roku was part of the streaming revolution in the second half of the 2010s and evolved into one of the leaders of the smart TV platform that brings together multiple streaming sources into one convenient location (your TV). Roku launched its IPO in September 2017 at $14 and began trading at $15.78. At the time, Roku had about 15.1 million active accounts, a 43 percent year-over-year increase, and logged 3.5 billion quarterly streaming hours, up 60 percent for the same period.[134] Roku was in a superhot industry with global potential and seemed to be dominating.

By Q2 2022, the company had over sixty-three million active users—as you can see from the following chart.

ROKU ACTIVE ACCOUNTS

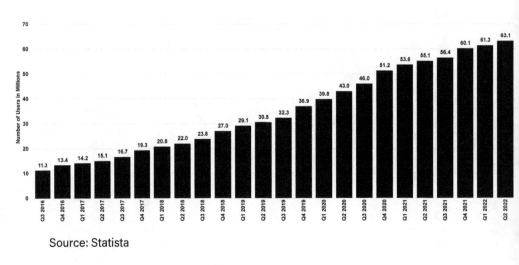

Source: Statista

---

134   Danny Vena, "If You Invested $1,000 in Roku's IPO, This Is How Much Money You'd Have Now," The Motley Fool, December 2, 2019, https://www.fool.com/ investing/2019/12/02/if-you-invested-1000-in-rokus-ipo-this-is-how-much.aspx.

Let's take a quick look at our checklist.

- Academically highly accomplished leader: CEO Anthony Wood is a pioneer in the streaming industry and a billionaire in his own right but not an academic standout in comparison to some of the others we have profiled. No.

- Hypercompetitive leader: One could argue yes to this and the next category—although maybe not at the Steve Jobs level—as all entrepreneurial start-ups require a good measure of both. Yes.

- Demanding, perfectionist leader: Same.

- Revolutionary product or service: Yes.

- Huge or global market potential: Yes.

- Rapidly growing revenues and market share: Yes!

- Hot IPO: Yes.

This one could be seen as checking almost all the boxes, so what happened to this hot IPO?

The stock was on a strong and consistent path for the first few years but then became another "round-tripper." This is another case of fast-growing revenues not equating to profits as a company fails to execute at expected levels. The buy-and-hold investor would not have made much at all. Let's compare that investor with our hypothetical algorithm.

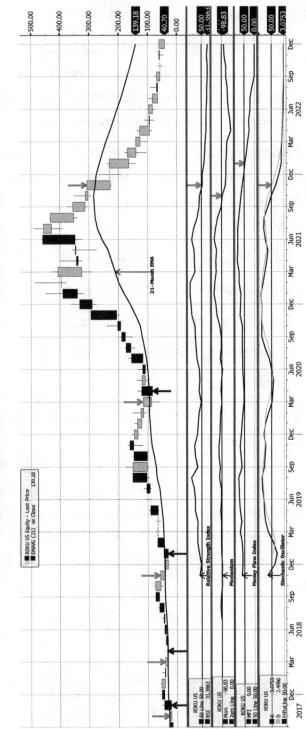

ROKU, SEPTEMBER 2017 TO DECEMBER 2022

ALGORITHM VALUE VS. BUY & HOLD VALUE: ROKU

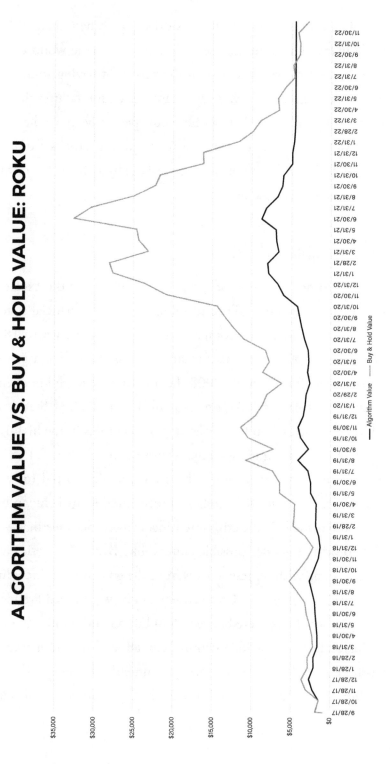

This is another win for a process-driven hypothetical algorithm. Clearly many companies that seem like they have the world by the tail don't end with success. That is the beauty of having some kind of process to help protect yourself against execution failures that are bound to happen somewhere within your speculative portfolio.

Now let's look at one of the most famous stocks from the 2008–2009 Global Financial Crisis to see if our hypothetical algorithm approach might have helped.

Lehman Brothers (LEH)

Lehman Brothers was one of the poster children for the excessive leverage that caused the GFC and almost broke our financial system as we know it today. The company had roots going back to 1847 and had been a Wall Street fixture since. It was spun off as a private company in 1994. Then, by 2008, Lehman Brothers Holdings Inc. was the fourth-largest investment bank in the United States. Its business was focused on heavily leveraging securities in the high-risk real estate and subprime mortgage sectors of the market. When the real estate market turned down there was literally no bid (or very low bids) left for billions of dollars of securitized loans Lehman had created and owned. As the crisis intensified, emergency meetings were called to bring together possible suitors, like Bank of America and Barclays, along with representatives from the government, including Secretary of the Treasury Hank Paulsen and New York Fed President Tim Geithner. There were between $50 billion and $100 billion of anticipated losses embedded within Lehman, and no suitor wanted to assume that risk without some government guarantees. The US government was not willing to provide those guarantees, so the talks failed, and on September 15, 2008, Lehman Brothers infamously filed for bankruptcy.[135]

So what were investors to do if they held this once "blue-chip" stock? We can see from the following chart that things had been going very well for years. But an investor had to be able to make an all-or-none decision extremely quickly under the circumstances surrounding the bankruptcy. If you didn't, you ended up with nothing.

Let's look at our checklist of subjective criteria first:

- Academically highly accomplished leader: CEO Dick Fuld was well educated but not gifted like some of the others we've profiled. No.

- Hypercompetitive leader: Lehman was known for its hyper-competitive culture. Yes.

- Demanding, perfectionist leader: Yes.

- Revolutionary product or service: Securitizing loans was not revolutionary. Leveraging them forty times probably was, but in a bad way. Warren Buffet has a famous line: "When the tide goes out, you see who is swimming naked." Leverage is only your friend when things are going up. No.

- Huge or global market potential: Yes.

- Rapidly growing revenues and market share: Yes.

- Hot IPO: No.

---

135 Kimberly Amadeo, "How the 2008 Lehman Brothers Collapse Affects You Today," The Balance, January 29, 2022, https://www.thebalancemoney.com/lehman-brothers-collapse-causes-impact-4842338.

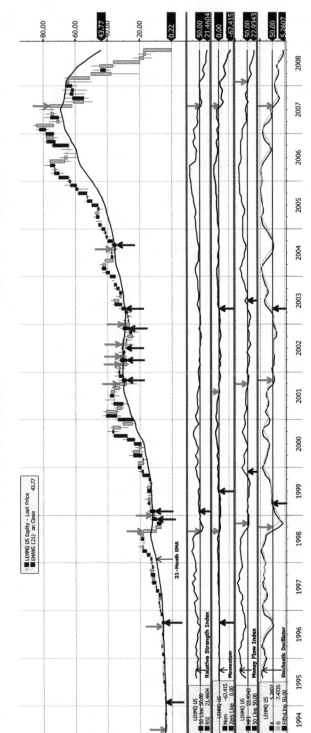

LEHMAN, MAY 1994 TO SEPTEMBER 2008

Because the checklist is highly subjective, an investor could have seen this mixed bag in a positive light. But that is all the more reason to couple the checklist with a powerful mechanical and *objective* algorithm. We can see how dramatic the chart tracking Lehman Brothers stock was at the end in the chart on page 298.

Wow, that's potentially a lot of emotion for an investor to deal with! Now what if we insert our process-driven hypothetical algorithm into the situation to see what could have happened here …

Using the algorithmic process, an investor would have been pretty dissatisfied for most of the time going all the way back to the first day of trading in 1994. When things got serious, this approach could have helped take a bit of the emotion out of the situation and given our hypothetical investor an opportunity not to lose everything. While LEH stock went to essentially $0 in bankruptcy, that same $1,000 invested initially would still have potentially been worth over $5,000. That's a huge difference and really a game changer in this situation ($5,000 is a lot better than $0).

ALGORITHM VALUE VS. BUY & HOLD VALUE: LEHMQ

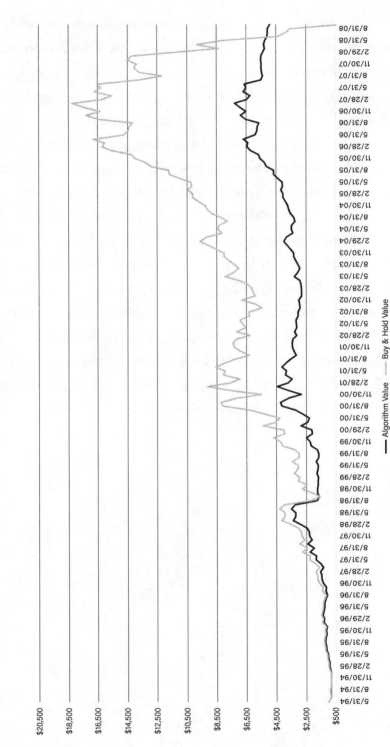

Enron Corp (ENE)

Enron Corporation (ENE) was ostensibly the greatest energy trading company in the world for many years. At the time, Enron had reached a market cap of about $70 billion, making it the seventh-largest publicly traded company on the NYSE in the year 2000. A lot of people owned this stock, which helps explain why the Enron scandal is one of the most famous in history. Lots of investors got caught up in the mess. What if you were unlucky enough to be one of them?

Essentially, Enron began losing money and used accepted and aggressive accounting methods, like mark-to-market accounting (unfortunately, the company used inflated estimates), and illegal methods like creating private shell companies and Special Purpose Entities to make sure that losses would not be discovered and could not be linked back to Enron. Analyst and investor scrutiny of Enron's accounting methods and financial statements began to intensify in the year 2000 and culminated in April 2001 with Jeff Skilling, Enron's CEO, calling analyst Richard Grubman an "asshole" on a public earnings call. We can probably file that occurrence under "red flag." By December 2001, Enron had filed for bankruptcy, and the entire fraud was publicly exposed. At the time, it was the largest bankruptcy in US history. The historic fraud led to the passage of the Sarbanes-Oxley Act in 2002, which enacted a comprehensive reform of business financial practices and put in place new standards for public accounting firms, corporate management, and corporate boards of directors at publicly held companies.[136]

Let's take a quick look at our checklist:

---

136 Simon Constable, "How the Enron Scandal Changed American Business Forever," *TIME*, December 2, 2021, https://time.com/6125253/enron-scandal-changed-american-business-forever/.

- Academically highly accomplished leader: CEO Jeff Skilling earned his MBA from Harvard Business School in the top 5 percent of his class. Genius, no. Smart, yes.

- Hypercompetitive leader: Definitely.

- Demanding, perfectionist leader: Definitely.

- Revolutionary product or service: Trading global energy markets and eventually other areas like broadband services was touted by the firm as revolutionary but probably doesn't check this box.

- Huge or global market potential: Definitely.

- Rapidly growing revenues and market share: Checked the box but was eventually revealed as fraudulent.

- Hot IPO: No.

Precisely because there's not much an investor can do if someone is lying, having a mechanical process like our algorithm in place could have helped in an extreme case like this one.

Here is the chart of Enron stock (ENE):

ENRON, JULY 1980 TO DECEMBER 2001

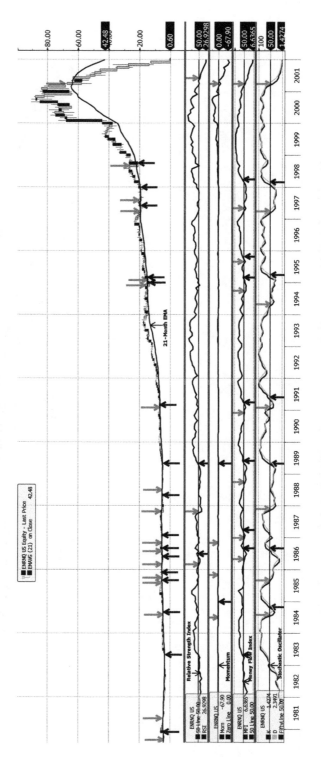

ALGORITHM VALUE VS. BUY & HOLD VALUE: ENRNQ

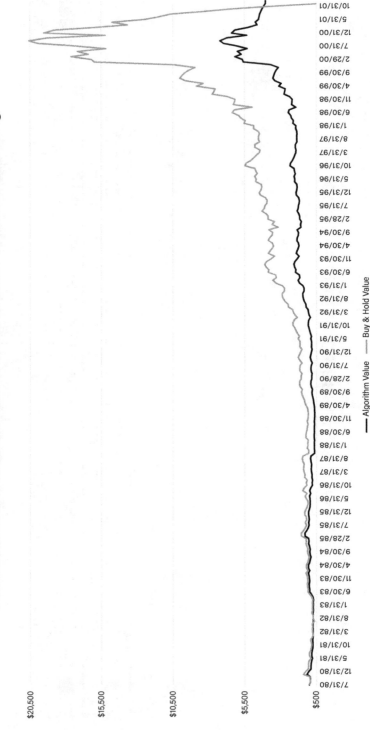

Algorithm Value —— Buy & Hold Value

You can see that ENE was a relatively successful stock, which then got turbo charged in early 2000. Unfortunately, the precipitous drop to $0 happened very quickly as well. The chart on page 304 shows our hypothetical algorithm applied to Enron with the benefit of hindsight compared to a buy-and-hold strategy.

As we can see, the buy-and-hold approach was winning, all the way up until it wasn't. There's an old saying about taking a stairway up and an elevator down that applies here. It's likely that a process that removed emotion from this volatile situation could have resulted in better performance. But in the case of Enron, anything would have been better than ending up with nothing.

JDS Uniphase (JDSU/VIAV)

The dot-com era ended abruptly in mid-2000. But the run-up to that peak was one of the most speculative periods in the history of the stock market. This was the period I mentioned earlier during which people were quitting their jobs to become day traders and looking to get rich quick. There were many stocks that were caught up in the technology/internet bonanza. JDS Uniphase was one of them. Jim Cramer of CNBC fame even coined the moniker "Just don't sell us" (J-D-S-U) because of the stock's relentless progress higher. A lot of investors owned this name. JDSU was at the forefront of the exciting fiber-optic components industry, which was being used to build out the World Wide Web and included advanced optical networks for the telecommunications and cable television industries. JDSU was right at the center of the entire infrastructure build-out for what was considered a "sure thing": the internet and the information superhighway.

Let's take a look at our checklist first to see how that shook out:

- Academically highly accomplished leader: CEO, Jozef Strauss, and his team at JDSU were all academically highly accomplished. Yes.

- Hypercompetitive leader: Nothing stands out here compared to some of our earlier cases. No.

- Demanding, perfectionist leader: Same.

- Revolutionary product or service: Yes.

- Huge or global market potential: Yes.

- Rapidly growing revenues and market share: Revenues were exploding higher through 2000. Yes.

- Hot IPO: JSDU was pretty sleepy until the dot-com boom hit, so this one is a no.

The checklist offers mixed results, but JDSU was generating massive revenues by the year 2000 (~$1.77 billion for the fiscal 2000 year). The company also enjoyed extremely positive analyst and press reviews. As late as August 2000, no less popular a source than the Motley Fool wrote the following:

> *JDS Uniphase's Growth Continues ... Sales growth of 10% or more on a comparable quarter basis—JDSU's top-line revenues are growing at a rate that puts it among the top tier of public companies. Its year-over-year sales growth came in at 119%. Its sequential quarterly growth of 25% easily passed our 10% target as well. Even if the impact of current acquisitions is excluded, JDSU grew revenues by more than 100% over the year-ago figure ...* [137]

---

137 "JDS UNIPHASE's Growth Continues," The Motley Fool, February 15, 2000, https://www.fool.com/archive/portfolios/rulemaker/2000/02/15/jds-uniphases-growth-continues.aspx.

This was a very popular stock at the time.

And you can see from the chart on page 308 that JDSU really caught the dot-com wave, with the stock going from single digits to over $500 in just one year. No wonder people thought they could get rich quick! Unfortunately, the company expanded aggressively and made expensive acquisitions right into the teeth of the dot-com crash. After posting massive revenue gains through 2000, by July 2001, they were posting losses of $50.6 billion(!), the largest annual loss ever reported in North American history up until that time.[138] This stock had a classic round trip: straight up, then straight down. A lot of investors got badly burned on the journey. A look at the following raw price chart makes that easy to imagine.

Now let's apply our hypothetical algorithm to this dot-com victim and see what could have happened.

The hypothetical algorithm on page 309 shows that it could have made, saved, and retained very substantial profits versus the buy-and-hold (and guess-and-hope) approach. We cut the analysis off when JDSU split into Viavi Solutions and Lumentum Holdings Inc. in 2015. But at that time, the hypothetical algorithm approach was at ~$85,000 while the buy-and-hold approach came in at just over ~$5,000. Clearly the technical approach could have saved the day in the case of JDS Uniphase, because "Just don't sell us" rapidly became "Get me out of this thing!"

---

138 "Sizing Up JDSU's Massive Loss," Light Reading, July 27, 2001, https://www.lightreading.com/sizing-up-jdsus-massive-loss/d/d-id/575080.

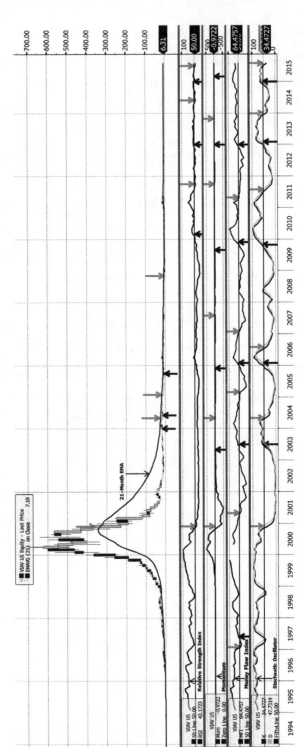

JDSU (VIAV), NOVEMBER 1993 TO JULY 2015

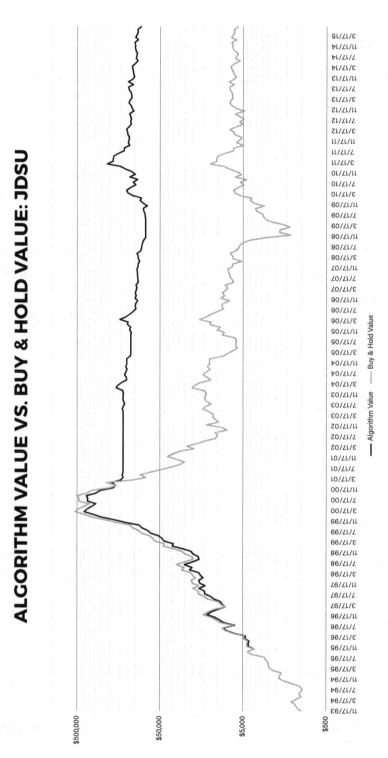

ALGORITHM VALUE VS. BUY & HOLD VALUE: JDSU

—— Algorithm Value   —— Buy & Hold Value

Pets.com (PETS/IPETZ)

Another memorable name from the dot-com era was Pets.com. Essentially, the story goes as follows:

- The market for pet products was a huge multibillion-dollar market.

- So getting rid of the bricks-and-mortar costs and moving the entire business onto the internet was a sure thing.

And Pets.com arguably had the most famous, now infamous, brand representative: a guy who had his hand in a sock puppet that looked like a dog. If you were around then, you remember it. If you were not, I have to assure you that this really happened, and the sock puppet logo was famous at the time.

So Pets.com basically had

- a sock puppet,

- a large potential market, and

- not much of a viable business plan, including solving for how to ship heavy bags of dog food economically one at a time.

What could go wrong, right? Again, it may seem hard to believe that this company was a phenomenon in the early 2000s, but it was so much of a phenomenon that Amazon actually purchased 30 percent of the business. The company went public in February 2000 and was completely liquidated 268 days later.[139]

Even though the company was truly a phenomenon at the time, when we review our checklist, it doesn't really pass muster:

---

139 JeffreyPowers, "November 7, 2000: Pets.com Closes," Day in Tech History, November 6, 2019. https://dayintechhistory.com/dith/november-7-2000-pets-com-closes-2/.

- Academically highly accomplished leader: Julie Wainright went on to some large successes later but doesn't really check this box like many of the others we have chronicled. No.

- Hypercompetitive leader: No.

- Demanding, perfectionist leader: No.

- Revolutionary product or service: This was more of a jump-on-the-bandwagon gambit. No.

- Huge or global market potential: Pet supplies is definitely a large market. Yes.

- Rapidly growing revenues and market share: Small revenues against huge costs. No.

- Hot IPO: Everything was "hot" in February 2000.

Sticking with one's process in all markets has a lot of merit. Starting with our subjective checklist might have helped an investor avoid this one even in the red-hot, emotion-filled dot-com period. On the one hand, "everything" was working at that time, but on the other hand, we can see from the next chart that this IPO went bad almost from the start.

PETS (IPETZ), FEBRUARY 2000 TO NOVEMBER 2000

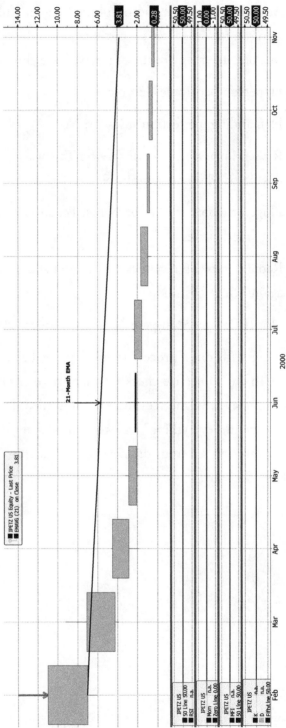

Most hot IPOs open above the initial offer price and stay up there for a couple of days at least, because of all the excitement. Pets.com went public on February 11, 2000, at $11 per share, went up to $14 on the first day, and then proceeded to go straight down. It is almost never a good sign when the price of an IPO breaks more than 10 percent below the actual IPO price (not the first trading price, but the announced IPO price). If you get stuck in that situation, it is probably a good sign to start legging out (i.e., selling). You can always buy back when and if the stock recaptures the IPO price. Hot IPOs often come back down below their first trade price, but should one get below 10 to 20 percent of the actual IPO price, it's usually worth considering taking some action.

Let's take a look at the hypothetical algorithm to see if we could have gotten some help there. Since the algorithm is heavily based on monthly data that does not kick in for the first twelve months, the short life of this stock is a reminder that we should have a plan in place for future potential Pets.com disasters. One approach could be to use price and earnings data until the stock has enough time to generate monthly data across all the metrics we have been using. To accommodate a stock that just blows up, I have adjusted the hypothetical algorithm on the following page to reflect only our price and earnings data weighted at 50 percent each until monthly is available.

You can see that in a worst-case scenario, the hypothetical algorithm did a little better, but nobody wins with a stinker that just goes straight down like this one.

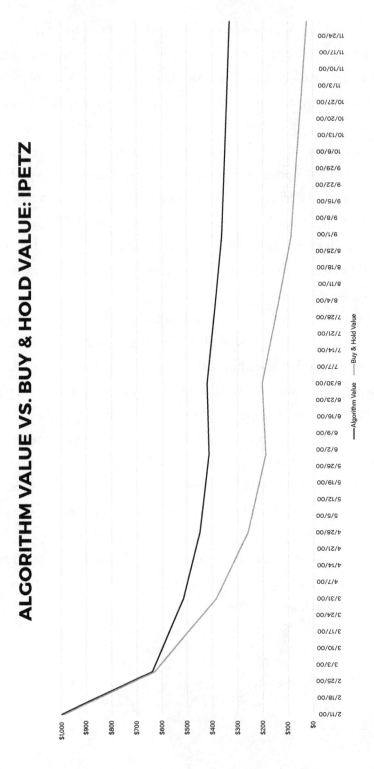

ALGORITHM VALUE VS. BUY & HOLD VALUE: IPETZ

Bitcoin

Yes, Bitcoin! It's not really a stock (and many people are not sure exactly what it is), but it definitely has been a huge moneymaking phenomenon. It doesn't check all our boxes, but it checks some of them in a big way:

- Academically highly accomplished leader: No one knows who, what, or "if" the famous inventor Satoshi Nakamoto is.

- Hypercompetitive leader: Same.

- Demanding, perfectionist leader: Same.

- Revolutionary product or service: Bitcoin is the very definition of revolutionary, and blockchain may evolve into other important use cases. Yes.

- Huge or global market potential: An alternate currency is the definition of global potential, and blockchain has other global applications. Yes.

- Rapidly growing revenues and market share: Ummm … Bitcoin has no "revenues," but it did essentially create the cryptocurrency market. Yes?

- Hot IPO: I'm not sure anything could be considered more "hot," since Bitcoin does not "earn" any money yet became a huge global phenomenon.

We can see that Bitcoin clearly does not resemble the great companies we have been looking at. What it does do is take the term "speculation" to a new high.

For the purposes of this examination, we are going to use the Grayscale Bitcoin Trust, since it trades in the US stock markets that most investors have access to. Let's look at this Bitcoin proxy and see what an actual investor could have done. Remember, until services like Robinhood (HOOD) came along, most average investors didn't have any idea how to buy, own, store, and transact in Bitcoin (I'm not sure people would agree that problem has been totally solved as of this writing, given the FTX collapse—ask Tom Brady …). Buying this Bitcoin proxy on the NYSE was the way most regular investors were likely to have traded Bitcoin.

Bitcoin was not "hot" when this proxy security launched, and GBTC actually traded by appointment on very low volume. We can see on the chart that volume didn't come into this stock until May 2017. I am going to use that date as the "start" date, since we are looking here at "hot" IPOs. Bitcoin enthusiasts will start screaming now, and I get that, but no one (except you early geniuses who all bought it at $2.50) was buying this stuff much before 2017, and we are trying to keep a consistent theme here, even with an unusual asset class. I am also going to assume a price for the GBTC stock of $2.00 per share as the starting point, because that was the price it was trading at during May 2017. If you are a Bitcoin enthusiast, please accept these conditions as one possible analysis approach.

We can see it has been a wild ride. Even using a relatively high starting price like $2, an investor could have gotten close to a 3,000 percent return at one point. The technical chart indicates multiple possible buy and sell points along the way.

Now let's see how our hypothetical algorithm might have helped now that the stock seems to be wanting to round trip. One side note before we review: Since Bitcoin/GBTC has no "earnings," instead of allocating a point for earnings, I made stochastics worth two points so that we could run the algorithm in a similar way to the other stocks we have been looking at.

GBTC, MAY 2015 TO DECEMBER 2022

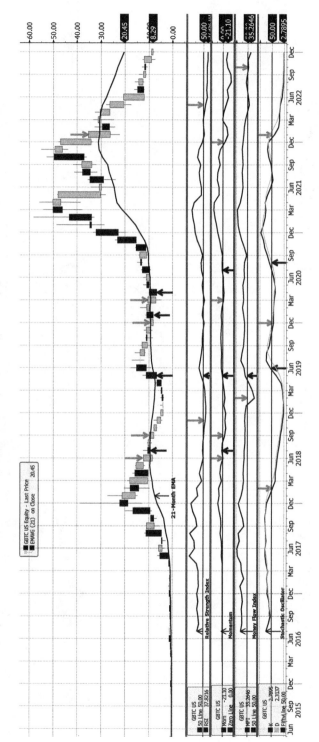

ALGORITHM VALUE VS. BUY & HOLD VALUE: GBTC

Legend:
—— Algorithm Value   —— Buy & Hold Value

Y-axis: $0, $1,000, $2,000, $3,000, $4,000, $5,000, $6,000, $7,000, $8,000, $9,000, $10,000

X-axis: 5/31/17, 6/30/17, 7/31/17, 8/31/17, 9/30/17, 10/31/17, 11/30/17, 12/31/17, 1/31/18, 2/28/18, 3/31/18, 4/30/18, 5/31/18, 6/30/18, 7/31/18, 8/31/18, 9/30/18, 10/31/18, 11/30/18, 12/31/18, 1/31/19, 2/28/19, 3/31/19, 4/30/19, 5/31/19, 6/30/19, 7/31/19, 8/31/19, 9/30/19, 10/31/19, 11/30/19, 12/31/19, 1/31/20, 2/29/20, 3/31/20, 4/30/20, 5/31/20, 6/30/20, 7/31/20, 8/31/20, 9/30/20, 10/31/20, 11/30/20, 12/31/20, 1/31/21, 2/28/21, 3/31/21, 4/30/21, 5/31/21, 6/30/21, 7/31/21, 8/31/21, 9/30/21, 10/31/21, 11/30/21, 12/31/21, 1/31/22, 2/28/22, 3/31/22, 4/30/22, 5/31/22, 6/30/22, 7/31/22, 8/31/22, 9/30/22, 10/31/22, 11/30/22

Bitcoin is obviously an odd security compared to the others we have discussed. But it is a huge phenomenon and may even become a new asset class. So we have to have a way to evaluate it from a process standpoint rather than just allow near-evangelical belief to help us overcome periods of relentless "FUD" ("fear, uncertainty, and doubt"—a popular crypto term used to encourage investors to hold their positions when controversy strikes). The supercharged volatility of Bitcoin (as shown through GBTC) is also reflected in the relative performance of the buy-and-hold versus the algorithmic approach. With a historic winner, we would expect there to be some advantage at times, or even most of the time, to the investor that just HODLed (that's more crypto slang for "hold on for dear life"). But as I write this, it looks like the two approaches are in a theoretical dead heat when it comes to this phenomenon of the twenty-first century. The crypto story is nowhere close to being finalized, but it is interesting to see how having a process could have fared against blind faith, at least so far.

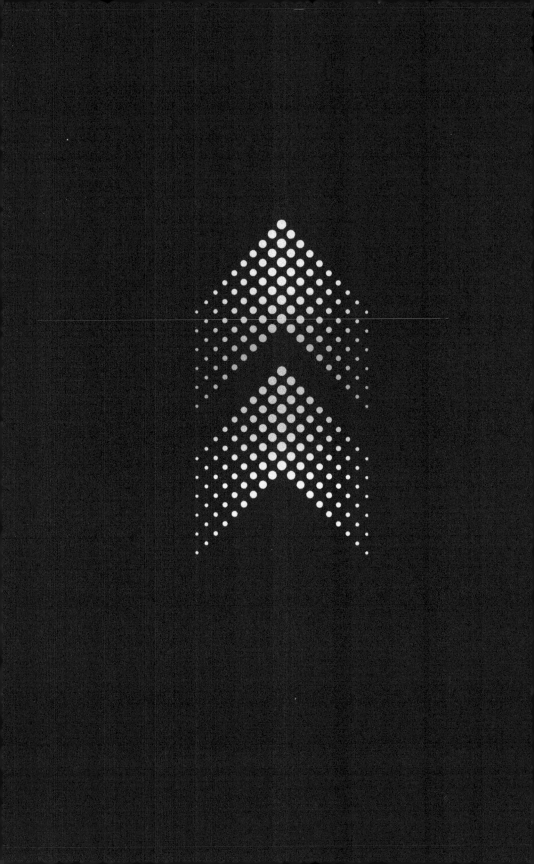

CONCLUSION

WE'VE COVERED A LOT OF GROUND and seen differing results. Here, at the end of our journey, I want to propose some ideas for blending the head and the heart. On the one hand, great companies can capture the imagination and make us believe that things that were not possible before are now possible. When business goals aren't executed according to plan, that wonderful ability to capture our imaginations can lead to acts of blind faith and horrible investment results. Add to that the difficulty faced by the average investor to really know what is happening inside a company. We read or hear the news reports, and if the facts are negative, then we almost certainly read or hear the positive spin coming out of the company. Given the companies we've reviewed here, one quick and obvious example should be all the negative news reports coming out surrounding Tesla's ability to meet production goals for its first breakout product, the Model S. Elon Musk and Tesla never wavered in generating generally overoptimistic positive spin, and they won out! Then, too, there was Enron: lots of negative reports alongside lots of positive spin coming out of the company—and all that spin turned out to be hiding fraud.

Below I present a table of the stocks covered in the preceding chapter that *didn't* work to show what could have happened if you hypothetically invested $25,000 in each one using either buy-and-hold or our algorithmic approach. As a reminder, we are no longer looking at the best stocks of all time; we are looking only at the stocks we reviewed that didn't work.

Here are the numbers based on this purely hypothetical exercise:

Ticker		Initial Investment	Start Date	End Date	Buy-and-hold	Algorithm
META	1	$ 25,000.00	5/18/2012	12/31/2022	$ 79,063.38	$ 58,079.22
UBER	2	$ 25,000.00	5/10/2019	12/31/2022	$ 13,725.15	$ 15,391.38
ZM	3	$ 25,000.00	4/18/2019	12/31/2022	$ 47,011.56	$ 204,131.99
PTON	4	$ 25,000.00	9/26/2019	12/31/2022	$ 6,844.28	$ 29,928.48
ROKU	5	$ 25,000.00	9/28/2017	12/31/2022	$ 72,649.50	$ 116,074.71
LEHMQ	6	$ 25,000.00	5/31/1984	9/30/2008	$ 1,194.33	$ 123,927.68
ENRNQ	7	$ 25,000.00	7/31/1980	12/31/2001	$ 3,529.20	$ 116,074.71
JDSU/VIAV	8	$ 25,000.00	11/17/1993	6/30/2015	$ 144,750.85	$ 2,124,650.92
IPETZ	9	$ 25,000.00	2/11/2000	11/30/2000	$ 25.32	$ 330.94
GBTC	10	$ 25,000.00	5/31/2017	12/31/2022	$ 38,954.71	$ 56,623.16
Total:		$ 275,000.00			$ 407,748.28	$ 2,845,223.00

Source: Bloomberg, December 31, 2022

The buy-and-hold approach ended up turning $200,000 into about $400,000 for this small sample of loser stocks over the selected time frame and our hypothetical process-based approach could have returned about $2,800,000. Yes, this is hindsight, and yes, this is a hypothetical approach. But it could have theoretically turned some of the worst losers ever into solid investment gains.

Ultimately, the lesson is that if you are *exclusively* going to pick the next crop of best stocks ever, you will make more money with a buy-and-hold strategy. However, if you factor in that you may invest in some names that do not end up working out, you should consider putting a process in place to manage risk. We have looked at some of the best-performing stocks of the last fifty-plus years, then some of the worst, to illustrate that the truth lies somewhere in between our gut feelings and an objective process that removes emotion. Clearly, the one approach we have been looking at, the hypothetical algorithm, could have acted like a good insurance policy. In other words, when things didn't work out, that approach—or a similar one that you come up with on your own—could have saved you some money. And let's be honest, if you pick ten companies today that you think (by whatever criteria you use) have the characteristics of the next great companies of the future, how many are going to work out? Realistically, none of us will go ten out of ten.

I propose to you that it makes sense to build an algorithmic approach and then determine what percentage of your investment in any highly speculative, aggressive-growth, early-stage company will be managed using that approach. We have focused on investing $1,000 at the IPO. But most people commit larger amounts to their speculative purchases. If you imagine a $50,000 or $100,000 initial commitment, the stakes are obviously a lot higher. That's the very situation in which some level of mechanical risk management makes more and more sense. One approach to consider is to manage 50 percent of your investment using a mechanical technical algorithm and manage the other 50 percent using fundamental analysis and not just your gut instincts. Clearly, you can adjust the percentages as you are comfortable, but adding a nonemotional, mechanical process can give you some measure of insurance against picking a bunch of stocks that could all end up not working. Also, when something is clearly not working, you will be

> It makes sense to build an algorithmic approach and then determine what percentage of your investment in any highly speculative, aggressive-growth, early-stage company will be managed using that approach.

freed up to cycle in new names. The ones that are working will take care of themselves by going up.

The final piece of the puzzle once you decide on your proportions is the most important: you have to stick to your plan and be disciplined. The market will *always* pressure you to add more when it is high and sell when it is low. That is the allure of the market and what I call the crucible of fear and greed: everybody wants in when prices are at their highest (irrational exuberance), and everyone wants out when things are at their lowest (or what legendary investor Sir John Templeton called the point of maximum pessimism). The technical algorithm is designed specifically to counter the powerful emotions with which you'll inevitably be confronted. So whether you allocate 100 percent of your investment to a mechanical approach or as little as 10 percent, you have to stick to your decision, or the emotions of the day will cause you to change your approach at just the wrong time and destroy any of the benefit of a process-based, technical algorithm approach.

Finding the Next Great Companies

While there is definitely a trend of the rich getting richer as existing companies dominate research into the great investment areas of the future (such as Microsoft acquiring ChatGPT), America is still the home of entrepreneurial capitalism. You can be sure there are really smart, competitive people out there who may be just about to drop out of college and start the next great company. I can't tell you who they are, but I can tell you where you might want to be looking in the years ahead.

The history of the stock market is the history of economic revolutions like the railroad bubble of the 1880s in the United States, the

Industrial Revolution and speculation that led to the roaring '20s, and then the internet boom in the 1990s. Great companies generally change the way we live or do business and provide large economic efficiencies. The areas I list here could yield explosive innovations and radical changes to how we live and enjoy our daily lives. These areas potentially include (but are not limited to) the following:

- Artificial intelligence (AI)

- Battery technology

- Biotechnology

- Carbon capture

- Cybersecurity

- Gene editing technology

- Low earth orbit (LEO) satellite communication for aviation, maritime, underserved, and military applications

- Quantum computing

- Robotics

- Self-driving cars and related technology

- Space exploration, tourism, mining, or propulsion/rocket and associated technology[140]

Here are some early thoughts on artificial intelligence (AI) and some of the implications for the broader economic landscape. In 2019, Microsoft invested $1 billion in a company called OpenAI, which is a research organization focused on advancing AI and is probably most known for its development of the GPT (Generative

---

140 "The Bubbles That Built America," CNNMoney, accessed March 12, 2023, https://money.cnn.com/galleries/2007/news/0705/gallery.bubbles/3.html.

Pretrained Transformer) models—specifically, ChatGPT—but is also involved in other popular projects, including text-to-image generator DALL-E (named for a combination of surrealist artist Salvador Dalí and fictional robot character WALL-E). The GPT models are large language models that are trained on significant amounts of text data and designed to generate humanlike responses. When ChatGPT was released in November 2022 Microsoft invested another $2 billion in the company and it was announced in January of 2023 that Microsoft would invest an additional $10 billion in the company, taking an aggregate 49 percent stake. It is still early in the development of this new technology, but like the computer revolution that began in 1977 at the West Coast Computer Faire with the Apple II computer and then the launch of the internet to the public in the early 1990s, AI has three important characteristics that may allow it to drive markets for years to come:

1. It promises massive productivity improvements for the overall economy.

2. It captures the interest and imagination of the public.

3. No one really understands its full potential at this point.

Just as with computers and the internet before, there will be amazing benefits, but there will also be major issues, and it will take a long time for this all to unfold (if it actually does unfold). There will be changes to the way elements of your life are conducted, and there will also be limitless scams around the new concept (remember the Nigerian princess many were asked to save during the early years of the internet and email …), so watch out for scams and promises of guaranteed investment returns generated by AI. Protocols still need to be embraced by the developers. Legislation will need to be put into place for issues that do not even exist yet. And, as has happened every generation, as new technologies emerge, jobs will be lost, and new jobs will be created. Currently in 2023, the companies with the largest number of employees dedicated to AI research are Amazon, Microsoft, Meta, Google, and Apple.[141] NVIDIA is also a company being rewarded in the marketplace initially, as it is recognized as the leader in AI processors. Elon Musk has even thrown his hat (back) into the ring with plans for a rival "maximum truth seeking" AI. The race is on and the ultimate winners in the space have yet to be decided. You can count on intense competition from the names we've mentioned as well as new companies that may not even exist yet as part of the ecosystem that may develop around this new technology.

NUMBER OF EMPLOYEES DEDICATED TO AI RESEARCH

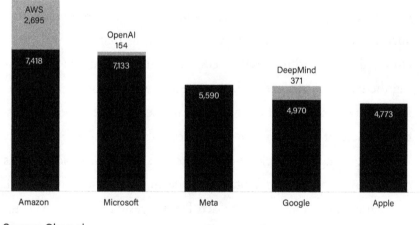

Source: Glass.ai

---

141 "Bloomberg Uses Glass.Ai to Write about the AI Armies of the Tech Giants," glass.ai, March 27, 2023, https://www.glass.ai/glass-news/code-red-the-ai-armies-of-the-tech-giants.

So the next time a hot IPO comes out that you have an interest in, first apply whatever subjective checklist you decide makes sense for you. Remember, here's the one we have been discussing:

- Academically highly accomplished leader

- Hypercompetitive leader

- Demanding, perfectionist leader

- Revolutionary product or service

- Huge or global market potential

- Rapidly growing revenues and market share

- Hot IPO

The more boxes you can check off, the better.

Then, determine not only how much you are going to invest but also what proportion you are going to manage with fundamental analysis and what proportion you are going to manage through an emotionless, algorithm-based process. All of the calculations determining the basic, unadjusted technical metrics we have used are located in the appendix of this book, so you can use what we hypothetically created here or create your own. I added a few tweaks to my process as I was writing this book, and I'm sure you will want to add tweaks of your own too. If there's one thing we all know, it's that there are no guarantees in life. The approach I've suggested here may end up not working for you, and you might still lose money. But if you look back at past investments that were managed solely through your gut instinct alone, I feel pretty sure you'd agree that a feature that counteracts emotions would be a welcome addition to your process. Investing is a pursuit of constant learning and improvement, so I want to wish you great success in your efforts to find the next great companies.

APPENDICES

Appendix A

THE FORMULA FOR THE RSI

The RSI is computed with a two-part calculation that starts with the following formula:

$$RSI_{\text{step one}} = 100 - \left[\frac{100}{1 + \dfrac{\text{Average Gain}}{\text{Average Loss}}} \right]$$

The average gain or loss used in the calculation is the average percentage gain or loss during a look-back period. The formula uses a positive value for the average loss. Periods with price losses are counted as 0 in the calculations of average gain, and periods when the price increases are counted as 0 for the calculation of average loss.

The standard is to use fourteen periods to calculate the initial RSI value. For example, imagine the market closed higher seven out of the past fourteen days with an average gain of 1 percent. The remaining seven days all closed lower with an average gain of 1 percent. The remaining seven days all closed lower with an average loss of –0.8 percent.

The calculation for the first part of the RSI would look like the following expanded calculation:

$$55.55 = 100 - \left[\frac{100}{1 + \frac{\frac{1\%}{14}}{\frac{0.8\%}{14}}} \right]$$

Once there are fourteen periods of data available, the second part of the RSI formula can be calculated. The second step of the calculation smooths the results.

$$RSI_{\text{step two}} = 100 - \left[\frac{100}{1 + \frac{(\text{Previous Average Gain} \times 13) + \text{Current Gain}}{(\text{Previous Average Loss} \times 13) + \text{Current Loss}}} \right]$$

Source: Investopedia, https://www.investopedia.com/terms/r/rsi.asp

Appendix B

THE FORMULA FOR MOMENTUM

Generally, market momentum can be defined from the following equation:

$$M = V - V_x$$

where:
V = The latest price
V_x = The closing price x number of days ago

Source: Investopedia, https://www.investopedia.com/articles/technical/081501.asp

Appendix C

THE FORMULAS FOR THE MONEY FLOW INDEX

$$\text{Money Flow Index} = 100 - \frac{100}{1 + \text{Money Flow Ratio}}$$

where:

$$\text{Money Flow Ratio} = \frac{\text{14 Period Positive Money Flow}}{\text{14 Period Negative Money Flow}}$$

$$\text{Raw Money Flow} = \text{Typical Price} * \text{Volume}$$

$$\text{Typical Price} = \frac{\text{High} + \text{Low} + \text{Close}}{3}$$

Source: Investopedia, https://www.investopedia.com/terms/m/mfi.asp

Appendix D

HOW THE STOCHASTIC MOMENTUM OSCILLATOR WORKS

Developed as a tool for technical analysis, the stochastic momentum oscillator is used to compare where a security's price closed relative to its price range over a given period of time— usually fourteen days. It is calculated using the following formula:

$$\%K = \frac{100 * (CP - L14)}{(H14 - L14)}$$

where:

C = Most recent closing price

$L14$ = Low of the 14 previous trading sessions

$H14$ = Highest price traded during the same 14-day period

A %K result of 80 is interpreted to mean that the price of the security closed above 80 percent of all prior closing prices that have occurred over the past fourteen days. The main assumption is that a security's price will trade at the top of the range in a major uptrend. A three-period moving average of the %K called %D is usually included to act as a signal line. Transaction signals are usually made when the %K crosses through the %D.

Source: Investopedia, https://www.investopedia.com/terms/s/stochasticoscillator.asp

Appendix E

HYPOTHETICAL AMZN TRADING ALGORITHM:

Date	% Below 52W High Score	21-Month EMA Score	RSI Score	Momentum Score	Money Flows Score	Stochastics Score	Earnings Score	Technical Score	Position Level
5/15/97							5	10	100%
5/30/97	0	5					5	10	100%
6/30/97	0	5					5	10	100%
7/31/97	2	5					5	10	100%
8/29/97	2	5					5	10	100%
9/30/97	2	5					5	10	100%
10/31/97	2	5					5	10	100%
11/28/97	0	5					5	10	100%
12/31/97	2	5					5	10	100%
1/30/98	2	5					5	10	100%
2/27/98	2	5					5	10	100%
3/31/98	2	5		1			5	10	100%
4/30/98	2	5		1			5	10	100%
5/29/98	2	5		1			5	10	100%
6/30/98	2	5		1			5	10	100%
7/31/98	0	2	2	1	1	1	1	8	80%
8/31/98	0	2	2	1	1	1	1	8	80%
9/30/98	0	2	2	1	1	1	1	8	80%
10/30/98	2	2	2	1	1	1	1	10	100%
11/30/98	2	2	2	1	1	1	1	10	100%
12/31/98	2	2	2	1	1	1	1	10	100%
1/29/99	0	2	2	1	1	1	1	8	80%
2/26/99	0	2	2	1	1	1	1	8	80%
3/31/99	2	2	2	1	1	1	1	10	100%
4/30/99	0	2	2	1	1	1	0		70%
5/31/99	0	2	2	1	1	1	0		70%
6/30/99	0	2	2	1	1	1	0		70%
7/30/99	0	2	2	1	1	1	0		70%
8/31/99	0	2	2	1	1	1	0		70%
9/30/99	0	2	2	1	1	1	0		70%
10/29/99	0	2	2	1	1	1	0		70%
11/30/99	0	2	2	1	1	1	0		70%

Date	% Below 52W High Score	21-Month EMA Score	RSI Score	Momentum Score	Money Flows Score	Stochastics Score	Earnings Score	Technical Score	Position Level
12/31/99	0	2	2	1	1	1	0	7	70%
1/31/00	0	2	2	0	1	1	1	7	70%
2/29/00	0	2	2	0	1	0	1	6	60%
3/31/00	0	2	2	1	1	0	1	7	70%
4/28/00	0	0	2	0	1	0	1	4	40%
5/31/00	0	0	2	0	1	0	1	4	40%
6/30/00	0	0	0	0	1	0	1	2	20%
7/31/00	0	0	0	0	1	0	0	1	10%
8/31/00	0	0	0	0	1	0	0	1	10%
9/29/00	0	0	0	0	1	0	0	1	10%
10/31/00	0	0	0	0	1	0	0	1	10%
11/30/00	0	0	0	0	1	0	0	1	10%
12/29/00	0	0	0	0	1	0	0	1	10%
1/31/01	0	0	0	0	0	0	0	0	0%
2/28/01	0	0	0	0	0	0	0	0	0%
3/30/01	0	0	0	0	0	0	0	0	0%
4/30/01	0	0	0	0	0	0	0	0	0%
5/31/01	0	0	0	0	0	0	0	0	0%
6/29/01	0	0	0	0	0	0	0	0	0%
7/31/01	0	0	0	0	0	0	0	0	0%
8/31/01	0	0	0	0	0	0	0	0	0%
9/28/01	0	0	0	0	0	0	0	0	0%
10/31/01	0	0	0	0	0	0	0	0	0%
11/30/01	0	0	0	0	0	0	0	0	0%
12/31/01	0	0	0	0	0	0	0	0	0%
1/31/02	0	0	0	1	0	0	1	2	20%
2/28/02	0	0	0	0	1	0	1	2	20%
3/29/02	0	0	0	0	1	1	1	3	30%
4/30/02	2	0	0	1	1	1	1	6	60%
5/31/02	2	0	0	1	1	1	1	6	60%
6/28/02	0	0	0	1	1	1	1	4	40%
7/31/02	0	0	0	1	1	1	1	4	40%
8/30/02	0	0	0	1	1	1	1	4	40%
9/30/02	0	0	0	1	1	1	1	4	40%
10/31/02	2	2	0	1	1	1	1	8	80%
11/29/02	2	2	2	1	1	1	1	10	100%

Date	% Below 52W High Score	21-Month EMA Score	RSI Score	Momentum Score	Money Flows Score	Stochastics Score	Earnings Score	Technical Score	Position Level
12/31/02	0	2	2	1	1	1	1	8	80%
1/31/03	2	2	2	1	1	1	1	10	100%
2/28/03	2	2	2	1	1	1	1	10	100%
3/31/03	2	2	2	1	1	1	1	10	100%
4/30/03	2	2	2	1	1	1	1	10	100%
5/30/03	2	2	2	1	1	1	1	10	100%
6/30/03	2	2	2	1	1	1	1	10	100%
7/31/03	2	2	2	1	1	1	1	10	100%
8/29/03	2	2	2	1	1	1	1	10	100%
9/30/03	2	2	2	1	1	1	1	10	100%
10/31/03	2	2	2	1	1	1	1	10	100%
11/28/03	2	2	2	1	1	1	1	10	100%
12/31/03	2	2	2	1	1	1	1	10	100%
1/30/04	2	2	2	1	1	1	1	10	100%
2/27/04	0	2	2	1	1	1	1	8	80%
3/31/04	0	2	2	1	1	1	1	8	80%
4/30/04	0	2	2	1	1	1	1	8	80%
5/31/04	0	2	2	1	1	1	1	8	80%
6/30/04	2	2	2	1	1	1	1	10	100%
7/30/04	0	0	2	0	1	1	0	4	40%
8/31/04	0	0	2	0	1	0	0	3	30%
9/30/04	0	2	2	0	1	0	0	5	50%
10/29/04	0	0	0	0	1	0	0	1	10%
11/30/04	0	2	0	0	1	0	0	3	30%
12/31/04	0	2	2	1	1	0	0	6	60%
1/31/05	0	2	2	1	1	0	0	6	60%
2/28/05	0	0	0	0	1	0	0	1	10%
3/31/05	0	0	0	0	1	0	0	1	10%
4/29/05	0	0	0	0	1	0	0	1	10%
5/31/05	0	0	0	0	1	0	0	1	10%
6/30/05	0	0	0	0	1	0	0	1	10%
7/29/05	2	2	2	1	1	0	1	9	90%
8/31/05	2	2	2	1	1	0	1	9	90%
9/30/05	2	2	2	1	1	1	1	10	100%
10/31/05	2	2	2	0	1	1	0	8	80%
11/30/05	2	2	2	1	1	1	0	9	90%

Date	% Below 52W High Score	21-Month EMA Score	RSI Score	Momentum Score	Money Flows Score	Stochastics Score	Earnings Score	Technical Score	Position Level
12/30/05	2	2	2	1	1	1	0	9	90%
1/31/06	2	2	2	1	1	1	0	9	90%
2/28/06	0	0	2	1	1	1	0	5	50%
3/31/06	0	0	0	1	0	0	0	1	10%
4/28/06	0	0	0	1	0	0	0	1	10%
5/31/06	0	0	0	0	0	0	0	0	0%
6/30/06	0	0	0	0	1	0	0	1	10%
7/31/06	0	0	0	0	0	0	0	0	0%
8/31/06	0	0	0	0	0	0	0	0	0%
9/29/06	0	0	0	0	0	0	0	0	0%
10/31/06	0	2	0	0	0	0	1	3	30%
11/30/06	2	2	2	0	0	0	1	7	70%
12/29/06	2	2	2	1	0	1	1	9	90%
1/31/07	2	0	2	1	0	1	1	7	70%
2/28/07	2	2	2	1	0	1	1	9	90%
3/30/07	2	2	2	1	0	1	1	9	90%
4/30/07	2	2	2	1	1	1	1	10	100%
5/31/07	2	2	2	1	1	1	1	10	100%
6/29/07	2	2	2	1	1	1	1	10	100%
7/31/07	2	2	2	1	1	1	1	10	100%
8/31/07	2	2	2	1	1	1	1	10	100%
9/28/07	2	2	2	1	1	1	1	10	100%
10/31/07	2	2	2	1	1	1	0	9	90%
11/30/07	2	2	2	1	1	1	0	9	90%
12/31/07	2	2	2	1	1	1	0	9	90%
1/31/08	0	2	2	1	1	1	0	7	70%
2/29/08	0	0	2	1	1	1	0	5	50%
3/31/08	0	2	2	1	1	1	0	7	70%
4/30/08	0	2	2	1	1	1	0	7	70%
5/30/08	2	2	2	1	1	1	0	9	90%
6/30/08	0	2	2	0	1	1	0	6	60%
7/31/08	0	2	2	0	1	0	1	6	60%
8/29/08	0	2	2	0	1	0	1	6	60%
9/30/08	0	2	2	0	0	0	1	5	50%
10/31/08	0	0	0	0	0	0	1	1	10%
11/28/08	0	0	0	0	0	0	1	1	10%

Date	% Below 52W High Score	21-Month EMA Score	RSI Score	Momentum Score	Money Flows Score	Stochastics Score	Earnings Score	Technical Score	Position Level
12/31/08	0	0	0	0	0	0	1	1	10%
1/30/09	0	0	0	0	0	0	1	1	10%
2/27/09	0	0	0	0	0	0	1	1	10%
3/31/09	2	2	2	0	1	1	1	9	90%
4/30/09	2	2	2	1	1	1	1	10	100%
5/29/09	2	2	2	1	1	1	1	10	100%
6/30/09	2	2	2	1	1	1	1	10	100%
7/31/09	2	2	2	1	1	1	1	10	100%
8/31/09	2	2	2	1	1	1	1	10	100%
9/30/09	2	2	2	1	1	1	1	10	100%
10/30/09	2	2	2	1	1	1	1	10	100%
11/30/09	2	2	2	1	1	1	1	10	100%
12/31/09	2	2	2	1	1	1	1	10	100%
1/29/10	2	2	2	1	1	1	1	10	100%
2/26/10	2	2	2	1	1	1	1	10	100%
3/31/10	2	2	2	1	1	1	1	10	100%
4/30/10	2	2	2	1	1	1	1	10	100%
5/31/10	2	2	2	1	1	1	1	10	100%
6/30/10	0	2	2	1	1	1	1	8	80%
7/30/10	0	2	2	1	1	1	1	8	80%
8/31/10	2	2	2	1	1	1	1	10	100%
9/30/10	2	2	2	1	1	1	1	10	100%
10/29/10	2	2	2	1	1	1	1	10	100%
11/30/10	2	2	2	1	1	1	1	10	100%
12/31/10	2	2	2	1	1	1	1	10	100%
1/31/11	2	2	2	1	1	1	1	10	100%
2/28/11	2	2	2	1	1	1	1	10	100%
3/31/11	2	2	2	1	1	1	1	10	100%
4/29/11	2	2	2	1	1	1	1	10	100%
5/31/11	2	2	2	1	1	1	1	10	100%
6/30/11	2	2	2	1	1	1	1	10	100%
7/29/11	2	2	2	1	1	1	1	10	100%
8/31/11	2	2	2	1	1	1	1	10	100%
9/30/11	2	2	2	1	1	1	1	10	100%
10/31/11	2	2	2	1	1	1	0	9	90%
11/30/11	0	2	2	1	1	1	0	7	70%

Date	% Below 52W High Score	21-Month EMA Score	RSI Score	Momentum Score	Money Flows Score	Stochastics Score	Earnings Score	Technical Score	Position Level
12/30/11	0	0	2	1	0	0	0	3	30%
1/31/12	0	2	2	1	0	0	0	5	50%
2/29/12	0	2	2	0	0	0	0	4	40%
3/30/12	2	2	2	1	0	0	0	7	70%
4/30/12	2	2	2	1	0	0	1	8	80%
5/31/12	2	2	2	0	1	1	1	9	90%
6/29/12	2	2	2	1	1	1	1	10	100%
7/31/12	2	2	2	1	1	1	1	10	100%
8/31/12	2	2	2	1	1	1	1	10	100%
9/28/12	2	2	2	1	1	1	1	10	100%
10/31/12	2	2	2	1	1	1	1	10	100%
11/30/12	2	2	2	1	1	1	1	10	100%
12/31/12	2	2	2	1	1	1	1	10	100%
1/31/13	2	2	2	1	1	1	1	10	100%
2/28/13	2	2	2	1	1	1	1	10	100%
3/29/13	2	2	2	1	1	1	1	10	100%
4/30/13	2	2	2	1	1	1	1	10	100%
5/31/13	2	2	2	1	1	1	1	10	100%
6/28/13	2	2	2	1	1	1	1	10	100%
7/31/13	2	2	2	1	1	1	1	10	100%
8/30/13	2	2	2	1	1	1	1	10	100%
9/30/13	2	2	2	1	1	1	1	10	100%
10/31/13	2	2	2	1	1	1	1	10	100%
11/29/13	2	2	2	1	1	1	1	10	100%
12/31/13	2	2	2	1	1	1	1	10	100%
1/31/14	2	2	2	1	1	1	0	9	90%
2/28/14	2	2	2	1	1	1	0	9	90%
3/31/14	2	2	2	1	1	1	0	9	90%
4/30/14	0	2	2	1	1	1	0	7	70%
5/30/14	0	2	2	1	0	0	0	5	50%
6/30/14	0	2	2	1	0	0	0	5	50%
7/31/14	0	2	2	1	0	0	0	5	50%
8/29/14	2	2	2	0	0	0	0	6	60%
9/30/14	0	2	2	0	0	0	0	4	40%
10/31/14	0	0	2	0	0	0	0	2	20%
11/28/14	2	2	2	0	0	0	0	6	60%

Date	% Below 52W High Score	21-Month EMA Score	RSI Score	Momentum Score	Money Flows Score	Stochastics Score	Earnings Score	Technical Score	Position Level
12/31/14	0	0	2	0	0	0	0	2	20%
1/30/15	2	2	2	1	0	0	1	8	80%
2/27/15	2	2	2	1	0	1	1	9	90%
3/31/15	2	2	2	1	0	1	1	9	90%
4/30/15	2	2	2	1	1	1	1	10	100%
5/29/15	2	2	2	1	1	1	1	10	100%
6/30/15	2	2	2	1	1	1	1	10	100%
7/31/15	2	2	2	1	1	1	1	10	100%
8/31/15	2	2	2	1	1	1	1	10	100%
9/30/15	2	2	2	1	1	1	1	10	100%
10/30/15	2	2	2	1	1	1	1	10	100%
11/30/15	2	2	2	1	1	1	1	10	100%
12/31/15	2	2	2	1	1	1	1	10	100%
1/29/16	2	2	2	1	1	1	1	10	100%
2/29/16	0	2	2	1	1	1	1	8	80%
3/31/16	2	2	2	1	1	1	1	10	100%
4/29/16	2	2	2	1	1	1	1	10	100%
5/31/16	2	2	2	1	1	1	1	10	100%
6/30/16	2	2	2	1	1	1	1	10	100%
7/29/16	2	2	2	1	1	1	1	10	100%
8/31/16	2	2	2	1	1	1	1	10	100%
9/30/16	2	2	2	1	1	1	1	10	100%
10/31/16	2	2	2	1	1	1	1	10	100%
11/30/16	2	2	2	1	1	1	1	10	100%
12/30/16	2	2	2	1	1	1	1	10	100%
1/31/17	2	2	2	1	1	1	1	10	100%
2/28/17	2	2	2	1	1	1	1	10	100%
3/31/17	2	2	2	1	1	1	1	10	100%
4/28/17	2	2	2	1	1	1	1	10	100%
5/31/17	2	2	2	1	1	1	1	10	100%
6/30/17	2	2	2	1	1	1	1	10	100%
7/31/17	2	2	2	1	1	1	1	10	100%
8/31/17	2	2	2	1	1	1	1	10	100%
9/29/17	2	2	2	1	1	1	1	10	100%
10/31/17	2	2	2	1	1	1	1	10	100%
11/30/17	2	2	2	1	1	1	1	10	100%

Date	% Below 52W High Score	21-Month EMA Score	RSI Score	Momentum Score	Money Flows Score	Stochastics Score	Earnings Score	Technical Score	Position Level
12/29/17	2	2	2	1	1	1	1	10	100%
1/31/18	2	2	2	1	1	1	1	10	100%
2/28/18	2	2	2	1	1	1	1	10	100%
3/30/18	2	2	2	1	1	1	1	10	100%
4/30/18	2	2	2	1	1	1	1	10	100%
5/31/18	2	2	2	1	1	1	1	10	100%
6/29/18	2	2	2	1	1	1	1	10	100%
7/31/18	2	2	2	1	1	1	1	10	100%
8/31/18	2	2	2	1	1	1	1	10	100%
9/28/18	2	2	2	1	1	1	1	10	100%
10/31/18	0	2	2	1	1	1	1	8	80%
11/30/18	2	2	2	1	1	1	1	10	100%
12/31/18	0	2	2	1	1	1	1	8	80%
1/31/19	2	2	2	1	1	1	1	10	100%
2/28/19	0	2	2	1	1	1	1	8	80%
3/29/19	2	2	2	1	1	1	1	10	100%
4/30/19	2	2	2	1	1	1	1	10	100%
5/31/19	2	2	2	1	1	1	1	10	100%
6/28/19	2	2	2	0	1	1	1	9	90%
7/31/19	2	2	2	0	1	1	1	9	90%
8/30/19	2	2	2	1	0	1	1	9	90%
9/30/19	2	2	2	1	0	1	1	9	90%
10/31/19	2	2	2	1	0	1	1	9	90%
11/29/19	2	2	2	1	0	1	1	9	90%
12/31/19	2	2	2	1	0	1	1	9	90%
1/31/20	2	2	2	1	0	1	1	9	90%
2/28/20	2	2	2	0	1	1	1	9	90%
3/31/20	2	2	2	1	1	1	1	10	100%
4/30/20	2	2	2	1	1	1	1	10	100%
5/29/20	2	2	2	1	1	1	1	10	100%
6/30/20	2	2	2	1	1	1	1	10	100%
7/31/20	2	2	2	1	1	1	1	10	100%
8/31/20	2	2	2	1	1	1	1	10	100%
9/30/20	2	2	2	1	1	1	1	10	100%
10/30/20	2	2	2	1	1	1	1	10	100%
11/30/20	2	2	2	1	1	1	1	10	100%

Date	% Below 52W High Score	21-Month EMA Score	RSI Score	Momentum Score	Money Flows Score	Stochastics Score	Earnings Score	Technical Score	Position Level
12/31/20	2	2	2	1	1	1	1	10	100%
1/29/21	2	2	2	1	1	1	1	10	100%
2/26/21	2	2	2	1	1	1	1	10	100%
3/31/21	2	2	2	1	0	1	1	9	90%
4/30/21	2	2	2	1	0	1	1	9	90%
5/31/21	2	2	2	1	0	1	1	9	90%
6/30/21	2	2	2	1	0	1	1	9	90%
7/30/21	2	2	2	1	0	1	1	9	90%
8/31/21	2	2	2	1	0	1	1	9	90%
9/30/21	2	2	2	1	0	1	1	9	90%
10/29/21	2	2	2	1	0	1	1	9	90%
11/30/21	2	2	2	1	0	1	1	9	90%
12/31/21	2	2	2	1	0	1	1	9	90%
1/31/22	0	0	2	0	0	1	1	4	40%
2/28/22	2	2	2	0	0	0	1	7	70%
3/31/22	2	2	2	1	0	0	1	8	80%
4/29/22	0	0	0	0	0	0	1	1	10%
5/31/22	0	0	0	0	0	0	0	0	0%
6/30/22	0	0	0	0	0	0	0	0	0%
7/29/22	0	0	0	0	0	0	0	0	0%
8/31/22	0	0	0	0	0	0	1	1	10%
9/30/22	0	0	0	0	0	0	1	1	10%
10/31/22	0	0	0	0	0	0	1	1	10%
11/30/22	0	0	0	0	0	0	1	1	10%
12/30/22	0	0	0	0	0	0	1	1	10%

ENDNOTES

Chapter 2: Amazon

"A Look Back in IPO: Amazon's 1997 Move." *TechCrunch.* Accessed March 10, 2023. https://techcrunch.com/2017/06/28/a-look-back-at-amazons-1997-ipo/.

"Amazon.Com Revenue (Annual)." Accessed March 10, 2023. https://ycharts.com/companies/AMZN/revenues_annual.

"Are Amazon's Stock Holders Doubting Jeff Bezos?" Accessed March 10, 2023. https://fortune.com/videos/embed/3e68d606-f2d1-447c-8ce4-236f1316eb62.

Aya, Adam. "How This Single Stat Helped Jeff Bezos Make $3,715 Per Second This Year." Medium. November 6, 2020. https://medium.datadriveninvestor.com/how-this-single-stat-helped-jeff-bezos-make-3-715-per-second-this-year-89ffc4e329c3.

CNET. "Barnes & Noble Launches Book Site." May 13, 1997. https://www.cnet.com/tech/services-and-software/barnes-noble-launches-book-site/.

DePillis, Lydia, and Ivory Sherman. "Amazon's Extraordinary Evolution." CNN. Accessed March 10, 2023. https://www.cnn.com/interactive/2018/10/business/amazon-history-timeline/index.html.

Stone, Ann Gehan, and Madeline Yoonji Han. "How Amazon's One-Click Checkout Patent Gave the Company an e-Commerce Edge That Competitors like Bolt and Shopify Are Still Trying to Overcome." Business Insider. Accessed March 10, 2023. https://www.businessinsider.com/amazons-1-click-patent-competition-shopify-bolt-fast-2022-4.

TIME.com. "TIME Magazine Cover: Jeff Bezos—Person of the Year—Dec. 27, 1999." Accessed March 10, 2023. https://content.time.com/time/covers/0,16641,19991227,00.html.

Chapter 3: Microsoft

"Bill Gates." History-Biography." Accessed March 10, 2023. https://history-biography.com/bill-gates/.

Biography. "Bill Gates—Microsoft, Wife & Children," May 3, 2021. https://www.biography.com/business-leaders/bill-gates.

Gates, Bill. "About Bill." gatesnotes.com. Accessed March 10, 2023. https://www.gatesnotes.com/Bio.

"Microsoft Founded." History. Accessed March 10, 2023. https://www.history.com/this-day-in-history/microsoft-founded.

"Microsoft Is Born." Microsoft. Accessed March 10, 2023. https://news.microsoft.com/announcement/microsoft-is-born/.

ThoughtCo. "Who Founded Microsoft and What Made It So Successful?" Accessed March 10, 2023. https://www.thoughtco.com/microsoft-history-of-a-computing-giant-1991140.

Chapter 4: Apple

"Macintosh by Apple—Complete History of Mac Computers." *History-Computer* (blog), January 4, 2021. https://history-computer.com/macintosh-by-apple-complete-history-of-mac-computers/.

"Macintosh Launched on Jan 24, 1984 and Changed the World—Eventually," January 24, 2023. https://appleinsider.com/articles/19/01/24/apple-launched-macintosh-on-january-24-1984-and-changed-the-world----eventually.

"Steve Jobs and the Early Apple Years." Accessed March 10, 2023. https://www.i-programmer.info/history/people/104-steve-jobs-apple.html?start=2.

"Timeline: The History of Apple since 1976." Mac History. December 16, 2022. https://www.mac-history.net/2022/12/16/timeline-the-history-of-apple-since-1976/.

Chapter 5: Google

"8 Search Engines That Rocked Before Google Even Existed." Accessed March 10, 2023. https://www.makeuseof.com/tag/7-search-engines-that-rocked-before-google-even-existed/.

"The Anatomy of a Search Engine." Accessed March 10, 2023. http://infolab.stanford.edu/~backrub/google.html.

"Google—Google Earth | Britannica." Accessed March 10, 2023. https://www.britannica.com/topic/Google-Inc/Google-Earth.

"Google Maps' Biggest Moments over the Past 15 Years." Accessed March 10, 2023. https://blog.google/products/maps/look-back-15-years-mapping-world/.

"Google to Reorganize as Alphabet to Keep Its Lead as an Innovator." *New York Times*. Accessed March 10, 2023. https://www.nytimes.com/2015/08/11/technology/google-alphabet-restructuring.html.

"Google's Incredible Growth: A Timeline." CNN.Com. Accessed March 10, 2023. https://www.cnn.com/interactive/2018/12/business/google-history-timeline/index.html.

"History of Google—From 1996 to 2022." *Mirror Review*. December 6, 2019. https://www.mirrorreview.com/history-of-google/.

"History of Google: Know About Google's History and How It Was Founded." Accessed March 10, 2023. https://interestingengineering.com/culture/almost-everything-you-need-to-know-about-googles-history.

"LYCOS." History of Domains. Accessed March 10, 2023. https://www.historyofdomains.com/lycos/.

Meisenzahl, Avery, and Mary Hartmans. "Sundar Pichai Was Awarded $281 Million in Compensation Last Year. Here's How the Alphabet CEO Got His Start and Rose to Become One of the World's Highest-Paid Executives." Business Insider. Accessed March 10, 2023. https://www.businessinsider.com/the-life-of-google-ceo-sundar-pichai-in-photos-2017-1.

"Short History of Early Search Engines—The History of SEO." Accessed March 10, 2023. https://www.thehistoryofseo.com/The-Industry/Short_History_of_Early_Search_Engines.aspx.

Stangel, Luke. "20 Significant Moments in Google's History, on Its 20th Birthday." CNBC. September 4, 2018. https://www.cnbc.com/2018/09/04/20-significant-moments-in-googles-history-on-its-20th-birthday.html.

"Sundar Pichai: Meet the New CEO of a 'slimmed-down' Google." *The Guardian*. Accessed March 10, 2023. https://www.theguardian.com/technology/2015/aug/10/google-sundar-pichai-ceo-alphabet.

"This Week 21 Years Ago, Google Raised $25 Million from Sequoia Capital, Kleiner Perkins." Accessed March 10, 2023. https://www.moneycontrol.com/news/business/companies/this-week-21-years-ago-google-raised-25-million-from-sequoia-capital-kleiner-perkins-5410441.html.

"TIME Magazine's 'Person of the Year' Is … You." NBC News. December 17, 2006. https://www.nbcnews.com/id/wbna16242528.

Turo, Jay. "The Story of Jeff Bezos' $250,000 Investment into Google in 1998." Growthink. September 25, 2022. https://www.growthink.com/content/story-jeff-bezos-250000-investment-google-1998.

Ward, Matt. "The Future of Google." *Matt Ward* (blog). August 31, 2018. https://mattward.io/the-future-of-google/.

Chapter 6: Tesla

"$35,000 Tesla Model 3 Deliveries Still Delayed." Green Car Reports. March 28, 2019. https://www.greencarreports.com/news/1122308_35000-tesla-model-3-deliveries-still-delayed.

"2012 Tesla Model S To Use Panasonic Lithium-Ion Battery Cells." Green Car Reports. Accessed March 10, 2023. https://www.greencarreports.com/news/1067252_2012-tesla-model-s-to-use-panasonic-lithium-ion-battery-cells.

"9 Things We Learned about Tesla's Plans for 2022 after a Blowout Year with $5.5 Billion in Profit." Fortune. Accessed March 10, 2023. https://fortune.com/2022/01/27/tesla-plans-2022-record-profit-optimus-robot-robotaxi-texas-factory-cybertruck-new-models/.

"A Timeline of Tesla's Self-Driving Aspirations—Consumer Reports." Accessed March 10, 2023. https://www.consumerreports.org/autonomous-driving/timeline-of-tesla-self-driving-aspirations-a9686689375/.

"Approach." Neuralink. Accessed March 10, 2023. https://neuralink.com/approach/.

"Building Model S: A Perfectionist Defines Tesla's Design Language." Tesla. Accessed March 10, 2023. https://www.tesla.com/blog/building-model-s-perfectionist-defines-teslas-design-language.

Bursztynsky, Lora, and Jessica Kolodny. "Elon Musk Wins Shareholder Lawsuit over Tesla's $2.6 Billion SolarCity Acquisition." CNBC. April 27, 2022. https://www.cnbc.com/2022/04/27/elon-musk-wins-shareholder-lawsuit-over-the-companys-2point6-billion-solarcity-acquisition.html.

Clifford, Catherine. "9 Years Ago SpaceX Nearly Failed Itself out of Existence: 'It Is a Pretty Emotional Day,' Says Elon Musk." CNBC. September 29, 2017. https://www.cnbc.com/2017/09/29/elon-musk-9-years-ago-spacex-nearly-failed-itself-out-of-existence.html.

Copeland, Cody. "The Truth About Elon Musk's Relationship With His Father." Grunge. October 1, 2020. https://www.grunge.com/254977/the-truth-about-elon-musks-relationship-with-his-father/.

"Elon Musk: Biography." Britannica. Accessed March 10, 2023. https://www.britannica.com/biography/Elon-Musk.

"Elon Musk Gives Update on Tesla Model 3." ABC News. Accessed March 10, 2023. https://abcnews.go.com/Technology/elon-musk-update-tesla-model/story?id=38893711.

"Fact #744: September 10, 2012 Average New Light Vehicle Price Grows Faster than Average Used Light Vehicle Price." Energy.gov. Accessed March 10, 2023. https://www.energy.gov/eere/vehicles/fact-744-september-10-2012-average-new-light-vehicle-price-grows-faster-average-used.

Ferris, Robert. "Tesla's Musk Pulled the Plug on a Settlement with the SEC at the Last Minute." CNBC. September 28, 2018. https://www.cnbc.

com/2018/09/28/teslas-musk-pulled-plug-on-settlement-with-sec-at-last-minute.html.

"Here's A Look At Tesla's Potential Future Projects." InsideEVs. Accessed March 10, 2023. https://insideevs.com/features/491964/tesla-potential-future-projects-revealed/.

Hern, Alex. "Tesla Motors Receives $10bn in Model 3 Pre-Orders in Just Two Days." *The Guardian*. April 4, 2016. https://www.theguardian.com/technology/2016/apr/04/tesla-motors-sells-10bn-model-3-two-days.

"History of Tesla: Timeline and Facts." TheStreet. Accessed March 10, 2023. https://www.thestreet.com/technology/history-of-tesla-15088992.

"How Elon Musk Managed to Secure Tesla's First Store with a Roadster and Patents." Electrek. Accessed March 10, 2023. https://electrek.co/2020/03/25/elon-musk-secure-tesla-first-store-roadsster-patents/.

Johnson, Eric. "Full Q&A: Tesla and SpaceX CEO Elon Musk on Recode Decode." Vox. November 2, 2018. https://www.vox.com/2018/11/2/18053428/recode-decode-full-podcast-transcript-elon-musk-tesla-spacex-boring-company-kara-swisher.

Kolodny, Lora. "Tesla Delivered 1,500 Model 3s to Customers Last Quarter, Says Production Numbers on Target." CNBC. February 7, 2018. https://www.cnbc.com/2018/02/07/tesla-q4-2017-model-3-numbers.html.

Lambert, Fred. "Tesla Was within Weeks of Dying Because of Model 3 Delays, Says Elon Musk." Electrek. November 26, 2018. https://electrek.co/2018/11/26/tesla-weeks-dying-model-3-delays-elon-musk/.

McFadden, Christopher. "The Short but Fascinating History of Tesla." July 5, 2020. https://interestingengineering.com/transportation/the-short-but-fascinating-history-of-tesla.

Merle, Renae. "Tesla's Elon Musk Settles with SEC, Paying $20 Million Fine and Resigning as Board Chairman." *Washington Post*. September 30, 2018. https://www.washingtonpost.com/business/2018/09/29/teslas-elon-musk-settles-with-sec-paying-million-fine-resigning-board-chairman/.

"Model S: Designing the Perfect Endurance Athlete." Tesla. Accessed March 10, 2023. https://www.tesla.com/blog/model-s-designing-perfect-endurance-athlete.

Pettitt, Lora, and Jeniece Kolodny. "Why Tesla's Solar Business Has Not yet Taken off as Elon Musk Promised." CNBC. October 6, 2021. https://www.cnbc.com/2021/10/06/why-teslas-solar-business-has-not-yet-taken-off-as-elon-musk-promised.html.

Rogowsky, Mark. "Tesla's Model X: Promises Kept And Broken." *Forbes*. Accessed March 10, 2023. https://www.forbes.com/sites/markrogowsky/2015/11/24/teslas-model-x-promises-kept-and-broken/.

Sari, Jessie. "Elon Musk: His Biography, Net Worth, Education, Spouse and Quotes." Toolshero, March 1, 2023. https://www.toolshero.com/toolsheroes/elon-musk/.

"SpaceX: Facts About Elon Musk's Private Spaceflight Company." Space. Accessed March 10, 2023. https://www.space.com/18853-spacex.html.

"The Spark of Invention." *TIME*. Accessed March 10, 2023. https://techland.time.com/2013/11/14/the-spark-of-invention/.

"Stunning Aerial Footage of Giga Shanghai." Torque News. Accessed March 10, 2023. https://www.torquenews.com/14335/stunning-aerial-footage-giga-shanghai.

"Tesla Could Start Cybertruck Deliveries in Mid-2023, Says Elon Musk." Business Standard News. Accessed March 10, 2023. https://www.business-standard.com/article/automobile/tesla-could-start-cybertruck-deliveries-in-mid-2023-says-elon-musk-122072100906_1.html.

"Tesla Explains Model X Production Delays as It Looks Ahead to Meeting Model 3 Demand." ABC News. Accessed March 10, 2023. https://abcnews.go.com/Technology/tesla-explains-model-production-delays-ahead-meeting-model/story?id=38163468.

"Tesla Model S: A Look in the Rearview Mirror." Consumer Reports. Accessed March 10, 2023. https://www.consumerreports.org/hybrids-evs/ tesla-model-s-a-look-in-the-rearview-mirror-a1010257349/.

"Tesla Model X and the Curse Of Gull-Wing Doors." Accessed March 10, 2023. https://www.fastcompany.com/1669083/tesla-model-x-and-the-curse-of-gull-wing-doors-2.

"Tesla Model X Is Named 'Standout Performer' in New Safety Crash Tests." Electrek. Accessed March 10, 2023. https://electrek.co/2019/12/04/tesla-model-x-stand-out-performer-safety-crash-test/.

"Tesla Model Y Crossover Will Have Falcon Doors, Deleted Musk Tweet Confirms." Auto Evolution. Accessed March 10, 2023. https://www.autoevolution.com/news/tesla-model-y-crossover-will-have-falcon-doors-deleted-musk-tweet-confirms-100783.html#agal_0.

"Tesla Raises $1.46B in Stock Sale, at a Lower Price than Its August 2015 Sale: IFR." Tesla. May 20, 2016. https://www.cnbc.com/2016/05/20/tesla-raises-146b-in-stock-sale-at-a-lower-price-than-its-august-2015-sale-ifr.html.

"Tesla Struggles to Meet Model 3 Deliveries Due to Production Delays." Endurance. March 21, 2018. https://www.endurancewarranty.com/learning-center/news/tesla-model-3-production-delays/.

"Tesla's History: From The Roadster to SEC Problems." CNN. Accessed March 10, 2023. https://www.cnn.com/interactive/2019/03/business/tesla-history-timeline/index.html.

"The Ultimate Tesla Autopilot Guide: How Has It Evolved Over The Years?." Inside EVs. Accessed March 10, 2023. https://insideevs.com/news/443886/tesla-autopilot-evolution-history-ultimate-guide/.

Thompson, Cadie. "21 Incredible Facts about Elon Musk's Gigafactory." Business Insider. Accessed March 10, 2023. https://www.businessinsider.com/tesla-gigafactory-facts-2016-9.

Thomson, Meg. "Tesla Stores: What Are They and How Are They Different Than Dealerships?." The News Wheel, September 26, 2017. https://thenewswheel.com/tesla-stores-what-are-they-and-how-are-they-different-than-dealerships/.

"Top Autonomous Vehicles Companies to Watch in 2023." AI Time Journal. Accessed March 10, 2023. https://www.aitimejournal.com/autonomous-vehicles-companies-to-watch.

"Twitter Takeover: A Timeline of Elon Musk's Bumpy Road." CNN Business. Accessed March 10, 2023. https://www.cnn.com/2022/05/17/tech/twitter-elon-musk-timeline/index.html.

"UPDATE 4—Tesla Prices at $17 in Upsized IPO—Source." Reuters. June 29, 2010. https://www.reuters.com/article/tesla-ipo-idAFN2724387520100629.

"Why Elon Musk Got Bullied in High School." Accessed March 10, 2023. https://futurism.com/elon-musk-bullied-high-school.

Chapter 7

"A Brief History of Enron—With Enron Stock Chart." Begin to Invest. March 6, 2023. https://www.begintoinvest.com/enron-stock-chart/.

Cohn, Scott. "Twenty Years after Epic Bankruptcy, Enron Leaves a Complex Legacy." CNBC, December 2, 2021. https://www.cnbc.com/2021/12/02/twenty-years-after-epic-bankruptcy-enron-leaves-a-complex-legacy.html.

"Enron Scandal." Corporate Finance Institute. Accessed March 10, 2023. https://corporatefinanceinstitute.com/resources/esg/enron-scandal/.

"History of JDS Uniphase Corporation." FundingUniverse. Accessed March 10, 2023. http://www.fundinguniverse.com/company-histories/jds-uniphase-corporation-history/.

"JDS Beats the Street—Oct. 26, 2000." Accessed March 10, 2023. https://money.cnn.com/2000/10/26/technology/earns_jds/.

"JDS Tumbles on Losses—Jul. 27, 2001." Accessed March 10, 2023. https://money.cnn.com/2001/07/27/technology/jds/index.htm.

"JDSU (Now Viavi Solutions)—Funding, Financials, Valuation & Investors." Crunchbase. Accessed March 10, 2023. https://www.crunchbase.com/organization/jds-uniphase-corporation/company_financials.

ABOUT THE AUTHOR

TODD R. WALSH is the CEO and Chief Technical Analyst at Alpha Cubed Investments. He began his professional career in 1986 at E. F. Hutton immediately after interning for various investment firms while attending UCLA. At E. F. Hutton, Todd managed risk-and-style-balanced investment portfolios for wealthy individuals, corporations, and retirement plans and then subsequently continued these endeavors at Paine Webber, Merrill Lynch, and LPL Financial Services. Prior to founding Alpha Cubed Investments in 2011, Todd was the managing member and chief investment officer of his eponymously named firm, TRW Investments.

Todd began applying technical analysis to his investment management process beginning in 1987, when he was introduced to the Investors Intelligence Newsletter Sentiment Index during the crash of 1987. Realizing its powerful utility as a contrarian indicator, he subscribed to the service and began handcrafting historical data and comparing it to market conditions over time (this was before ubiquitous computer graphing and analysis was available, so it had to be done by hand). Building on this research, Todd went on to develop over thirty technical analysis tools over the years that are used daily at Alpha Cubed Investments to help determine current market conditions.

Todd enjoys educating investors about the processes of long-term investing, technical analysis, and general business development in the financial services industry through speaking, writing, and media appearances. He is the proud father of five children, graduates from UCLA, UC Santa Barbara, UC Irvine, and UC Berkeley.

ACKNOWLEDGMENTS

WRITING THIS BOOK was a lot like agreeing to run a marathon that is a year away: It seems like a great idea in the moment, but at some point, you start realizing that the actual amount of work involved is overwhelming. I want to thank my entire team at Alpha Cubed Investments for helping in different ways throughout the writing of this book. Primarily, though, I want to thank and acknowledge our portfolio associate, Connor Keim. Connor holds the Chartered Financial Analyst® designation, and he worked side by side with me to do the heavy lifting of building out the hypothetical algorithm discussed throughout the book as well as building all the stock market charts used to illustrate the book. He is a Cornhusker alumnus and is very proud of his Nebraska roots—so much so that his idol is Warren Buffett. Who knows? Maybe he will surpass him someday.

CONTACT TODD

Todd R. Walsh is available for media appearances at
https://www.toddrwalsh.com/
to provide his expert commentary on the following:

- Current market conditions

- Fundamental news impacting markets

- Technical analysis of markets

- Stock market entry and exit targets

- Bull and bear market conditions

- Management and leadership topics

Printed in the USA
CPSIA information can be obtained
at www.ICGtesting.com
JSHW021544111223
53613JS00002B/4